the FUTURE FORMULA

Stop repeating the same old steps. Change something! Will Mattox, in *The Future Formula,* tells us that we cannot make a mistake, and then shows us the path to change. Change that will result in the bright future we have searched for. Read *The Future Formula*, embrace the principles, do the exercises, and you'll find yourself living that brighter future.

Dame D.C. Cordova, CEO of Excellerated Business Schools

Will Mattox fills in the missing puzzle pieces between ideas, principles and actions. After you read 21 Principles your beliefs and actions will line up in a straight path all the way to the bank.

Jay Conrad Levinson, The Father of Guerrilla Marketing
Author, "Guerrilla Marketing" series of books

I've had the pleasure of being a student of Will's and when I found out he was writing a book, I couldn't wait to get my hands on it. *The Future Formula* is exactly what I was hoping it would be. A straightforward how-to for living a life with purpose and achieving your dreams, written by an expert who has helped thousands of individuals do exactly that. Although I had heard much of this information through sitting in on Will's events, having the opportunity to read and absorb it made so much more of it click for me!

Melissa Tosetti, Bestselling Author of Living The Savvy Life

Will Mattox has a deep understanding of the Universal Principles and how they impact our world and our lives. He teaches a simple (but profound) Future Formula that allows you to easily move toward your goals with ease and grace rather than stress and pain. Will is the "Coaches Coach" and has mentored and coached some of the top leaders in the world. He generously shares his strategies and principles so that any reader can apply what he's taught others for ultimate growth and prosperity.

Ursula Mentjes, Bestselling Author of Selling with Intention

the

FUTURE FORMULA

21 Powerful Principles to Achieve the Life of Your Dreams

WILL MATTOX

NEW YORK

the FUTURE FORMULA
21 Powerful Principles to Achieve the Life of Your Dreams

ISBN 978-1-61448-348-9 paperback
ISBN 978-1-61448-349-6 eBook
Library of Congress Control Number: 2012944114

Morgan James Publishing
The Entrepreneurial Publisher
5 Penn Plaza, 23rd Floor,
New York City, New York 10001
(212) 655-5470 office • (516) 908-4496 fax
www.MorganJamesPublishing.com

Cover Design by:
Rachel Lopez
www.r2cdesign.com

Interior Design by:
Bonnie Bushman
bonnie@caboodlegraphics.com

In an effort to support local communities, raise awareness and funds, Morgan James Publishing donates a percentage of all book sales for the life of each book to Habitat for Humanity Peninsula and Greater Williamsburg.

Get involved today, visit
www.MorganJamesBuilds.com.

Habitat for Humanity®
Peninsula and
Greater Williamsburg
Building Partner

CONTENTS

Acknowledgments   vii

Authors Note   ix

Foreword   xi

Introduction   xv

Chapter 1: Your Thoughts Create Your Reality   1

Chapter 2: Free Will Means We Get to Choose   12

Chapter 3: True Fulfillment Comes From a Life of Purpose   23

Chapter 4: We are Spirit, Mind and Body in That Order   34

Chapter 5: You First, Then Others   46

Chapter 6: Maximize Your Strengths   53

Chapter 7: Your Ego is Your Unseen Partner   64

Chapter 8: You Are Your Own Expert   76

Chapter 9: Gratitude and Stewardship   89

Section One Summary: You Work On You   98

Chapter 10: Exponential Growth/ Compound Effect   105

Chapter 11: With Freedom Comes Responsibility   113

The Authors Encouragement   127

Chapter 12: Experiences And Relationships, The Catalyst For Change 128

Chapter 13: Radical Acceptance Allows the Ideal Outcome   142

Chapter 14: You Have to Create Space   155

Chapter 15: Communication Happens at Three Levels   167

Chapter 16: Understand Failure, Embrace the Positive   179

Chapter 17: Time And Velocity   190

Chapter 18: Full Engagement Theory   202

Chapter 19: Growth is the Natural Order of the Universe   214

Chapter 20: Leverage and Multiplication of Efforts   228

Chapter 21: Balance is Essential   241

Summary   *249*

About The Author   *253*

Special Offers   *255*

ACKNOWLEDGMENTS

I HAVE BEEN BLESSED to have many encouraging supportive people in my life, without who's help I would not have finished this book. They talked me into taking 300 pages of ideas that had been sitting on my shelf, reworking it, and getting it out to the world. I want to thank the many fellow coaches, teachers, and speakers that went before me publishing amazing books, for guiding me through the writing/publishing maze with insights and connections that were invaluable.

I want to thank my first editor, Cliff McMurray, who was given very raw pages to make readable. Also, thanks to my friends and family with common sense edits and changes that made the book more understandable and practical.

I want to especially thank the hundreds of clients that I have had the pleasure of working with, for their teaching, challenging, and inspiration. I learned from all of them and every encounter brought me lessons for much of what I am sharing in this book. Thank You!

Also, I want to thank my great family! I really have been blessed to have their love and support for whatever I have taken on over the years. They are the motivation for my doing everything else.

Finally, a very special thanks to my wife Virginia, who is has always been the love of my life, and without who's help I could not do most of what I do. Thanks for keeping me grounded and for inspiring at the same time!

Author's Note

I WANT TO MAKE three quick comments regarding the content of this book and the source of the ideas that I share. These principles came to me through a lifetime of interaction with my family, my friends, my businesses, and coaching clients, as well as a personal desire to understand how life works. After coaching the accelerated growth of both businesses and people for over 15 years, I have always, and continue to want to know more about how life works, and our relationship to A Higher Power, and our purpose on earth, and more… Like all of you I have formed certain opinions and beliefs from my years of life experience. That is what I am sharing in this book. The opinions, ideas, and beliefs are strictly my own and now yours if you choose to believe them.

It is not my intention or desire to give specific legal or financial advice. Please do not read anything between the lines in that regard and always go to your personal advisors and team to get professional support for any financial or legal decisions before you make them.

This book is not written to support a specific religion or spiritual doctrine but instead recognizes the creative power of God and his universal energy. I want to challenge each of you as the reader to not get caught up by any specific language that may seem to represent a religious view that conflicts with yours. Instead, understand that my intention is to share generalized, powerful principles that can be utilized and implemented physically, mentally, and spiritually to support your growth and help you achieve your goals.

Finally, as you will notice, there is a lot of repetition in this book. I don't apologize for the repetition because I understand from years of working with clients that we all hear things differently. We will all hear things when we are ready to and not before. By sharing the principles with stories and examples in many different ways I hope to reach more of you reading this book in a way that makes sense to you. If some of the points that I am making seem redundant, please know that my intention is to develop a deeper connection with as many readers as possible.

My only intention for you is to help you remove obstacles, go to your next level, and reach your life goals. Success on your terms is my hope for you.

Will Mattox

FOREWORD

by Loral Langemeier

WATCHING WILL MATTOX WRITE, *The Future Formula*, had such a deep meaning to me. You know how you are able to read people's energy? With Will, that's how it was. We read each other's energy and instantly knew something. Something deeper. Something spiritual. We knew the instant we met that we had known each other for lifetime's past. That's how we felt on our first day together and not too much has changed since then.

We met in 1997, over 15 years ago, at the Coaches Training Institute. As part of that program, we met with the group three-to-four times each year. Will and I quickly bonded. We were the only two people in the group who understood money and finance. We connected instantly even though we were at very different places in our lives. Will was entering into his first retirement from a pottery business he started at age 17. I was just transitioning out of Chevron where I had been a successful intrepreneur having quit only to return the next day as a coach making five-times the salary I made as an employee.

That is where our story began and we have since shared a tremendous journey together. Coming out of the Coaches Training Institute, we understood there was a huge need for financial coaching. None of the teachers even had tremendous knowledge surrounding money and finance.

Cute, right? Well, by then I was working for Robert Kiyosaki as a master distributor. Will and I decided to pitch Robert the idea of a coaching company – sort of the "how to" companion to the books he was writing. I would build the relationships and Will would write the programs. Unfortunately this idea was considered too much of a liability. Shortly thereafter we went to work for my dear friend, Bob Proctor, and three or four other nationally known speakers. Basically, we took their intellectual property and created programs out of it. It was clear that this was not a great model, so Will and I looked for other things to do. For those of you who know me, you know that I always say "Yes! now and then figure out how." Well, Will and I were about to do just that in a HUGE way.

We decided one day to purchase about $12 million dollars worth of apartment complexes in Oklahoma City. It was time to burn the boats. We had just said yes to buying all these apartments. Now we had to figure out what to do with them. We did. We renovated them and raised money for them. We made money on two-out-of- three of them. Success! This experiment led us to create our Financial Foundations Coaching Program. We'd realized the investors we were working with on the apartment complexes needed this program. It was a ten week course that became the foundation for my Sequencing Blocks I teach. Our ultimate goal with this was to create a community of informed investors, similar to what the Live Out Loud, Inc Alumni group is today.

What I am about to share with you now is HOT. In fact it is a story of the origins of my company Live Out Loud, Inc. After five years of partnering together, Will and I met for breakfast in Scottsdale, Arizona. We were there working with Bob Proctor. We met this early morning at a diner – I think it may have been Denny's or something similar. At breakfast I looked across the table at Will and told him, "this is not working." I told him we should stop doing it for other people, use our energy and start our own company. We would call it Live Out Loud. We would work really hard to build the brand, build our own database and present all over the world. Will's response to my plan? Well, he looked back across the table at me and said, "Loral you go ahead and start Live Out Loud and I will start my own company called Live Quietly and Leave Me Alone."

To make a long story short, I did start Live Out Loud, Inc; a company that today has become a multi-million dollar global enterprise. Will did start his own company, Coaching Services, but I did not leave him alone. In fact, we continued on our journey together with Will running the coaching arm of Live Out Loud. Today he is still the lead coach and has helped me train over 150 coaches for my company. Will has been instrumental in setting the tone and helping me maintain the Live Out Loud, Inc quality that our community has come to expect over the past 11 years.

Have we had our conflicts? Sure, but all good business partners do and should. Having a team around you to hold you accountable and offer a different perspective is crucial to any business. Every successful entrepreneur understands that. In fact, there was even a time during our journey together that Will left Live Out Loud, Inc. Will and I have drifted in different directions, but never apart. It was during one of my early Alumni events in San Mateo, California, that he came back. Will showed up at the event – in shorts and a T-shirt – and sat in the back of the room. During this time, I asked everyone in the group what they wanted and their response, for Will and me to be their only coaches, was profound. That day we signed-up 25 people and made $250,000. That is the extreme energy that Will and I have. Even to this day, Will is the only person I have complete confidence in letting coach my Alumni community.

So how does this close business relationship Will and I share impact the rest of our lives? Well, Will is like my older brother. He is 15 years older than me. My kids, they love him! Both of them have always called him, "Uncle Will." I cannot think of anyone I would have rather shared this amazing journey with than Will Mattox. At the beginning of this forward, I told you we had shared lifetimes together and I believe we will share many more. We have parallel energy and we've known that all along. I recently autographed a copy of my latest bestseller, Yes! Energy: The Equation to Do Less, Make More, for Will. I wrote simply, "Looking forward to what's next partner because I am sure we will be together for many years to come."

This is why I am so pleased Will has written the book you are about to read. It has been six years in the works and now he has a chance to share it with you. You will now have the opportunity to read about the principles that Will has used in his own life, shared with me and compelled success in the lives of so many others. When Will asked if I was willing to write the forward for this amazing book, I said "Yes!" Yes! is always the answer, but in this instance it was also an honor. I want to support Will in this endeavor the same way he has supported me over the years in Live Out Loud, Inc and as a dear friend. So to my friend, business partner and "Uncle Will," here's to your success and the rest of our journey! Ready – Set – Go!

Loral Langemeier.

INTRODUCTION

FOR THE PAST 15 YEARS I have worked with thousands of clients as a business and personal coach. Eventually, every client I've ever worked with has run into personal challenges to their beliefs. They have run into limiting beliefs, beliefs that limit their future. As a coach, I have found it to be a universal truth that each client will run into those limiting beliefs and limited future potential at some point. Many of you have experienced the results of limiting beliefs yourself. You may have been stopped, or distracted, or had limited results because your beliefs would not let you move forward.

The principles of this book are designed to expand and challenge your beliefs, and allow you to have a brighter, fuller future. **A single idea or principle, when part of our beliefs, will change the course of life from the moment it is accepted.** Doors are opened or closed. Futures are defined or lost.

Be very clear about this: I'm not here to give you the answers. I'm here to give you the questions. I'm here to increase your awareness, to raise the bar. The answers will come from *you* and this book will draw them out!

We each come from a different background. We are of different ages, cultures, past experiences, and we're in different current life situations. No two of us have had the same experiences, background, and opportunities. As a coach, I know that there is no one application of principles that is universal, no magic formula for happiness. There is no one set of ideas or beliefs that will move every person forward and allow them to have that brighter future. All of you reading this book and indeed, everyone on the planet, will eventually run into their limiting beliefs. Examining those limiting beliefs will cause you to make choices and when you make those choice, your life will change and take a different course.

Each chapter is focused on a single basic principle designed to challenge your thinking. Some of these principles will just plain not fit at first. They'll be concepts and ideas that seem too different or too strange for you to accept at this time. Others will be pieces that do fit, principles you can understand and grasp immediately. So each of the principles will actually challenge you take an idea and put it into action in your life in some way.

From the very first chapter you may feel challenged to believe or trust the validity of the principle that I am offering. The challenge I chose for the first chapter in this book was chosen intentionally to hurtle you forward, to expand your faith in these principles and to challenge you to believe that everything else in this book will be of benefit to you as you integrate those principles. I'm asking you to develop and build trust, trust in your beliefs, knowing that they are creating your current reality and defining your future. As you begin to trust that process more and more, it will be easier and take less and less time to make changes that propel you forward. It will become an automatic part of your operating procedures. It will be a natural part of you. But you need to grow that part of you.

This book may appear to be about principles, ideas, and beliefs, but it is in fact about you! It is about the choices you will make when you are confronted with principles, ideas, and potential beliefs. Many of these simple principles will be easy for you to accept. Indeed, they may be part of your belief system already, and as such they are supporting your choices and not limiting them. Those will be the easy chapters for you! There will also be chapters which, as you think about them and study them or do the small homework assignments associated with them, you will be able to embrace and believe the principles they introduce, and they will be added to your belief system. And finally, there will be chapters that you will find very difficult to process into your own belief system. They may introduce a principle that is outside your past experience or may even fight with your current beliefs. This book may ask you to make hard choices, to believe things that fight with your current beliefs. Some of the principles found in these chapters may take you a long time to work through. In some cases it may not be as simple as just accepting the idea or belief or principle.

I believe that life is like a jigsaw puzzle with thousands and thousands of pieces, and we're constantly looking for the one or two pieces that allow us to continue to build our individual puzzle. We're constantly picking up pieces, trying them in one place and then another, turning them, adjusting them, and looking at them from every angle. We're holding them up to the light for inspection, looking at their shapes and contours. We're looking at the implications, or looking at how those little pieces of the puzzle will touch our lives. Do they fit together or do they not fit?

In this search to find the missing pieces of our puzzle, every person's puzzle is different. As we look for pieces of the puzzle we find them laying everywhere. Every conversation we have with someone on the street, every book we pick up and read, every time we turn the television on and hear something on the news, every time we browse the Internet, every time we open a letter from a friend or every time we let our mind wander to new areas or new thoughts. In each of these instances we are basically defining, picking up, looking at some potential piece of our puzzle and our puzzle is developing slowly over time. We came into this life with only one or two pieces of our puzzle. Two things we knew from birth were that we had a fear of falling, and we had a fear of loud noises. Falling and loud noises were both bad things. From there, everything else was learned and added as pieces of the puzzle we picked up and tried to fit together.

Some people never build a very big puzzle, or it's never very complex. They live a very small puzzle life you might say. Other people are intent on adding to their puzzles constantly, always looking for new things, seeing how they fit, trying on new ideas and thoughts. Some thoughts and ideas immediately fit into place. Other ideas and thoughts seem logical, as though they might fit, but they don't quite mesh. Maybe we're not quite ready, maybe our puzzle needs a couple of other pieces before it's ready for that piece to fit.

Sometimes we go through life and for a long time we seem to be on a plateau. We're not growing, not moving forward, and we're not filling in our puzzle. We're not developing our picture. At other times, information seems to be coming at us in a steady stream and we are rapidly developing our puzzle and growing – sometimes so fast we can barely keep up!

One of the intents of this book is to offer you lots of pieces for your potential puzzle to try on for size. As I present different principles, I'm asking you to lift those puzzle pieces up to the light and examine them from every side. I'm asking you to look at those contours, and shapes to see if there's a fit. How and where does it fit? See how many more puzzle pieces you can add in once you put just one new piece of your puzzle in place.

KEY:

I cannot change you. I can barely change me!
Only you can change you. Be very clear about this:
I'm not here to give you the answers. I'm here to give
you the questions. I'm here to raise the challenge, to
raise the bar. The answers come from you!

Fundamentally, I am committed to continued change and growth in myself, and supporting the change and growth in those around me. I am not attached to a specific belief in this book or to any specific principle, and I don't care which ones you choose to embrace. I am not trying to direct the course of change in you. I'm hoping to plant a seed or two that may allow you to make positive choices and move you forward in your life, business, family, and in every other area.

I have always been an entrepreneur. I haven't worked for anybody since I was 17 years old and have always valued creativity, contribution, and relationships. You could say those are my highest values and another part of the reason I have written this book. I have always been blessed with both left and right brain. Perhaps you were, too. However, most of us are dominant in one or the other.

We are either highly creative, intuitive, impulsive, or we are calculating, linear, and logical. I have always operated at the polar extremes, being both highly creative and very logical. I look at principles, ideas, and new thoughts from the extremes to see how they will fit with my current established beliefs. I encourage you do the same as you read. Try these ideas and principles on, wear them for a little while in your mind, and see how they fit in the life puzzle you are building.

You can only look at them from your own perspective coming from your current beliefs. These beliefs are layered over your past experiences which your mind then analyzes. Therefore each of you reading this book will take away different bits and pieces. More than once in the course of this book, you will hear me describe it as *building your personal puzzle*, and indeed if you are able to add one or two pieces to your puzzle in the process I will feel my purpose in writing this book has been fulfilled.

The principles are generalized, but the answers are specific to you and your circumstance, in this moment, right now. Listen to what they're saying to you. Listen to how your body mind and spirit speak to you through these principles. I challenge you to throw out the excuse: "This does not apply to me, that is not something I can do." Instead ask yourself, "What can I do with this principle? Where is this principle *not* showing up in my life? What would the first steps be?"

This is not a book that is designed to be read in two or three hours, or two or three days, or even two or three weeks. It's a book that is designed to be used as a workbook and maybe something you carry with you for the next year, adding more principles, challenging yourself at deeper and deeper levels. It should be a book that creates noticeable, profound change in your life for the positive. Immediate results should include increased fulfillment and happiness in your life!

As a coach, I have seen clients make amazing forward strides when they accepted a simple principle into their lives and added it to their belief system and then acted on it. It is often like unlocking a door to a secret room that they didn't know existed. As a coach is fun to be part of that process. It's rewarding for me to be a part of someone else's success and feel that I have contributed to their personal or business growth. It's the reason I coach, and it's the reason I'm writing this book.

It might also be good for you know the manner that this book was written:

Because my fingers are not as fast as my mouth, I spoke this book into being. It has only gone through very light editing, and is therefore very conversational in tone. Many phrases are repeated for emphasis, and I would like you to imagine us in conversation as you read. Speak back to the pages. Argue with the ideas and be in dialogue with me as you read this book. I have intentionally written the book in that style, as a conversation. I intend it to be a dialogue between the two us, as opposed to a lecture from me.

Embrace and enjoy the process of change. Change will happen to you regardless, you cannot avoid it, so you might as well participate in it proactively.

principle n. 1. a general truth or law, basic to other truths: 2, a law or rule of personal conduct. 3, moral standards collectively. 4. That which is inherent in anything determining its nature or essence. 5. A source or cause from which anything proceeds; a fundamental cause.

belief n. 1. Acceptance of the truth or actuality of anything without certain proof; mental conviction. 2. That which is believed; something held to be true or actual. 3. A tenant or body of tenants; doctrine; or creed.

Chapter 1

YOUR THOUGHTS CREATE YOUR REALITY

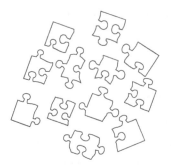

The first principle is that your thoughts create your reality, IF you will move those thoughts into action. We hear that concept in a lot of different ways from a lot of different people, and the truth is that when we have a thought, we have to go beyond just thinking about it.

As a coach, I am often asked for the "Formula" for success. It would be very convenient and easy for everyone if we could simply do A, B, and C, and then get D. But it doesn't work that way because we are all different and in different circumstances. There is, however, a process that I have found works with everyone. It works with each of us because we apply it to ourselves in unique ways to achieve the results we are looking for. The process will be different for each of you!

It is a *process for creating your new future* and I therefore call it **"The Future Formula™"**.

The basics are this: at first we have the thought. It may be in the form of a goal, or it may be in the form of an idea for a new product, or a new process or system, or something we want to integrate or move into our lives in some way. Maybe it's something we want to achieve, and we set this as our goal.

Secondly, we have to be able to believe that this is absolutely possible for us! We have to see that the thought, or the belief, or the goal is believable. That it is a belief with possibility. Once we actually can believe it, then we have to be able to visualize it.

So, step one is to set the goal. Step two is to be able to believe in the goal, absolutely believe it is possible for you – not for someone else, but for you. Step three is to be able to visualize yourself at the point of the goal.

In other words, if your goal is to retire at the age of 50, you have to actually be able to picture yourself sitting on a porch and retired at the age of 50, or living on the beach, or going to the movies with your wife, enjoying time with your children, or whatever represents your vision of what retirement is like at the age of 50. *It's very important that you are able to visualize it with you in the picture.* It is not about visualizing that you're home when you're 50 years old. It's a matter of visualizing you at the point of having achieved your goal, in other words you *are* retired.

If you can absolutely visualize yourself there, and you can believe it is possible, and that you have set the goal for yourself to do that, then you are ready for the most important step.

The next step, after you can absolutely visualize yourself there and believe it's possible, is that you should start to *expect* it. That is one of the keys! Step four is to be able to expect the goal to come true. Sometimes people do that through a series of affirmations, or through reminding themselves of their goal, or through actions that focus their attention on their goal daily. **Expectation is belief without doubt!**

Once we expect it, we discover that opportunities show up that will accomplish our goal for us. They are opportunities that lead us to the goal! This can be expressed as a 7 step process, or *Future Formula*™, to meet your goals:

1. Set one specific **Goal**
2. **Believe** it is possible for you
3. **Visualize** that goal with clarity
4. **Expect** it to happen

5. Watch for **Opportunity**
6. Take strategic **action** on the opportunities
7. Track the **Results** and adjust

Often we set goals and we have no idea how they're going to come about. You may be sitting reading this book at the age of 45 years old and say, " I want to retire by the time I'm 50 years old", and you don't have a clue how that is possible.

Trying to figure out *how* something is possible is not your job.

Your job is to decide WHAT you want and not HOW you're going to get it. And that is the very best kind of goal, because it is not limited. You're leaving it wide open. You're going out and taking a step of faith to believe that this is possible for yourself. That's when it's hardest to believe, but it's also when your goal has the most power and possibility because you are not limiting how it comes about.

Imagine you set a goal to retire by the time you're 50, or whatever other goal you have in your mind, and at the age of 45 you don't know how that's possible, but you still believe it *is* possible. You can visualize it for yourself, and you start to expect it because you talk to people about it and continue to visualize it. You reaffirm it with yourself. You may focus on it through a single daily action or some small event that you choose to do to remind yourself that you're going to retire by the time you're 50. Once you expect that, you start watching for opportunities to show up to fulfill that goal and that belief. It's amazing but true – once you create something through your thought pattern, then heaven and earth move, the universe shifts, and God brings opportunities for you to meet your goals.

How To Think BIG

Our reality is created by our thoughts!

Everything that is in reality now was first a thought. Everything that people have designed and created, they first had in their minds as an idea. Later in this book, we will discuss some of the other pieces that have to go along with this idea, but this is the central theme that we'll keep coming back to over and over. Your thoughts *do* create your reality! So be careful what you think, and think big!

Thinking big is one of the key elements in goal-setting and, in fact, is a key to achieving things in life.

Those who think big, achieve big. Those who think small, achieve only small things. But one of the challenges we face is that people have a problem thinking big. I find this with people that I'm working with all the time. They're able to think slightly bigger than they are right now, in the moment, but they're not able to take leaps of faith. Belief is a huge step toward a big goal. It is something that really stretches them, something that's unbelievable to them. But being able to fully put their faith and belief in their goal so that they can have that goal attracted to them is what needs to happen. It's the belief that allows the opportunity to show up.

So how do we think big? Thinking big is an exercise. **Thinking big is also a habit** that we develop, a muscle that we grow over time. We do not immediately have the ability to do this. The people who are already able to think big have been growing and developing, and moving into that ability to think big in other areas of their lives. So thinking big is a habit. If I asked you to imagine your annual income from this past year, and now to think about the coming year, and to then set a goal to make it bigger, how big could you make your new goal? For many of you, it's probably only 10% bigger than what was last year's income. If your annual income was $50,000, most of us can imagine $55,000 or possibly $60,000. Very few of us can imagine $500,000 if we made only $50,000 last year.

And yet, what are the limitations on our goals? What are the limitations of what's possible in this world? Most of the limitations in our lives are self-imposed. Do you want to limit your beliefs and grow slowly, or do you want to be able to use this principle of 'thinking creates reality?" Do you want to take a leap to the beliefs that you really want – that you want in the very depths of your truest self?

Whether it's financial income, personal health, good relationships, spiritual life, a better environment, or any other goal; each of us have those areas in our lives where we would like to see a big change. In those areas, do you want to limit yourself with a restricted belief system that says; "I now make $50,000 I probably can only make $55,000 in the next year if I work really hard?" First of all, who says you can only make $55,000, and secondly, who says you have to work really hard?

You are imposing your old beliefs on the goals that you're setting for yourself and therefore limiting your results.

KEY:

You cannot base your new expectations on your past experiences or you will get what you have always received. Always!

New Habits Of Thinking

One of the challenges we have is creating habits that produce results. There are many areas of our lives where we are asked to do things that are very challenging for us, and then we have to create a habit of being able to do those things. Setting goals is one of those areas. Believing for large things, having faith, or what is sometimes called trust – trusting the process, trusting that our goal is possible and believing in the possibility without being able to see it – these are some of those areas of challenge. It's a habit we can develop, like responsibility. Responsibility is not something that somebody has immediately. It's something that they develop. Don't we always hear the phrase, "they developed responsibility or they became responsible," implying that it happened over time? It wasn't something they were born with.

EXAMPLE:

Let me give you a quick example of how our habits of thinking can change: If you agree to start getting out of bed on the other side tomorrow morning, most of you will be in the shower or eating breakfast before you remember that you didn't do it. You will recommit and on the second day you will be walking to the bathroom before you remember because your old habit is so strong. Studies show that it will take you 3-4 weeks of determined effort to change that *habit of thinking*. Eventually you will be getting up on the other side and it will be automatic. You will have changed that habit and you can do the same with any habit from your past that is holding you back.

Trust or faith in our ability to leap to larger goals for ourselves is something that we have to grow and develop as well. Start by believing for small things and grow your beliefs.

If we challenge ourselves to believe small things that seem impossible at first and then move those beliefs to larger and larger things, we can develop that habit of being able to leap to larger beliefs. Perhaps you cannot imagine your income going from $50,000 to $500,000 as in the example I was using a moment ago. But perhaps you could imagine finding a dollar bill somewhere today, and you can actually picture that. Say you believe it is possible that out of the blue and for no apparent reason, you could find a dollar bill. Not because you know how it would happen right now, but that you would find a dollar or in some other way have a dollar bill given to you today in a way that is totally unexpected. You may be thinking, "Oh, that's happened to me! I've had that exact same thing happen! I've had an idea in the morning that something was going to happen, and before the end of the day, it actually happened." You created an unconscious belief that actually came true.

I'm asking you to take a leap of faith and believe, for instance, for something like a dollar bill to show up in your life today, or for a front row parking space at your supermarket for you today when you go shopping, or for small things to happen like that, so you can develop the habit of belief–a habit of trust.

As that shows up, I want you to notice, and to acknowledge that it has happened. If you notice and acknowledge, pretty soon you will develop a habit of faith growing for you. You will become a believer in larger and larger things, and eventually become a believer in big things for yourself. You will be able to imagine yourself retired at the age of 50 if you're now 45. Not because you'll know how to retire at the age of 50, but because you *want* to retire at the age of 50. You will now be in the habit of knowing that what you choose to believe actually comes true. Our habits support our learning and doing greater things. The people in the world who are capable of huge leaps of faith haven't gotten there overnight. They've developed that habit of belief! The *habit of belief* is a way of thinking that is foreign to most.

I'm asking you right now to take a very, very small leap of faith and believe in a small thing for today. Right now, today! Take a leap of faith, for instance that a dollar bill will show up in your life today from some unexpected source. Or believe that some other small event will happen in your life today that's totally unexpected, even when you have no idea how it is going to happen. It's not that you're believing it because you see it happening already. If you will take that small step today, and continue to do that every day, you will slowly develop the habit of being able to believe large things for yourself. You'll be able to picture yourself in the beach house at the age of 50, retired, and be able to have that dream, or any other dream, come true for yourself.

And now I have a challenge for you. The idea of challenging ourselves is what this whole book is about. If we take the "thoughts-create-reality" principle and challenge you with it, it will have to be something that specific and personal to you. Everybody's level of challenge will be different based on everybody's experience with using this concept in their lives previously. If you're very used to this, it will take a big challenge to be something that will move you beyond where you have been in the past. That's the whole purpose of what we're talking about and what we're doing. It is to take you beyond where you have ever been before.

If you take this principle of "your thinking creates your reality" and you have never done this before in your life, then I encourage you to start with some small example like we talked about a moment ago. The challenge you need to set for yourself is one with a measurable result. In other words, I want this to be a short term challenge. And I mean very short term. I want the short-term challenge to be as short as an hour, or at the most a day. This will be the first step for people who are not used to creating their reality with their thinking.

THE EXPECTATION EXERCISE

I want you to choose to believe something, it could be in the area of personal health, finances, relationships, business, etc. Remember the Future Formula™ we talked about before; believing, seeing yourself in the picture, expecting a result, and watching for opportunity and taking action? I want you to choose something very small that you can believe will come true for yourself in the next six hours or less. If you're reading this in the evening I want you to do this first thing in the morning. Choose a thought for yourself that you completely believe will come true within six hours, but NOT because you know it's going to happen automatically or you've already scheduled it. In other words, you're not allowed to choose a belief that the sun will come up tomorrow. I encourage you to choose to believe in something that you have no idea how it is going to happen. Choose something you would like to see happen, that you believe is possible, that you can imagine or envision happening, and that you can now expect to happen because you can imagine yourself in that situation. Take whatever action you need to make that happen and then watch to see if and when it happens. Notice how opportunities show up. More about this in the up-coming Quick Exercise...

The next challenge I have for you is going to be growing the size of the challenge you're capable of taking on. Again, I encourage you to choose a challenge that is just beyond the level of your current belief system that you've used before to create reality from your thoughts in the past. Choose something that is going to stretch you a little bit, that you're going to be able to achieve, but not with ease. Choose something that's going to make you bigger.

This is a growth process! In other sections of this book we will talk about you working on you and what areas of you can be worked on and what effect it will have. One of the best places that you can work on yourself is to stretch what's possible for you to believe.

It's a combination of believing what's possible for yourself as well as seeing it happen. Growing your belief system is a process that is going to take place over time. It is not going to happen instantly. You're not going to go from believing for a small thing like a parking space and move right up to having $500,000 annual income if it's 10 times the size of your current annual income. You are not going to make that happen in a couple of days. But it is possible for you to move rapidly from one small challenge to a larger and larger challenges and eventually create the habit of believing for very large possibilities.

QUICK EXERCISE:

Right this moment I want you to identify some small goal. I want you to write it down on a piece of paper, then spend five minutes after you've written it testing yourself. Ask yourself if you believe this is possible? If you can convince yourself that it is possible for you, then imagine it happening to you. Physically close your eyes and imagine yourself in that situation, whether it's finding an empty parking space, a larger income, or somebody congratulating you for something you did well at work. It doesn't matter what the challenge you set before yourself is. Spend five minutes seeing if it's possible, asking yourself if you can believe it. Spend another five minutes envisioning that happening for yourself. Actually imagine yourself finding a dollar bill on the street. Imagine somebody congratulating you. Close your eyes and see it happening in your mind's eye.

The challenge for many of us is to see if we are also in that picture. This is very important. It's easy to believe these things are possible for someone else. I want you to notice if it's you bending down to pick up the dollar bill. Notice if it's you getting a handshake and being congratulated for job well done at the office. See if it's you pulling into the parking spot in your car. Whatever the challenge you set for yourself, the thought you choose to believe and create in reality, check to see if you are in that picture. If you are not in that picture I challenge you to work on that visualization until you can put yourself in that picture.

I work with clients all the time on the idea of retirement. Many people want to retire to a sunny place by the beach. I often ask them to imagine themselves in their sunny place on the beach and then describe it to me. That's the exercise I want you to do for yourself with your goal. Describe what the situation is like that you've chosen to believe. When you ask yourself, "Is it me in the picture?" I want you to actually pull away and look at the scene. See who's driving the car into the empty parking space or who's picking up the dollar bill. If it's not you, I want you to change the image, and remember you get to choose. Choose to insert yourself in that scene. You need to be able to picture yourself in that scene if you want to be able to expect it to happen to you, after all this is all about you. As soon as you can envision yourself in that scene, the next step is to repeatedly go back and imagine that scene with you in it. *Repeatedly* imagine yourself in that situation. Through repetition you'll start to expect that to happen for yourself.

Even in a quick expectation exercise, there's plenty of time for this whole process to take place for reality to unfold before you. This really is different than what would've happened to you if you had not had that thought, believed it, imagined it and expected it to happen.

Opportunity will show up to allow your thoughts to become reality!

So, one last time before you turn the next page, I want you to challenge yourself right now with a new reality you would like to bring into effect. Write it down on a piece of paper, spend five minutes believing it, five minutes envisioning it, and start to expect it. Watch for the opportunity to show up that will allow it to happen. Six hours from right now, check in with yourself and see if this thought became reality. Be honest with yourself. Is this exactly what you had hoped would show up? If it is not, notice what's different. If it is, notice that it is what you asked for. This is the challenge: at the end of that time, I want you to ask yourself what worked and what didn't work. What did I get, and what didn't I get? Did you chose a bigger belief for the first time, a bigger thought to try and create into reality. Or did you chose a smaller thought to create in reality, and you got everything you asked for?

If you truly want your life to GET EASY, then use the Future Formula™, do the exercises, and take action. That's the only way it happens!

In chapter 2 we will be talking about the power and impact that *choice* has in our life, that we are always free to choose. We do have free will and we have free choice. That's the opportunity we have for implementing any of the principles in this book. In future chapters we'll talk about other concepts which will relate back to this idea of your thoughts becoming a reality. We will talk about the speed with which reality shows up. And we will talk about its relationship to beliefs without doubt.

Chapter 2

FREE WILL MEANS WE GET TO CHOOSE

"Two roads diverged in the woods and I, I took the road less traveled by, and that has made all the difference." —Robert Frost, 1910

This chapter, and indeed this whole book, is about the choices we make and the roads we go down. As individuals, we are constantly asked to make choices that will affect our future and the futures of many of the people around us. You are already making those choices, and as you will see, those choices will shape who you become.

This principle simply states that *we all have free will.*

By that I mean that we are all the ones who get to make the choices for our own life. Our life is the result of the choices that we make. If we don't like our life, we can only blame ourselves for the choices that we have made up till now. We are, in this moment, the result of all the choices that have been made for us, or by us up to this point. We either allow change to happen to us, or we are proactive and make the choices for ourselves.

Your Path Is Always Dividing

When we are very small children, all of our choices are made for us—when we eat, when we get changed, when we get picked up, when we get held. We have very, very few choices that we get to make on our own when we are still infants. The more we grow, the more choice we can implement in our own lives and the more choices we make for ourselves. Many people, however, don't like to take responsibility for their own choices. There are many people who don't want the responsibility of answering questions like "What if I do it wrong? What if I choose the wrong thing?"

The principle of free will and the principle of choice are, for some people, one of the very hardest principles to grasp. There are many areas of our lives in which we have taken responsibility and exercised our free will, but there are also many areas of our lives were we have not. There may be areas of our lives where we haven't wanted to, or haven't felt confident in making our own choices, and so we've delegated those choices to someone else in our life. This may be a husband or wife, or even an attorney. It may be a financial planner or tax consultant or friend. It could be a brother or sister, or anybody else in our life.

This is an insidious habit! It's a habit that sneaks up on us, and we may not realize that we have given away a responsibility. It may be more comfortable for someone else to be responsible for the choices of our life. We then have someone we can blame. We can say "It's not my fault, I didn't vote for him" or "It's not my fault, I didn't dent the car." Or "It's not my fault, I didn't pick this place to live." And so, in case after case, we give over our choices to other people. We then get to feel as though we have an independence of the responsibility, when in fact the bottom line is—and this is a key principle–we are responsible for our own lives.

We are responsible for the choices that are made, *whether we are active in those choices, or whether those choices are made by somebody else for us.*

Today You Are The Result Of Your Past Choices

One of the defining features of the transition from being a juvenile to that of adulthood is that when we cross into adulthood it is assumed that we are at that point of taking responsibility for all of our choices. It is at that moment in many people's lives when we leave home for the first time. When we go to college, or when we get our first apartment away from our parents we are saying, in effect, "I'm taking responsibility now in all the bigger things of my life not just the small things. Not just how I dress, or what I eat for breakfast, but where I live, what I do for a living, who I associate with, and what I envision and dream and believe for myself is possible." When we make these choices, the bigger choices in life, and we take responsibility for them, we are said to have "grown up". We are said to be "mature". We are crossing a threshold, the doorway that most of us never go back through. Actually, this is a series of doorways, a series of moments, when we are asked to make choices in different areas of our lives.

Some of the choices that we avoid making are things to do with life and death. Many people put off those choices and their responsibility in this area, until at a very late age they're forced to make those choices. Many people are forced to make very difficult choices based on circumstance. For instance, they couldn't send their children to college because of insufficient income, or they couldn't make their house payments, or medical emergencies arose in their family and they hadn't made a choice to put away money for those situations. Often something happens that make the choice for them and they lose the opportunity to make their own choices.

Please understand what I mean by events in time making those choices. If we are not proactive in making a choice, a choice is automatically made.

A small example would be if we think, "I would love to take a vacation this Christmas and go to Maui and spend a week in Hawaii." We have two ways of approaching that choice. We can be proactive and make a decision by scheduling the time off from work and booking flights and a hotel room. Those would be proactive choices; taking responsibility for making the trip happen. The other alternative is not to do anything and allow the choices be made for us. If we don't book the room, don't buy the plane tickets, we don't arrange time off from work, then pretty soon the choices are made for us. They are made by the passage of time and the occurrence of other events caused by the choices of other people. We then get to say, "Oh, I just didn't get it planned, so it didn't happen," and we don't go to Hawaii.

People are often reluctant to make choices. This is a huge, huge concept! **People are often reluctant to make choices because it involves change**. People resist change! It is much safer to stay where we are than it is to move. At least that's our perception. We know where we are, but we don't know where we're moving to. We know what we have in the moment, but we don't know what the new choice will create for us. We know what our finances look like with this job even though our paycheck may not be enough, but we don't know what our paycheck will be if we quit and try to get a new job. We can imagine. We can believe. We can have a thought or expectation. But there is a lot of fear associated with change from where we are now to something new!

Often people will tell me "I don't like my job, but it's my job, and I know how to do it. You know what I mean—I don't like my situation, but it's my situation." In other words, there is a certain safety in staying where we are. We have an internal resistance that makes it hard for us to take major steps of change. And yet, we also know that people who are willing to embrace change, to examine things with a willingness to change, are the people who actually create huge change in their world and the world around them. In fact, the world in general changes as people make individual changes.

People who are willing to embrace big ideas and make radical changes are the ones who actually get things done. They are the inventors, the leaders, the ones who seem to be what we call "Type-A personalities". They're very active, very willing to step out there and take a risk. So that's another thing we have to look at; the comfort of not changing as opposed to the risk of changing. What is your risk tolerance for change?

Making Choices Means That You Are Taking The Responsibility

It's important to remember that responsibility goes hand in hand with the choices you make. It's true that you get to make the choice and get to be the creator of your own life, but at the same time you also have to take responsibility for the effect and the result of those choices.

So free will has a little bit of a price tag. The Bible talks about free will and our power of choice, as do many other religions. When we talk about those powers of choice and free will what we are really saying is that God is letting us have some control over our own destiny, of our own lives and futures, and that it's not preordained. This is a principle that a lot of people shy away from. A lot of people can have the sort of vision that we talked about in Chapter 1; they can have a belief or a vision for themselves, and they can actually expect things to happen for themselves, and yet they will still not make the choice. They will not act on their own free will. Instead, they will say "If it's God's will, it will happen, or it must have been fate for that to happen or it wasn't destined to happen to me". And yet we all know that we are given free will, and are given the power of choice. It is absolutely up to you to do your part.

The principal of choice has two prongs: one is that if we do choose, we have a responsibility associated with that choice. Secondly, any choice we make will involve change.

What's interesting is that changes are happening to us all the time, regardless of our choice (or failure to choose) to direct them! If you want a voice in the change that is happening around you, then you have to realize that "I'm in charge of making the choices of my life and I'm willing to take responsibility for it in order to move forward and create the dream, the vision, that I expect to have happen to me. I have to be willing to grasp the power of free will and choose for myself and be willing to change from my present position."

Why We Resist Change, The Price Tag Of Free Will

The principle sounds so simple. It sounds as if it ought to be very easy and not even a challenge. But I'm here to tell you that this principle is one of the most challenging principles of all.

You have the power of free will and the power to choose your own life! You also have the power of choice over other people's lives at times. But in such cases it's always given to us temporarily, and it's always our responsibility to give the power of choice back to the individual as soon as possible. For example, as you are raising your children, it's imperative that you give your children the power to make small choices in their lives so that they can learn to take responsibility. That is how they learn to be good stewards over the choices they make in choosing their life path. Choice is something that should be taught by our parents, our teachers, and the people around us as we grow up.

So, sometimes we have a responsibility for other people's choices when they're young or very old, or when they're infirm, or have a serious health issue. Again, it is always our responsibility to give the power to exercise free will back to the person who owns it as soon as possible.

Okay, so that was the explanation of the principle that we all have free will. Now let's talk a little bit about the challenge that I want to put out to you associated with the principle of free will and having choices in our lives. This is that we get to choose our own destiny, our own future, just like we have chosen the past that delivered us to this moment.

The first step in taking on any new challenge is to understand where we are now. We are not challenging ourselves and growing if we follow the same path we've taken many, many times before. On the other hand, we don't want to challenge ourselves with something that is such a huge step from where we are now that we can't do it. So the challenge for you is going to be individual just like every chapter in this book. You'll have to find the challenge that is right for you and the level of change that's appropriate as your next step. Some people can take large steps. Other people are not used to taking any steps at all and therefore have to take very small steps at first. The first step is to determine where you are now. Do you make your own choices? Have you been exercising free will to any real extent? One way to measure it is to honestly ask yourself if you are a responsible person. Have you taken responsibility? If you have taken on responsibility in many areas of your life, then I'm sure you have taken the responsibility for your choices and the results of those actions.

Notice what responsibilities you have right now. Then notice what choices created those responsibilities. Where did you exercise free will in your choice? As you ask yourself these questions you may notice that you do not make your own choices. You may notice that you have not taken responsibility, but instead delegated that responsibility to somebody else.

EXERCISE:
Tracking your responsibilities, notice, then choose

The first request I have is for you to carry a piece of paper and for two or three days start writing down all the areas in which you have responsibility. Here's a very, very simple and obvious one: do you drive? Have you taken the time, the energy, the responsibility of getting your drivers license? For most of you the answer is probably yes. For some of you, it may not be yes. You're letting somebody else make your choices in terms of the time it takes to go places, including how you get there, bus schedules, and more. You have allowed yourself to be subject to someone else's choices. You're letting somebody else take that responsibility for getting you from place to place. You are not taking control in that area of your life.

None of us have control over every aspect of our life. I'm not suggesting that you have to be responsible for every single action. But ultimately, you are responsible. As Robert Kiyosaki has said in his books, "Make no mistake, the business you are in is the business of you. You are your own business." You are the one who is ultimately responsible for you. Even if you work for somebody else as an employee, you are still responsible for yourself. You may feel that you've given over responsibility for your welfare somewhat, given over some of the choices about how your life is structured. You have surrendered some free will about what happens between those 9-to-5 hours. If we give that over to somebody else, we sometimes believe that we are working for them. But ultimately that's just a choice we're making—working for them in order to support ourselves, and that is how we've chosen to do it. In the end, we are really always responsible for ourselves.

Remember, *the first step is simply to notice* and start writing down all the places that you make choices and take responsibility. You are standing here today as a result of the choices you have made in the past up to this moment. What have you chosen in the past?

Who Are You Today Is A Result Of Your Past Choices!

When you see good results, notice what kind of good choices you made. By good choices I mean choices that really serve you and support your values. Choices that really move you forward in life. These positive choices are really going to serve you in the long run and bring you to those life dreams and goals that you have for yourself.

EXERCISE:
Taking responsibility consciously

Now is the time to start taking responsibility!

Pull out a sheet of paper. Start writing down as many things as you can think of right now, and write more down as they come to you during the day or this evening, or when they wake you up in the middle of the night. Within a day or two you will have noticed all the places where you are making choices for yourself and exercising your own free will.

In that process, as I stated a moment ago, you will also start to notice where you didn't make conscious choices. Places where you haven't exercised free will and where you haven't taken responsibility. Some of those you may choose to leave just the way they are. In other cases you may choose to make a different choice, to exercise your free will in one more area of your life. Remember that each of us is ultimately responsible for our own life and what we have created.

The second step in this process is to ask yourself, "What will I now choose for myself that I haven't before?"

It may be a very small step. Maybe you will choose to start being responsible about how you eat. I am not suggesting that this is a small step. For many of us that is a very, *very* large step. It is an intimate emotional issue, and it may be very difficult to take responsibility for how you eat. Perhaps a beginning choice is to take responsibility in a smaller area and take a different step, for instance; "I will clean my desk, and I will keep it neat and orderly." Now for some of us again, that is not a small step. For some of us that is a very major step. It may go against a lifelong habit of lack of organization. Okay, the area you may choose to take responsibility in today may be as simple as mowing the lawn or washing your car if that is something you have left up to somebody else, or to events and circumstance. Have you waited for the world to make those choices for you?

You have choices on the table in front of you right this moment. Take responsibility! A lot of people will want to say; "Well, why would I want to take responsibility for all these things? Why wouldn't I just let somebody else carry the responsibility, and shoulder that load for me? Let them help me go through life without having to carry all that responsibility." After all, that's how it is when we are children. Our parents shoulder the responsibility for what happens to us, when we're young they make the choices for us. We don't have free will in many areas of our life. But as adults, ultimately we have to hold ourselves responsible for the choices we have made up to this point.

Please take responsibility. Take responsibility in areas of your life where you haven't already done so. Notice where you haven't taken responsibility and start making choices for your future.

Here are the benefits: choosing will put you in the driver's seat, and you will have more control over your life in every way. If you combine the principle from chapter 1 that says *"your thoughts create your reality"* with taking responsibility for your own choices, knowing that you have free will, you will soon be able to direct the path of your life. You'll start noticing that you are accomplishing those things that have only been dreams and goals for many, many years.

KEY:

As you take responsibility and control, there is another side benefit. **Control reduces stress!** That's a huge benefit. People who are under stress, are feeling stress because they're actually out of control.

EXAMPLE:

Recently I was coaching a client that was in total overwhelm with multiple deadlines for work and lots of other demands on their time from family and friends. Some of you can probably relate? They were VERY busy but were unable to be productive due to the level of stress that caused them to lack the focus to complete even the simple things. I asked them to do just one of 3 things: Either clean off their desk, clean up the kitchen, or simply make the bed. When they spoke to me later they told me that the simple task that I had them complete affirmed their ability to be in control and complete tasks. They were then able to go on to larger and larger tasks and become productive again. Their stress was dramatically reduced by simply controlling a very small task. Remember that *stress is always about lack of control...* go control something!

If you're feeling stressed out simply make a plan for your future, and it will reduce the stress. Making a plan means that you're thinking about what *you're* going to do. It is the act of you taking control, choosing to exercise your free will and take responsibility for something. You then just have to follow your plan and follow through with your choices. When you've made plans your stress level will drop immediately. The stress in a situation will go away when you take control, and you take control by making choices. You get to choose. Whenever you're feeling stressed it's a good indicator that you haven't taken control in some area of your life, That there is something out of control and you need to make some choices.

You only need to choose what you want for yourself, create a plan, and begin to execute it, and your stress will be lessened considerably. Then simply follow the plan!

The challenge in this chapter is to notice where you're making choices and where you're not making choices. Identify where you want to make choices. Notice where you're being stressed and that may be the target point for where you want to make some choices. Make choices and take the first steps and you will see the stress level drop immediately. See if it doesn't give you a sense of control in your life. Making conscious choices will put you back in the driver seat of your own life! Remember that we are responsible for ourselves. You are responsible for you. No matter who we think we work for, we work for ourselves. You work for you! And by work I don't mean your 9-to-5 job, I mean you work for your own benefit, your own welfare, and your own growth.

Become Responsible And Make Your Own Choices!

Let me leave you with one final thought . This chapter has been all about exercising free will, making your own choices, and taking responsibility. It's a simple and natural principle. People sometimes overlook it because it's *too* simple.

The inquiry I leave you with for this chapter is to ask yourself: what am I choosing?

Please ask yourself this right this moment: what am I choosing? You are constantly making choices. You're driving to work in a certain direction, you're getting dressed a certain way. What are the implications? Where am I choosing? What am I choosing? And the larger question underneath that you should spend time journaling or meditating on is: how do my choices serve me?

Please go onto the next chapter only after you've spent some time doing these exercises. This idea of free will and the power of your choices is the key to much of the rest of this book. Enjoy the process. Do the work, and challenge yourself.

Chapter 3

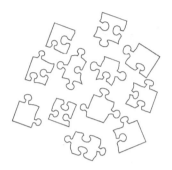

TRUE
FULFILLMENT
COMES FROM A
LIFE OF PURPOSE

The third principle is that if you live a life of purpose—a life *on* purpose, you might say—that is where you will find your true fulfillment, happiness and reward. That's where satisfaction lies for you.

It's almost like the notion that each person has one true love. Each person has one true purpose. There is a true purpose for you, at least in this moment. That purpose may be a lifetime purpose, or it may shift many times for you, but in the moment there is only one true purpose, and that's where you will find reward, satisfaction, and contentment. When you find that, you will be able to be there knowing that that's where you were supposed to be, doing what you're supposed to be doing, and that's moving you forward on your spiritual journey in this life.

Life Purpose Comes From Your Spiritual Core

Please don't read anything into that except what I said. Finding your life purpose is one of the keys to fulfillment because it comes from your spiritual core self.

So, if finding our true purpose and living it is where our reward is, then the first thing that gets in the way of that for most people is knowing "what is my true purpose?".

People always tell me: "I could do anything if I only knew what it was." Many people have that problem with their true purpose. They don't have any idea what their true purpose is, and they feel as if they're stumbling around most of their lives trying to identify it. That's where the true challenge comes in!

Another challenge in finding your true purpose is knowing when you've really found it. Really believing it and accepting that it is your true purpose.

The third problem that people have in living their true purpose is that other things get in the way. Specifically, money–the challenge to make an income, to make a living, to provide for our families, sometimes gets in the way of our true purpose. Sometimes our family themselves get in the way of our true purpose. True purpose is sometimes held in check by all of the challenges of the world, all the things going on in our lives. Perhaps it's personal health issues, perhaps it's relationships, or finance, or mental strength. Perhaps our one true purpose seems like too big a challenge for us. But I'm here to tell you that these things are all part of the true life purpose challenge. Finding your true purpose in order to find fulfillment in life is one of the greatest challenges that we have. Many people live their entire life feeling like they never found their true purpose. They stumble along or feel that they are struggling because their true purpose is this elusive thing that is very very hard to identify. Don't let that be you!

I'm going to give you a few steps to enable you to identify your true purpose. The first step is to go back to chapter 1. The principle that I challenged you with in that chapter was that our thoughts create our reality. What is the reality we are looking for in this chapter? The reality we're looking for is that we identify, accept, and step into living a life of purpose—our own individual highest purpose. We know that's where fulfillment, reward, satisfaction, and contentment will be found. We also know that's what moves us ahead spiritually. Chapter 1 tells us that we must first set a goal for what we want. We must then believe it is possible for us.

Is it possible for you to find your true purpose? Absolutely! Many people do. Many people accept that they have a true purpose and thereby start living a life of purpose. Secondly, can you imagine your true purpose? Can you imagine yourself living a purposeful life? Can you imagine yourself being satisfied? Being fulfilled? Feeling that sense of fulfillment that you're living a life with a calling? If you can, then absolutely you can have it! If you believe it, and visualize it, then you will begin to expect it.

But instead of simply expecting in this case, I want you to *accept*. No, I'm not asking you to settle for what you already have, but to accept that you are in the right position right now, and that your life purpose will show itself to you as you start expecting it to. Simply accept that what you have and what's showing up in your life is your purpose. Because as soon as you accept that that is your purpose and start living that way, living a purposeful life, the things you are doing will bring you fulfillment, happiness, reward, satisfaction, closer to your spirit of truth and spiritual growth. As soon as you start believing that and accepting it, it will happen for you. It shows up. Your thoughts will have created your reality once more. Much of this simply boils down to acceptance.

I know this sounds contradictory and I am going to try to explain how both your acceptance, and your creativity can work together. It is important to first accept your current situation and circumstance rather than deny or fight against it. When you acknowledge that it is part of who you are now, it will then be easier to build on that to become the more complete person you want to be.

When we're living a purposeful life, what are we looking for? Again, we are looking for fulfillment, we are looking for reward, satisfaction, contentment, and something that draws us closer to our spiritual selves. Those qualities create spiritual growth, and grow the true you. We're also looking for something that's meaningful. Now, what do I mean by that? A meaningful life makes us all feel that we are making a difference. When we say "I'd like to do something that has some purpose," what we're really talking about is something that has some positive impact on other people. That positive difference that is flowing from our actions gives a reason for our lives.

"How do I know"

KEY:

Accept this principle before reading further. In your center, in the spirit and soul part of you that inhabits your body, you know your true life purpose. You know what you came into this life to accomplish. You chose it! You chose your body. You chose your situation. So If you chose your body and situation, then it follows that in your heart, in the deepest core of your being, you know your true life purpose.

Your obligation at this point, and the challenge I am offering you, is to find that life purpose and start living it.

I want to stop for just a moment. I want to challenge one more piece, and this is probably the biggest piece for some people. Many people will say "Well, I know what my true life purpose is, but I can't do it because I don't have enough money. My financial requirements keep me at my job, keep me from living a purposeful life." These are all nothing but excuses. Living a life of purpose isn't necessarily something you drop everything to do. You don't have to leave your family or quit your job. You don't have to join the Peace Corps and live in Africa helping people build huts or put in water systems. That may or may not be your true life purpose, but if it is and you identify that as your true purpose, then there will also be an opportunity that will allow you to live your true purpose. Remember we talked about the "Future Formula" in chapter one, about beliefs, visualization, expectation, and opportunity.

There Will Always Be Opportunities For You To Live A Purposeful Life!

They may be challenging opportunities, they may be very difficult. They may be something you've chosen for yourself that other people could not accomplish. They may be things, specifically that you and you alone are capable of doing.

This is a process of identifying *your* true purpose, not somebody else's. Living a life of purpose may not be easy, it may not be without challenge, but it will be very rewarding!

When I talk about *Life Purpose*, I am not saying the you have one purpose. I am saying that you have one current *Life Purpose* and as you fulfill that purpose, your next purpose will show up. Through your lifetime you may have many different purposes that enable you to continue to evolve while contributing to others in the process.

Start Noticing And Learn To Question Yourself

I want you to take a moment right now to simply be aware, start noticing, and start asking yourself this simple question: what is my life purpose?

The next step is to notice what shows up in the form of an answer. Listen to your inner voice. When you say: what is my life purpose? What is the thought that pops in your mind? Answer that thought. Learn to converse with your higher self, or inner self, or even your inner critic. Learn to access your inner self to identify your true purpose. Be willing to go there. Accept what shows up. It may be very, very simple—as simple as accepting that "acceptance" is your life purpose. Learning to be accepting of other people in other situations, and accepting of your own situation.

Identify What Is Your Life Purpose And
Accept What Shows Up. You Cannot Be Wrong!

If you are not clearly on target, you're going to be centered and re-centered toward your target or life purpose. This will happen as long as you continue to notice and to seek your life purpose, and are willing to change. It's as if you are a marksman shooting an arrow toward a target, and you are standing many yards away from the target. You're shooting toward the target, and the arrows are going roughly the right direction. As long as the arrows are flying, an arrow will eventually find its mark. Many people never shoot the first arrow. Many people never asked the question "What is my purpose? What am I on this earth for? What am I intended to be doing?"

It's very, very difficult for many people to identify their life purpose. Sometimes we want to believe that our life purpose is saving a species, or saving mankind from nuclear holocaust, or some other huge thing that will impact millions of people. But sometimes our life purpose is about developing our own strengths, our own internal growth. In this book one of the themes is that you work on you. You work on *you*! Very simple! Your life purpose may be as simple as learning to accept yourself, to let go of anger and accept other people, or learning to give freely and be charitable. Listen up—these are just as important as saving the world from nuclear holocaust!

Finding your true life purpose and acting in a purposeful way in this life is not only fulfilling, rewarding, and satisfying. It also brings you contentment as you draw closer to your spiritual core and spiritual self. Finding your life purpose moves you forward in your spirit, soul and body. You lead by example! Often the greatest leaders, the people who create the greatest change, are not people who go out and do something dramatic. They're not always great inventors. But they're almost always people who lead by example. They're people who have done the work on themselves. That may be what your life purpose is about. I don't know. Only you know! If you ask yourself, and listen for the answer, the answer is there.

Please ask yourself right now. The question again is; What is my life purpose? What am I intended to be doing?

Pretend that you have the answers

If you don't have any answers show up, pretend. That's right pretend! When we pretend, we take the pressure for the result off of ourselves. So ask yourself again, what is my true life purpose? Pretend that whatever shows up is the right answer. It doesn't matter because it doesn't have to be your final answer, it's just pretend. Pretend this is something that shows up for you. Remember that this answer is just for fun. It is just pretend anyway! What is my true life purpose? Be silent for a moment. Give yourself time for the answer to float to the surface. Things don't always pop into our minds instantly but if you continue to ask, your life purpose will be revealed from your spirit.

EXERCISE:
Learn to talk and listen to yourself

If you've never spoken with yourself and given yourself permission for those thoughts to come out, an excellent tool is to journal. A journal simply means that you take the time to write, a little time each day, every other day, whatever is appropriate for you and ask yourself a question. In this case at the top of the page, write: *What is my life purpose?* Then start writing whatever thoughts pop into your mind. Write until you filled up one page. Don't try to edit it. Do not try to control your thoughts. When you're finished, set it aside and forget about it for the rest of the day. Tomorrow spend a few minutes and do the same thing again. The best time for you may be in the morning, or in the evening before you go to bed. Whatever time you choose, try to be consistent. Do that every day for a week and you'll notice a pattern of thought showing up. That is your spirit and soul trying to speak through your thoughts, trying to come out and make sense for you on a physical level. Your inner knowledge from your spirit and soul will begin to clarify your conscious physical thoughts. Listen to that. Go back and read what you've written in your journal at the end of the week, or maybe even at the end of the month. A theme will show up. A life purpose will come out if that's what you're seeking. "Seek and you shall find," remember? What are you seeking? If you're seeking your life purpose, your true life purpose will show up.

I want to make some distinctions between life purpose and what your skills are, or what you're good at. A lot of people find their best jobs based on competency tests or aptitude tests to find out what they're very good at. That doesn't necessarily even mean that you enjoy it. You may be exceptionally good with numbers, but you might hate being an accountant or CPA, working in an office all day. So your skills do not necessarily define your purpose. They may be part of your life purpose, or you may be very talented in some area, and you may have some purpose associated with that, but very often skills have nothing to do with your true life purpose. Remember, life purpose is the goal that's going to move you forward spiritually, and move you on your path doing whatever you're supposed to be doing on this Earth at this time. Conversely, if you have no idea what your true life purpose is, I often find that giving back what you have been given is a great place to start finding fulfillment and will often uncover your true life purpose. Often sharing your gifts and talents with others leads to rewarding and purposeful opportunities. You will start to recognize it as you do your part and take action. It's going to be the piece of your life that's really rewarding for you, that feels really good, that has your juices running first thing in the morning and gets you out of bed. You know exactly what I mean!

Life purpose is also not necessarily what your friends tell you that you should be doing. But sometimes it's exactly that. Sometimes your friends can see something in you that you can't see. But it is not necessarily the case. Just because they say "Oh, Jimmy, you ought to be doing this, you'd be perfect for it," doesn't mean you should follow their advice. Sometimes it's worth listening to those comments to see if they're indicators that are pointing you toward your true life purpose. But always question them. Hold them up against the question of your true life purpose. Only you know your true life purpose!

You Have To Seek And Look If You Want To Find

There are always indicators and signs as well as opportunities for us to jump into our true life purpose. Maybe you've been missing them, not seeing them or not recognizing them. Maybe you're not certain you have found your true life purpose. Many people are challenged to know that they have found their true life purpose. Remember my telling you at the beginning of this chapter, the primary indicator of life purpose is that it's going to be something that's very fulfilling, rewarding, and will bring you peace and contentment. If you're not experiencing those things, then you probably have not found your true life purpose, and you need to keep looking.

Our life purpose is found only when we are looking, when we are seeking. In the bonus chapters I'll talk about movement and how movement creates opportunities. But one of the things I want to mention to you right now is that if things seem to be taken away from you all the time, opportunities don't turn out to be anything, or you keep going down a lot of what seem to be *blind tunnels*, then consider these indicators.

If you think you've found life purpose and it turns out that is not what you thought it would be, or opportunity knocks and then you answer the door but there's nobody there, then you are being told that you have not found your true life purpose.

If that's the case, often what is happening is that you're going through a learning series that is setting you up for your life purpose to be revealed to you and giving you small bits of information and skills. If you look back on each of these opportunities that didn't work out, you'll realize that in each case some little skill was picked up, some relationship made, or something was learned. You read something, you connected with somebody, or put yourself in a situation, and got some tools or some piece that you're going to be able to use in the future.

Another thing to remember is that not everything is right for you. And until you find that right thing, you maybe trying so hard that you're finding things that are not right for you.

Often when that happens, God or the universe, or providence, or whatever you choose to call it, takes those things away from us if they're not right. A quick example: have you ever been in a position of looking for a job? Often you get rejected from job interviews for the *perfect job* (or you don't even get the interview), only to find a much, much better job later on. This sort of thing is very common but actually helps us in finding our true purpose. Don't be discouraged if you have a few doors shut, or a few doors opened with nothing on the other side. Its part of your search, part of your process.

In some ways people are like a piece of property. You may have heard realtors say, "That property is not meeting its highest and best use". Each property has its ideal use or purpose. That means that you would not want to put a horse pasture in a downtown location. You wouldn't want to put a high-rise building out in the country. They would never flourish and thrive. It's very much the same with finding true life purpose. A lot of times it involves trying different things on, and seeing what really is a fit for you. Seeing what is your highest and best use. There are natural laws of attraction and growth which we'll talk about in later chapters. These laws of attraction draw us toward what's going to be rewarding for us and what is going to move us ahead and allow us to grow spiritually. There is a natural tendency for this to happen. Events will occur, opportunities will show up, and people will come into our lives to lead us toward our perfect life purpose.

Our job as individuals on this Earth who really want to find their true life purpose, is just to notice. Be aware. Pay attention and see what shows up in your life. If you start noticing all the opportunities and all the things that are showing up in your life as you are seeking your true life purpose, you will find it.

As a coach, I often work with clients to **create a resource list**. A resource list is a list of all the people you can call on, not just friends and acquaintances, but people with skills and knowledge in certain areas. Information sources such as books and websites can also go on your resource list. It includes tools, skills, and aptitudes that you have, and all the things that you can call on to move forward or to get a job done. When my clients created their resource list, we noticed that often those resources are a direct result of destiny, or God's hand intervening to bring their life purpose and life work to them. There is an attraction between us and our true life's work like the force of gravity that pulls us together. When we're not sabotaging that attraction or getting in the way of it, we are going to find fulfillment and success there.

Don't put this book down until you have asked yourself "What is my true life purpose?" Listen, accept, and trust the answer. An answer will show up for you. Everybody has a life purpose. You have a life purpose, beyond any doubt. Find out what it is! Life can be fulfilling, rewarding, and satisfying. Your true life purpose will move you forward in your spiritual life, your intellectual life, and your physical life.

LIFE PURPOSE EXERCISE:

Journal daily for 7+ days asking the simple question "what is my life purpose". Don't edit your answers or even think about the spelling or grammar. The idea is to let the ideas and responses spill freely out of you onto the paper. After a week look at all the pages and circle the statements that are the same or similar. What are you trying to tell yourself? What is a question that you need to ask yourself for the following week to get more clarity? Continue with this process and purpose will unfold from you to you.

Powerful Questions: *Trust the first answer that shows up and then go deeper…*

1. What are the special gifts or talents that you have been given?
2. What can you do to share those gifts? With whom? When?
3. How do you feel when you are "Fulfilled"?
4. When have you had that feeling of fulfillment ? Tell me about it, write it down.
5. What should you start doing today, right now, to start a life of purpose?

Chapter 4

WE ARE SPIRIT, MIND AND BODY IN THAT ORDER

T his principle simply says that we are body, mind, and spirit, but in reverse order. In other words *we are spirit, mind, and body,* and by mind, I mean our intellect or soul. That is our true nature. That is the most important part of who and what we are. Our body is actually just a vessel that holds us for this lifetime in the physical world.

Getting The Order Correct

Without getting into a lot of spiritual argument that would cause you to put this book down or skip over this chapter, I want to toss out a few ideas. My premise is that we are spirit, mind, and body, in that order. And if you pay attention to that priority it will serve you well. The challenging part for most of us is that most of us have the order backwards. We all experience life through our physical body, and so we put our body first. We put intellect and knowledge second. And finally we put our spiritual self third.

When I talk about your spiritual self, I want to be clear that I am *not* speaking about religion. This has nothing to do with religion. Religion is man's attempt to control spiritual beliefs, and to structure it, and to bring it to the people. I am talking about personal relationship with your spiritual self, God within you, the energy within you that drives you. I am speaking about that spiritual essence that actually chose the life that you are living now, that chose the body you live in and the family you came into. This spiritual core being is going to go on beyond this body—beyond many bodies, if you believe in multiple lives. I'm speaking about the part that is actually made in God's likeness—the part that is all-knowing as God is, that has God dwelling within it and cannot be separated from God. That is our spiritual core, our spiritual self. When we're speaking with our spiritual self, or higher self, we are communicating and listening more carefully to the spiritual side of ourselves. That spiritual side is always ever present with us. We are never within only our body and mind and without our spirit. We are never in our body without our mind. Some people might say, "well, I did it without thinking", but you still have your spirit and soul residing within your body.

So how does that challenge us?

KEY:

The challenge is to simply reverse the worldly order. Reverse the body, mind and spirit order and live a life based on principles, and make decisions based on the fact that we are spirit, mind, and body in that order!

So what does that mean? This is going to mean that you make decisions based not on "I'm hungry, or I want that, or I'm cold, or I'm greedy, or me first and you later." Instead, you're going to start looking at things from a totally different perspective. The perspective I challenge you to shift to is a perspective that holds you as a spiritual being that happens to live in a physical body. If that is the case, what would you do? What actions would you take, what would you say to people, how would you show up differently in this world? I suspect for most of us, if we truly embrace this principle, our lives would be radically different. I suspect we would see other people in a totally different light. And by that I mean, if you are spirit, mind and body, you'll start thinking about the answers to questions like "Who am I? Who is he? Who is she? Who is my spouse? Who are my children? What's the nature of the relationship I have with them?" For those of you who believe in multiple lives, what is the relationship you had before? What is it that you chose to come into this life to do? What's your true mission on Earth or life purpose? If you accept it as true, this principle raises many, many questions.

Our True Life Purpose

We spoke in earlier chapters about finding our true purpose. Our true purpose is what we came into this life to do. Pursuing our true purpose will develop our spirit and soul, that true permanent essence of who we are. It causes that part of us be elevated and moved forward. Most of the time we're focused on elevating our physical bodies, and our stature among our peers. We are concerned with who we are in the world, what people think of us, and what we can physically achieve. You and I, like most of the people in the world, focus almost all of our time, energy, and money in creating a personal physical image.

Most of us focus completely on who we are in the world, and how we show up in the world. Our physical bodies, our appearance, our prestige, and our egos get in the way of spiritual considerations. Our egos drive us to believe that our physical self and how others perceive us is the most important piece of our lives. The important piece is actually how God sees us, and how the spiritual being in each of us sees each other and sees ourselves. That spiritual part of us must be inside laughing at the things we do in the physical realm, because so much of what we do does not serve the spiritual or intellectual soul. It's as if we chose to come into this world and take a physical form, a physical body, so that we can learn lessons, but in the process we go through the stupid tunnel. The stupid tunnel leads from the spiritual world to the physical world. We actually unlearn what our spirit and soul know. Our connection to God and our spiritual selves is lost. We come into this world with fear of falling, and fear of loud noises, and that's it. We are born with only a very few instinctive things and a few genetic things, and everything else we have to learn or relearn. What this chapter really is all about is relearning the importance of spirit, mind, and body, and to start living a life based on that knowledge.

> # KEY:
>
> The key to your life is not what you know, it's not even what you do, it is who you are at your spiritual core. It is taking actions and doing things from that spiritual center. When you connect with your spiritual higher self, your impact in the world and on the world will be completely different.

If you say to me right now; "Oh, I knew that. I knew I was spirit first, then soul, then body. That makes good sense to me. Right. Now I gotta go, because I'm hungry, and need a bite to eat," you should hear the irony in what you're saying. We pay attention to our physical bodies and are driven by them 99% of the time. We spend very little time focused on our spiritual selves.

How do we focus on our spiritual selves? That's a great question. We focus on our spiritual selves *simply by noticing*.

SINGLE DAILY ACTION EXERCISE:

Just take a moment in the morning, or before you go to bed, or whatever time of day you choose, to stop and simply notice your internal focus. Devote yourself to that simple act one or two times a day. Spend a moment or two to simply notice and reorganize your thoughts, putting spirit first. In coaching we would call it a single daily action. A **single daily action** simply focuses your energy. It is something you agree to do every single day. Take on the single daily action of devoting yourself to notice whether you are acting from spirit first. This single daily action doesn't have to take more than a minute or two, although you can take longer if you wish. As you focus on putting spirit first, you may spend time redirecting the focus of your energy, or meditating, or in prayer. You may spend that time walking. You will know what action is correct for you. Later, you can take that habit of a single daily action and apply it to business, personal, or health issues.

In this specific search for answers your single daily action, whether it is meditation, prayer, or a walk in the park should focus on the question of who you really are. Your spiritual self knows who you really are. I'm not giving you any new information. A powerful question that you can ask yourself is "Who am I really? Who am I in my spirit? Who am I at my core?" Have a conversation with your higher self. If you have never done it before it can be both scary and challenging, because the higher self is there and ready to speak back to you and your thoughts. Most of us never take the time to listen, or even to ask the questions, because we're not ready to hear the answers and learn. Most of us are not in the habit of learning and most of us do not know how to trust that inner voice, or trust that higher self. This is a practice and habit you can develop like many other things. **The ability to communicate with your Spiritual Self is something that you can develop so that when you ask the question you get a very clear and immediate response.** The answer is simply a thought that pops into your mind in response to your taking the time to ask the question. With practice you learn to trust those thoughts. And you learn to tap into that part of you which is your higher spiritual self.

Confusion With Internal Communication

Sometimes, in the beginning, you'll have confusion, doubts and anxieties about who is talking to you because sometimes the responses are obviously not spiritual, not godly, not even intellectual. Some of those thoughts that bounce back to you are your Ego (we'll discuss the Ego in Chapter 7). As you practice this process you'll learn to discern those thoughts which are from your higher spiritual self and those which are coming from old tapes from your past experiences in your life. You will develop the ability to speak with your higher spiritual self in a powerful way and get the spirit filled answers to the questions that you have. When you start shifting your focus to living a spirit-based life as opposed to an earthly-based life, there will be a powerful impact. You will have the support and the power of God, and the entire spiritual world at your fingertips. You will have spiritual power instead of just worldly power. That will be your new perspective. You know what I'm saying? You will know the difference. Spiritual power is the power of God in the heavens and with that power and knowledge miracles can happen. The worldly power is "I've gone to college, I have 3 degrees, and am well respected in my profession, and so you'd better listen to me." Which would you rather have? One is available to you for free and the other is a long and expensive process of education. One is permanent and goes with you throughout all time, even after death. The other is something you have to develop over a lifetime and then instantly lose when pass away. I'm not saying that we lose the intellect that we developed in the knowledge that we learned. I believe that part goes with us in our soul. That's what our soul is; it's our intellect and our decision-making processes and all the combined intelligence part of us. But, I don't think that knowledge has the importance in the spiritual world that it does on Earth. I don't think God or our higher self cares that so-and-so has a doctorate in whatever. I don't think it's important because our spirit is all knowing. What *is* important is the development of our spiritual selves, and how we interact with our fellow spirits to nurture, and honor, and support each other. Those are the things that we're going to take with us, and we're going to recognize those people who develop this side of themselves as powerful people. The powerful people are the ones that honor their spiritual side first, and then their soul, and then their body. And, they act on this Earth from that perspective.

At this point you may be saying to yourself, "It sounds as if you're asking me to be like Gandhi and give up everything in this world and to live a life of poverty or to go become a monk and live on a mountaintop in Tibet." That's not at all what I'm asking. What I'm saying is: if you go off and live in a mountaintop in Tibet, great! Good for you, if that's what you're truly called to do by your spirit and soul. But if you truly want to have an impact on yourself and on the world, live the spirit filled life starting from your current situation.

> ## KEY:
> It is not an accident that you are where you are at this moment. Live in your current situation, and grow from there.

I'm not asking you to sell your house and give your money to the church or anything like that. I'm asking you only to spend a moment each day to ask yourself "What am I supposed to be doing?" Go back to your life purpose again from the last chapter. "What is the spirit in me asking me to do?" I'm asking you to take a moment when you're in the middle of a discussion or an argument with somebody and ask yourself "What's the right thing to do or say in this case?" not in order to get your way, but for you to honor the spirit in yourself and the other person that you're in dialogue with. I'm asking that you ask that question in situations when you're making major decisions. I'm asking you to honor the spirit in other people and in your family and your co-workers, and the people that you come across in every walk of your life. Even if it's while pumping gas, grocery shopping, or in the middle of other daily tasks. If we look at other people in that regard and we say: "this is a spiritual being living in this person's body. I don't care if he's an accountant, doctor, PhD, janitor, or manual worker. That person is first a spiritual being!" This allows us to look at other people (and ourselves, too!) in a totally different light. It lets us look at everyone with forgiveness and with compassion. It lets us see who we truly are at our core—who we are inside the body, not just the body.

ARGUMENT EXERCISE:

I want to challenge you to stop yourself in the beginning of the next argument that you get into and take a moment to remember that you, and the person you are arguing with, are both spiritual beings first and foremost. Stop defending your physical position and need to be *right*, let yourself see a bigger picture of who you each are in this world, and then respond from your spirit. What you will find is that as you shift to that perspective, so will the person that you were arguing with. Your higher spiritual self wants to find a solution and resolution but *you* must be willing to notice and shift yourself!

Many of you are unhappy with some aspect of your physical bodies or physical circumstance. As you read this, you're saying "I would never have chosen this body or the circumstance, you got me wrong. This cannot possibly be true. I would not have chosen this. I have freckles. I'm too short. I'm too heavy. I have a stutter. I have a disease. I have no money. I have nobody in my life right now to love me. I hate my job. I have a disability." If you are reading those words and some of them ring true for you, just know that you have chosen that situation and choosing those tough situations is where your learning and life lesson are. This is where you chose to come into this life in order to learn that piece which is next for you. If it seems very difficult, it's only because you are ready for the very difficult. That may be where you're purpose lies. **It is definitely where your spirit wants to grow**. In daily conversation and especially in coaching, we often talk about finding our next level, moving to our next level and growing as people, and moving forward. I'm sure that's a common conversation that you've participated in in the past. We all want to move forward, we all want to grow and develop, and be more than we are currently. We especially want that on the physical plane, for our physical bodies and lives.

The average American has a 76 year life span, and each of us wants to spend those 76 years getting better, stronger, more powerful, and more knowledgeable. And we want the entire world to see that in us. Our ego is asking for these things. I'm not saying that all those things are bad. More power, more money, and more knowledge are all great tools. All those physical things that we can work hard for are tools we can use to be more of who we are in the world. But they are only tools, and tools are morally neutral. If at your core you act unselfishly, and with generosity of spirit, then power and money are tools that will allow you to leave a bigger footprint and do more good. However, if your true nature is bad, or greedy, or selfish, then having those tools of money and power that you've worked for in the physical world will also allow you to become more of who you are. You'll leave a bigger footprint in a negative way.

Most of us will easily accept that we, personally are spirit, mind, and body, but most don't realize that the trilogy also carries over to our communication (we'll talk about that in a future chapter) and every other aspect of our lives. These principles apply to every aspect of your life, even finances and business.

> EXAMPLE:
>
> I am often hired to help someone move their business off a plateau and recently had an experience that illustrates the importance of working on all three aspects of your business. The client that hired me could not identify why their business had stopped growing because they were *doing* all the right things but it clearly was not enough. All that we "do" in our business is the physical or *body* part of the business. When we did a clear assessment of the business looking at all three aspects, it became clear that while the body of the business was being worked on diligently, the mind of the business, which included all the planning, strategy, and communicating those elements to the entire team was very weak. More importantly, the spiritual aspect of the business was lacking altogether. There was no business mission or business purpose that should have flowed as an integrated reflection of the founder, owner and CEO's spiritual beliefs. We shifted our focus, strengthening the mental aspects of the business, and integrating the spiritual aspects as we continued to find the solution to the stymied growth. The response was radically positive as we brought the business back into balance. I have since worked with many other companies to find that integrated balance in the business between spirit, mind, and body.

At the end of this chapter I will offer a short exercise to identify the seven key areas of your life where you need to focus to bring balance of spirit, mind, and body.

Having our focus on the physical world, on money, and our physical bodies is always counterproductive to our true spirit and mind/soul growth and development. Looking first to our spiritual selves always focuses us in a way that supports and builds us up. It is automatically going to move us forward and help us to grow on every level. Some people say: "The reason I work so hard is to make money. If I just had more money, I could be a better person. I wouldn't be so selfish. I wouldn't have to work so hard and be so focused on myself and getting ahead."

KEY:

Your nature without money won't change when you have money. You will just be more of who you are. Money is simply a multiplier.

Take The Challenge To Shift

I want to challenge you right now to start taking that single daily action to focus on your spiritual self. I want you to ask your spiritual self for instruction. I want you to ask "what is the single daily action that I should undertake for at least the next seven days as a trial that's really going to support me and focus me on who I really am, my true spiritual self?" Again, that *single daily action* may be as simple as five minutes of meditation or journaling or prayer, or one of many other things that will help you hold that focus on your true spiritual self. Some of you may choose to carry a tangible reminder, like a string around your finger, to remind you of your true nature.

EXAMPLE:

On my 50th birthday a close friend gave me a small silver cross and I started carrying it in my pocket as a reminder of who I truly am. For me it was the tangible reminder that kept me focused on my higher self, my spiritual self. I carried that cross in my pocket for many years. I rarely showed it to anybody. It wasn't for others, it was only for me. I didn't wear a large cross around my neck, and I don't have any religious symbols on my body because it's not important for the world to know about my focus on my spiritual self, but it is important for me to know. I carried it in my pocket until it almost wore out. It helped me maintain the focus on my Spiritual self. I'm only sharing this with you as an example and not as a specific thing you need to do. You know what you need to do. Your higher self knows what that reminder or single daily action needs to be.

The single daily action or physical reminder will enable you to touch base with your true self at least once every day. The truth is, we need these reminders to be ever present. We don't need them to just alter our decisions occasionally, but to affect our decisions constantly. The silver cross in my pocket was never enough, but it started my habit of thinking. That habit allowed me to make decisions from my higher spiritual self, and it allowed me to see the spiritual side of other people as I focused on the spiritual side of myself.

So, before you read further, I urge you to embrace this idea, try it on, challenge yourself to establish the *single daily action* or find a physical reminder that you can carry with you daily. Ask yourself: "what is that thing for me, the single daily action for me, or physical reminder that's going to keep me focused on who I am as a spiritual being? What will keep me focused on spirit first, then mind, then body?" As your higher self reveals those actions to you, make an agreement with yourself to take a single daily action or to carry the reminder for at least a seven day trial. If it's not effective after seven days, go back to your higher self again and revisit an alternative daily action or physical reminder..

Spirit, Mind, and Body
AWARENESS EXERCISE:

I want you to rate yourself from 1-10 on your attention to spirit, mind, and body in the seven categories below:

Physical Health
Relationships and Family
Environment and home
Business or Job
Investments and Finance
Recreation and Fun
Your Spiritual Life

List these seven categories down the left column on a paper. Beside them add 3 more columns to rate yourself. Finally in an additional column on the far right I want you to write down the *single daily action* or physical reminder that you will use to draw your attention back to those weak areas where you had low numbers. The intention of this exercise is to bring your awareness of Spirit, Mind, and Body to every aspect of your life.

You are establishing a new habit of being! I guarantee you it will change who you are!

Even a five minute process in the morning will change who you are and how you show up in this world. You will become slightly more spirit-based, more spirit focused. Your internal order will slowly shift from body mind spirit, to spirit mind and body. I challenge you to do that right now. Put this book down and at the end of this chapter spend whatever time it takes to identify that single daily action or physical reminder and commit to taking the action to put yourself first—your true spiritual self. The challenge is to shift your spiritual nature. This is one of those seemingly small things that will have a profound effect on you for the rest of your life.

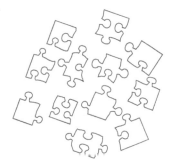

Chapter 5

YOU FIRST, THEN OTHERS

The principle in this chapter may seem at first glance to be very selfish. It could be best summarized simply as **"Take care of yourself first, and then take care of others."** This is an idea that seems foreign to many people, especially the people who have achieved success and have met their goals. Generally these people are at a point where they are often becoming altruistic and wanting to help and support others and share what they know with the world. Sometimes however, people become so focused on others that they exclude themselves and do themselves a huge disservice. If you truly want to be in service to others, and share what you know, whether it's in the financial, emotional, or intellectual realm, you need to be powerful first. You need to be strong in your knowledge first. You need to be grounded, centered, and powerful so that you have something to give. You need to be in balance yourself. You need to be healthy for yourself. And if you have not spent time and effort in a balanced way to maintain yourself, then you are not going to have much to share with other people, and it's not going to be very effective for you to try to share. You will be unable to lead *by example*, which is one of the strongest ways to share with others.

Leadership By Personal Example

Let's talk about leadership for a moment. Who are the strongest leaders? Who are the people in your life that stand out as leaders? Who are your heroes? Generally, if you think about that for a moment and make a list of who those people are, you'll notice that they are people who *walk their talk*, people that *lead from the front*, by their *personal example*. We were inspired by their example as much as what their message was. Mahatma Gandhi said: "my life is my message." By this he meant that he absolutely tried to live the message that he was sharing with his people. Peaceful coexistence was Mahatma Gandhi's message, and he lived that principle and exemplified it to the world.

If you work on yourself first, you then inspire others to follow your path. Surely it's obvious that if you want to have power to be able to help somebody else, you have to be able to have your own power.

EXAMPLE:
Imagine that you are climbing a mountain with a team strung together by ropes. The reason you're strung together by ropes is to be able to catch your teammate if they happen to slip. But if everybody lets go of their grip to be able pull on the rope to support one person when he falls, the entire team falls. What makes a team strong is the combined strength of each individual in the team. The chain is only as strong as its weakest link. You don't want to be the weakest link. You want to be the strongest link. You want to show how strong it's possible for a single link to be.

When you lead by example, and walk your talk, what you're doing is taking care of yourself in a balanced way. The principle I'm challenging you with in this chapter is "you work on yourself first, and then you can help others," as opposed to helping others to the exclusion of yourself. Balance comes in knowing when to help others and when to help yourself. Knowing when to help others is a critical piece. We'll talk more about this in later chapters. It's called: "caring about and not caring for." When you care about somebody else you have their best interest in mind and you want to support their moving forward. You do not want to take away their opportunities to grow. You don't want to eliminate all their challenges and enable them to get by without growth. You want to care *about* them and not *for* them. How many times have we seen the parent sacrifice for the child and in the end the child is the one who winds up having to support the parent? Often parents put aside money, scrimp and save so the children go to college. And it's true, the children do move ahead and benefit from the parents sacrifice, but it may be at a high price to the parents that they may never be able to recover from.

As a coach I'm occasionally confronted with clients whose adult children are draining them. I often give them the council we just discussed: simply care *about* your children, but stop caring *for* them. This is so important that we will devote a future chapter to the subject.

EXAMPLE:
On every commercial airline flight the flight attendant tells you during the preflight briefing that "In the event of cabin depressurization, the air mask will drop down from the ceiling. Please put on yours first and then help your child put on their mask." Why would that be? It is the same principle in action. If you don't take care of yourself first, you're not going to be able to take care of others. Without your own oxygen you will not have the ability to help your child beside you or the people around you.

Another example: if you don't maintain your health, you will absolutely live a shorter life. If you don't work to do what you can to maintain your health, then you won't be here to support others, to share with others, to nurture and raise your children. You'll have no opportunity to participate in life in a balanced and meaningful way. Only by keeping yourself healthy will you be able to give back to life and to other people. So, this principle of "you work on yourself first" is a very critical one.

> # KEY:
> It's very, very important that you see that you need to live your life in a balanced way and take care of yourself first.

Now, what is the challenge in that? I suspect there is a place in your life where this is challenging you. I don't know where that is. Again, everyone has their own individual levels of challenge. The thing that is challenging to one person may be easy for the next, and vice versa. So maybe for you it's in the area of personal health. Maybe you're a person who puts off their own health because you're too busy helping others. Or, maybe it's in the area of spiritual development. Maybe you've been so busy working to make money to be philanthropic, to give it away or to support your own family, that you've neglected your own spiritual growth. In that case you're actually not moving ahead, and I will guarantee that you will become ineffective. Your power will be diminished!

Achieving The Balance Between You And Your Business

One of the most powerful people I know is a person who works very, very hard at their business and has become very successful in a business way. And yet, I see them being a fraction of their potential because they refuse to work on their personal issues. They are unable to lead by example. People see very little in that person except his business skills, he is very one dimensional. He is totally out of balance, focusing on one area of his life so that he won't have to focus on the rest. And when a person is out of balance they're out of strength. If you move out of balance and stop taking care of the total you, you take away energy that can be directed toward your being powerful, being a natural leader and living a life of purpose.

Consider yourself as a complete whole being much like we describe in the last chapter. Now, imagine that this holistic being has it all together, has nurtured and strengthened every part of themselves. All the components of your life are working together in harmony in a fully balanced way. When you have it all together in this way, you will show up powerfully in the world. You can't help it. Your example will be a strong one. You will lead from the front. People will be attracted to your presence, want to be near you, and automatically follow.

With balance you will have that powerful, charismatic leadership potential.

CARING *FOR* VS. CARING *ABOUT* EXERCISE:

It's time to notice the places where you're giving too much away, and as a result are out of balance. Make a list of the 7 key areas of your life:

Physical Health
Relationships and Family
Environment and home
Business or Job
Investments and Finance
Recreation and Fun
Your Spiritual Life

Ask yourself what are you neglecting, which areas are you weak and need to be strengthened. Notice where you're caring *for* others more than you're caring *about* them. Notice also where you are caring for others more than you care for yourself. Identify the areas that you will recommit to working on within yourself. It may be just a few things, or it may be quite a few things. Make a list before you go to the next chapter and commit to at least a small action toward working on yourself. Write down the action that you will take and then start right now, make the list today, take the first actions today.

Don't Stop Giving And Sharing With Others

I am not saying to stop sharing with the world or to stop giving, or to stop being generous with others. I am not saying to become selfish or egocentric. I am only challenging you to notice the areas where you are out of balance. I applaud your efforts in the areas of leadership, sharing, and giving and encourage you to continue to share what you have with the world. But what you'll notice is that your ability to share becomes natural–get this, this is important–sharing and giving will be natural by-products of you taking care of you first! Your sharing with others and being an example, a leader, will be a natural by-product of you taking care of yourself. You will then have the capacity, the ability, and the qualities needed to share with other people in a powerful way. Again, It's you working on you. Only you have the power to change you!

You don't have to tell yourself "Okay, now I'm going to be balanced, now what can I give to the world?" Instead, the world will automatically be coming to you, following you and being nurtured by you when you are in balance. You will automatically be sharing. Opportunities will come to you.

Again, where is the challenge for you? In what part of your life are you supporting others and not supporting yourself? Where in your life are you saying "they need that" and keeping a blind eye to what you need yourself? As you ask yourself these questions, answers will pop in your mind. Add them to the list you created of where you need to work on yourself.

What Are You Seeing In Life's Mirror?

As a coach, I often find my own issues reflected in my clients. Sometimes it's enlightening to become aware of an issue as you see it in somebody else. It's often very hard to see that issue in your own life. The simple solution is to start to notice the things that bother you about other people. In some way, these are your issues. These may relate to the areas that you need to work on. We're all blind to what we don't see!

There are thousands of trite sayings reflecting this, such as: "We can see the splinter in someone else's eye but not the log in our own," or "You can't see the forest for the trees." Again, you don't know what you don't know and you can't see what you can't see. So that person that you have an issue with is actually holding up a mirror. There's something in that reflection for you to see—not about them, but about you.

Again, I'm saying these things to help you notice what the area is in which you're out of balance, giving away too much and not taking care of yourself? What is the area where everyone else has an oxygen mask except you? Are you still trying to help others put on their mask? Are you running out of breath? Are you not being very effective? Maybe it's time to take a break and save yourself first, *so that you can then save the world.*

As this chapter ends, go back to the list you started of all the areas you need to work on in yourself and start. Just start! Start right now!

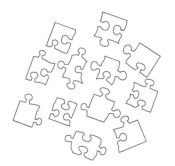

Chapter 6

MAXIMIZE YOUR STRENGTHS

I n this chapter we will talk briefly about a principle we often overlook. It's the obvious. It is simply to **"play to your strengths."** What are your special gifts? What are your highest abilities? Where have you had success in the past? What are you good at? What do you like? What serves you? What supports you and your values? What is a fit for you? I know you're thinking: "So many questions, and for what?" But these are the kinds of questions you need to be asking yourself. If you boil it down to just one question, the one you would come down to is—what are your strengths or special gifts? And don't tell me you don't have any. Everyone has certain talents and abilities that are beyond the average. Everybody has certain areas of aptitude that they excel in. Very few people excel in every area—very, very few! But almost everybody excels in at least one area. What is the area that you excel in or where you can show up as excellent with little effort?

Where Are You The *Expert?*

> # KEY:
> The challenge is to identify the areas where you show up as excellent and magnify or amplify those areas. Focus on those areas. Develop your business, habits, skills, enjoyment time, and more, around them and magnify your success in the world.

It would be totally inappropriate for an introvert or a person who has a very difficult time expressing himself to be in a high-pressure sales position or work as a door-to-door salesperson. An introvert does not make a very good used-car salesman or infomercial presenter. On the other hand, this person may make an excellent accountant, or may excel in an internet business.

I sometimes talk about overcoming the things that are really challenging for you and about pushing out your limits into new directions, and that is important. But this particular challenge is about finding out where you fit best. **What is the highest and best use of *you*? Where is your "sweet spot"?**

What sort of skills do you have that you could utilize in business that could really amplify or magnify the level of your success? Based on what you *inherently* bring to the table, what you are capable of doing that's unique to you? You may have some skills that are absolutely unique to you—and I don't mean just in your workplace. You may have some talents and abilities that nobody else in your field has, and that puts you in a very unique and powerful position. These skills can differentiate you and set you apart from your competition.

Often people say to me, "That may be true, but I don't know how to identify the special talents or abilities that I have. I don't feel as if I have any special talents or abilities". If we look way back, we often find that our special talents and abilities are things that showed up in our childhood and have carried all the way through with us. Some people have artistic talent. Some people have a speaking or communication talent. Some people have the ability to connect with others. Some people have a special talent that others see in them, but they may not see in themselves. They may have the ability to have everybody perceive them as a nice person. That's not a trivial ability! How do you use that? Where is it showing up in your business? Where is the evidence of your special talent? How can you leverage and magnify that?

Sometimes we have a special talent that is so special we don't want to utilize it for business because it ruins it for us. It may be something we definitely enjoy and gently try to use in our work or as a basis for business, but we find that it puts pressure on that gift and distorts it. It puts it in a box, and tries to make it conform to a certain work model. To try and generate income from it feels almost like prostituting your special gift or talent. If that has been your experience, and if that's what you are noticing, I encourage you to rethink the business. Those things in life that bring true enjoyment are special and need to be held apart so that we can continue to enjoy them.

EXAMPLE:
One of the most talented artists I have ever known tried for a decade to develop and build a business utilizing their talents as the income generator. They tried to sell their art but continued to run into the ongoing issue of having to compromise their creativity to satisfy the clients desires and the frustration ruined the enjoyment of the business. They quit the business and developed income from alternate sources to bring back the satisfaction and reward they received from creating art without the clients demands.

However, I also encourage you to look for ways that you can express yourself with that special talent that don't put you in a box and that don't put pressure on you. Ask yourself how you can utilize those special talents and still enjoy it.

This is not about taking something that's a gift that you have and making money from it. That is not what I'm asking you to do. I'm only asking you to notice where your strengths are. Let me use myself as an example. I'm pretty good at math and running numbers in my head, and can generally hold my own in that department, but I've noticed that I really, seriously do not like doing accounting. I'm not very good at it. It requires a level of detail that causes me to quickly lose interest. I don't follow through on things requiring that level of tedious detail. It requires a level of concentration and a dedication that I find monotonous and do not enjoy. When I noticed that about myself, I hired someone to do those tasks for me. So for me, I know that doing detailed financial work such as accounting is contrary to my own best use.

I did notice that one of my special gifts is broad based creativity like coming up with ideas and thinking outside the box, finding solutions where other people can't find a solution. I *love* that! I love it, and I'm really good at it. Does it make sense for me to be spending my time in accounting? Or should I be spending my time and energy coming up with new ideas or solutions to challenges or identifying creative investment strategies? It just does not make sense for me to spend my time focused in the areas that I'm not very good at. Especially if it takes away time and energy from things that I'm really good at, and that are going to propel me ahead in life.

What Is Your Highest And Best Use?

I'm not just speaking about business. What I'm talking about is noticing where your strengths are in your home, with your children, and in every other area of your life. If you grew up sailing and love that sport, it may not be appropriate for you to try to play football with your children. And if football is something you were never good at, never understood, never enjoyed, then football would not be a good subject for you to focus on.

Play to your strengths! This entire chapter is about playing to your strengths, learning to swim with the current and not against the current.

So what is the challenge in this? You might be saying to yourself, "Oh my gosh, this is a challenge that's easy for me. I have no problem with this. This is what I do already!" But like most of the challenges in this book, this one has many levels. I'm asking you to go to the next level in utilizing your strengths. I don't know what that next level is for you. Again, this is unique to you. Your strengths are not the same as my strengths. They're not the same as your brother's strengths, or your coworkers' strengths, or your husband's or wife's strengths. Your strengths are unique to you.

STRENGTHS, GIFTS, AND TALENTS EXERCISE:

I want you to take out a piece of paper and identify what you would consider to be your unique strengths, gifts, or talents. Make a list. You will come up with a few very easily. And then I want you to spend a little more time and go into the next level and say to yourself, "What am I good at that I have never acknowledged?" Ask yourself, "What are my hidden talents? What are the talents I have that only I know that I have"? Once you increase that list beyond the initial two or three talents, when you've gone to the deeper level and uncovered a few more talents you may have 5 to 10 talents that you think are special talents unique to you. Second step is to simply ask yourself, "Where am I using my talents? In what way can I implement this latent talent today that I haven't yet used?"

Multiplication Of Your Talents

I want you to take those talents, especially the ones you haven't used, and multiply them times each other.

EXAMPLE:

This is a huge idea, the *multiplication of talents*. Here's an example of what it might look like. Multiplying your talents is like taking a special gift you have with art then multiplying it times the special gift you have in public speaking. If you took public speaking and art and you multiplied those talents, what would you be? Maybe an art historian, or a lecture speaker about art, maybe an art auctioneer, or perhaps there would be opportunities for you to implement that in a business that you're already doing.

If you've identified your special talents and you notice ways to multiply those talents, finding two or three on your list and combining them, it actually has more power than using any one of them without the other. The more talents on your list that you're taking advantage of and using, the more powerful you're going to be, and the more successful you will be in every situation.

If you have 5 to 10 talents on your list, start a little game with yourself. The challenge is to see how many of those special gifts or talents you can use in one business or one setting, or one scenario at a time. That may look something like this: maybe the artist who is a gifted public speaker is also good at thinking off the top of his head, is also quick-witted, has a knack for chemistry, and he's a science fiction reader. How do you use all of those special talents in one specific business? Combine those talents. Combine your strengths. It's not enough for you to use just one strength anymore. It's not enough for us to rely on what we learned in school and not combine it with our own strengths and talents.

This unique combination of talents and gifts is what differentiates you from everyone else on the planet so you no longer have to compete at the more basic levels.

KEY:

We need to focus on stepping to our next level by *playing full out*. What does playing full out mean? It means using all our energy, doesn't it? When we play full out we are using all of our energy. What is our energy? How do we define energy? One definition of energy is our strength. But our energy is also our essence. It's who we are at our core. Playing full out means using all of our energy, all of our special talents, all of our gifts and playing from our center. Playing from our core and who we are at our deepest level.

So what we are talking about in this chapter is finding your "sweet spot." That is, finding your highest and best use that makes it easiest for you to reach your peak potential. It will be uniquely you. Your most efficient and uniquely powerful self.

But we cannot talk about reaching your highest level of success without also talking about what serves you. That brings up a discussion about your *true values*. In coaching we talk a lot about values and findings those things that support one's personal values. There are personal values, there are business values, there are even corporate values. I remember growing up hearing on television about General Electric, seeing their logo, and their slogan was "people are our most important product." That was a value they were expressing to the world. What does that even mean? It means that people are important to them and they're going to build products that are people-oriented and that serve people.

Understanding Your Personal Values

What are your personal values? Values are intangible and they are not things. You can't say, "Well, I value my car". Sure, you value your car, but it's a personal asset, not a personal value. What does your car represent to you? That might be the bigger question and bring you closer to your values. What is it about your car that you value? "I love the feeling of sitting inside of it (comfort or security). I love the way it makes me feel (pride of ownership). I love the smell of the leather." You may have a value centered around prestige, or comfort, or luxury, or around impressing others. These are all values.

At the end of this chapter I will give you a values exercise to help you deepen your understanding of yourself and what is important to you. If you will combine the insights from this exercise with the journaling that you started to do after chapter 3 you will begin to get a deeper look into what's truly important to you. Through this process I want you to start noticing what your personal values are. **When you know what your personal values are you can use them as a yardstick to help you make decisions.** As you begin to make new business decisions or life decisions I want you to start asking yourself, "How is this serving my values?" In order to do that you will have to have a clear sense of what your core values, your most highly held values, really are. Do the exercise at the end of this chapter and combine those results with the journaling work from chapter 3. I want you to identify your highest three values, the three values that if you had to, you would say "These are the three values I cannot live without." For example, I know that I personally, cannot live without creativity in my life because creativity is one of my highest values. Creativity is one of those values that motivates me and drives me in this world. I love coming up with new things, new ideas, new thoughts, solving problems, and being creative. I use that value and others to help me make decisions about what I say yes and no to in life. Creativity expresses itself in many ways in my life, and permeates almost all aspects of what I do. I recognized long ago my need for creativity in my life, and it has shaped my decisions in almost all areas.

What are your three highest values? Identify them using the values work we are giving you and post that list of values where you can easily refer to it. Read that list regularly, especially the top three values, and notice that they ring true. Notice that they feel right. Imagine them being taken away or not being available to you. How would that impact your life? How would that feel? I'm asking these questions because I want you to realize how important your personal values are to you.

Finding out what your core values are and then combining that with your special gifts or talents is extremely important. It has direct relationship to the purpose and passion of your life that we talked about in chapter 3. **If you're doing something that does not support your core values, basically what's happening is that you are out of personal integrity and not being fully honest.** I don't mean that you're lying to your boss. I mean you're lying to *yourself.* I don't mean that you're stealing from the company or robbing them. You are robbing from yourself. You're robbing yourself of the opportunity to live a more fulfilling life if you do not live a life that supports your most important values.

> ## KEY:
> If you don't notice, identify, and support the values that are important to you, then by default you are living, supporting and honoring somebody else's values instead of your own. That's not a very fulfilling life.

That is not what's going to help you move to your next level. And it's not rewarding. It won't make you feel happy and you'll wonder what is missing. If you notice that you are unhappy or that you're struggling, then you have probably moved away from your own values or from your own special gifts and talents. Again, and this is an important thing to notice: if you notice that your life is a struggle or that you're unhappy there are two simple places to look. Identify and honor your values, and your strengths! Are they being utilized? If you're unhappy or life is a struggle, you need to make some changes. You need to identify some choices for yourself. What can I choose to do differently? What can I choose to change? The old saying says that one of the biggest mistakes we can make is to believe that if we continue to do the same thing that we may get a different result. Einstein called that the definition of insanity, yet many people go through their life not knowing how or when to change.

> ## KEY:
> If you notice that life is a struggle, it's often because you are living outside of your talents and gifts. If you notice you're unhappy, it's often because you are living outside your values.

To conclude this chapter I would summarize what we've been talking about like this: if you want to create more fulfillment, more reward, more satisfaction for yourself, then identify your special gifts and talents and combine them with your core values. There is no simpler process than this to start living the life of your dreams: both rewarding and fulfilling! Create a new business and/or lifestyle utilizing this process and watch yourself leap forward. This is literally a key to your kingdom!

VALUES IDENTIFICATION EXERCISE:

I want you to take 15 minutes with 2 sheets of blank paper. First I want you to imagine a time in your adult life when you were very very happy. Close your eyes and recall that time with as much detail as you can. Spend 2-3 minutes back in that time and place, notice how it felt and how it made you feel. Do that now and then open your eyes again.

Ok, write down on your first sheet of paper what it was about that experience that made it a happy time. For instance if you were recalling a tropical vacation, then it may have been the lack of responsibility or knowing that you had no schedule, etc. Write down as many things about that happy experience as you can recall.

Now find the value in each of those things. For instance the lack of responsibility or schedule may be about having "Freedom" or "Independence". Those are both values. Write down the list of values on that same piece of paper.

The second step is the reverse. I want you to recall a very difficult unhappy and bad time in your life. Again I want you to spend 2-3 minutes with your eyes shut being there and feeling all the emotion and challenge of that time. Do that now and then open your eyes...

Again write down what you did *not* like about that time and place on the second sheet of paper. Perhaps it was a time when you were all alone and went through a scary event. Write down as many things as you can about that event. This time you will look for the value that was *not* being honored in that event. For instance, if you felt isolated and alone you might realize that "companionship" or "love" are very important values to you. In this exercise you are looking for the value that was missing in that bad experience. Write a list of those values on that same paper.

You may now have 10 or more values including both experiences. I want you to now rank them by comparing them to each other asking yourself "If I could have this but not that, which would I choose?" Compare all the combinations until you find your most important values and arrange the list in that order. Your top 3-5 values are the critical ones for you to pay attention to because if you are not being true to them, you are not being true to you! They are the values that you could truly not live without.

Values are your best measuring stick to gauge decisions and to make choices that will serve you best. Post your new top values list everywhere to support and define the choices that you make from now on.

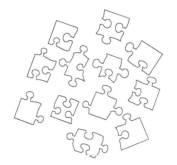

Chapter 7

YOUR EGO IS YOUR UNSEEN PARTNER

I n this chapter the challenge will be to manage your unseen partner, your ego. Your ego is always working on your behalf—or so it thinks. In many cases we need to learn to negotiate with our ego in order to be able to move forward. Our ego is always interfering in what we do. Your ego is like a spoiled child demanding attention, and that spoiled child interferes in one of two basic ways that we'll talk about in this chapter.

There are many subtle ways that the ego is at work in all aspects of our life. The two that I want to focus on in this chapter are two areas where your awareness has the ability to change the impact that your ego has on decisions and choices that you make. Let's call them the *small ego* and the *big ego*.

Ego Creates The Fear Of Change

First I want to talk about the positive role that the small ego plays to keep us safe. The way our ego "keeps us safe" is by keeping us from ever changing. There is a certain safety in our current position, no matter what it is. In other words, **the ego sees all change as a risk, because all change has an associated risk.** Our ego wants us to stay where we are, doing what we're doing, and staying safe. In this case, our ego usually shows up expressed as fear. Fear of change. Fear of doing something different, because in our current position we know what to do. We can look good there. We know how to act in that position. The larger the change the more fear will show up, and in many cases that fear will keep us from moving forward. Fear will keep us from making a change, from growing and moving toward our potential.

KEY:

Your small ego expresses itself as fear in order to force you to negotiate.

That unseen partner is always on your shoulder, in your mind, and rides with you. As you become aware and notice where fear is causing you to act small, you will be able to negotiate with your ego to allow you to do what's necessary in order to grow, even if they are scary. In some cases our ego is protecting us appropriately, and as we examine the fear we may become aware of a bad choice we were about to make. But in other cases our ego is manifesting as fear to keep us from making choices or changes that we know are necessary or appropriate. In those cases, we need to negotiate. When I say negotiate I mean to have a conversation with our small ego to dispel the fear.

KEY:

Fear is always caused by unanswered questions! Fear will be reduced and the ego satisfied when we have all of our questions answered. In many cases, we don't know the critical questions that require answers in order for the fear to be reduced. Therefore, our first task is to identify the questions.

EXAMPLE:

Imagine you're offered a new job that requires you to move to a different city. Immediately both excitement and fear will show up. These are natural functions of your small ego protecting you and keeping you safe. In this case there are probably many questions to answer to reduce the fear and allow your ego to accept the move. Those questions might include: Where will we live? Who will our neighbors be? How will we get to work? Is it safe? Will we be okay? And dozens of other questions. If we have the answers to all of these questions our fears will be dispelled and we will be left with only the excitement. We will move forward easily and without resistance from our unseen partner the ego. Remember that our ego is trying to protect us, trying to keep us from change, trying to avoid risk, thereby continuing to look and feel good.

ANSWER THE FEAR EXERCISE:

Stop for a moment right now and write down any major decision you are considering, and what fears you have about the choices you could make. Notice what the fear is. Very often we can say. "I would have no fear if I knew this..." Identify the question, or questions. Write them down, then identify *who* has the answers, and get them answered. You will quickly see the fear diminish and you will have a clarity about the decision you're about to make. Whether you go forward or decide to remain where you are, at least you will have examined your options. You will be able to come to a decision that is not limited and controlled by the fear that your small ego brings. Start using that process anytime fear shows up. Make a list of the questions that need to be answered, get the answers, and reduce the fear so that you can move forward.

Remember, fear is always a result of unanswered questions.

You could make incredible change if fear did not hold you back—if your small ego was not trying to keep you safe at all times. The problem is that the small ego does not have all the information you need, and that is why we need to ask and get answers to the right questions. Only then will our small ego let us comfortably move forward.

For some of us that unseen partner, our small ego, keeps us from making any change at all. The process just described to reduce the fear will definitely break that cycle.

In many cases, fear raised by the small ego is a good thing. It keeps us from making mistakes both large and small, and helps us avoid costly or painful mistakes. That is why I refer to negotiating with the ego. In some cases it is very important for you to listen, and to hear what the ego is afraid of. Don't just discount it out of hand. Examine where the fear is coming from and why it is present at all.

Our "Big Ego"

The second role of the ego is almost exactly opposite to what we have been discussing. That is the traditional role of the *big ego*, which gets us into trouble by believing we can do all things. The big ego believes that nobody can do it as well as we can, no matter what "it" is. In many ways, that part of our ego is just as restrictive and limiting as the small ego. Your big ego is also like a spoiled child demanding attention, saying things like "Let's do it our way, we have a better way to do it," or "I know I can do this. Let's go ahead and push through it. Let's not accept defeat, period. Let's make it happen." The big ego even more boldly says, "I'm the *only* one who can do it. If it wasn't for me, nobody could get this job done." the big ego is really close to being a great driving force. It's really close to bringing us complete confidence. The big ego is also supporting our desire to try new things and is constantly fighting with the small ego that's trying to keep us safe. Big ego wants us to step out of little ego's box!

How do we know? How do we define the difference between ego interfering and our being challenged to go ahead and take the next step or push through something? Sometimes the only way we can know is if we check in with ourselves. At this point you've heard me reference that idea of checking in with yourself in previous chapters because we have the ability to tap into our own buried knowledge. We have our own answers, and we know now that sometimes we just don't ask the right questions. When I talk about checking in with yourself to know if this is your ego or if this is a true opportunity, distinguishing the difference may be as easy as asking a few simple questions: "What's happening? What am I afraid of? Is this just my ego interfering?"

In some situations it's really best for us to step out of our own way. Many people are entrepreneurs, and as an entrepreneur they often believe that they are the only one that can get the job done and do it right. They often believe that nobody can do it as good as them, no matter what the job is. This is almost always wrong. If one person can do the job and do it right, there's probably at least one other person on the planet that can do it as well, or possibly even better. And there may be many others that can do it as well as them. There may be people in your office, your family, or in your town, etc. There will probably be people in the phone book or available through the Internet that can do just as good a job as you can. They may be able to do it better, faster, and for less money than you. But in some cases you may be reluctant to let that go and delegate because you believe you're the only one that can do it and *do it right*. This absolutely limits your growth as a business, as a person, as a family member, and in many other circumstances. You won't be able to use the simple principles of leverage, efficiency, and systems. You will be taking your time away from what you do best because you believe what your big ego is saying: "I am the only one that can do this! No one else has ever been able to do it!"

That brings up a great point. There may have been a time when your big ego was absolutely right. In the past, maybe nobody was able to do it. In the past you may not have been ready to let go of the big ego. You may not have been ready to move on to a higher level, to let go of some things and delegate to other people that can do them for you. This allows you to focus on what you love to do and become more efficient.

The last chapter was all about finding your strengths and skills and doing what you do best. Sometimes our ego tells us that we have to do it all. **The biggest saboteur to our moving ahead sometimes is our own ego. Sometimes things will work better if you don't get in the way.** Do you know what I mean? If you can just stay removed, detach, step back, be rational, let go, accept what is happening, and delegate to other people, your progress will accelerate. But all of these things are counter to your big ego. Your big ego is saying: "I'll do it! I'm the only one! I've got to do it myself. I've got to be in the middle of it! It's my job! I'll control it!" All those comments and arguments are from the big ego.

Sometimes the big ego can work for you. Sometimes you get more done. Sometimes the big ego is a motivator which causes you to take on things that you might not otherwise take on. In those ways it can sometimes be good. But, here's the big challenge… you have to be really careful to distinguish when ego is interfering and limiting you, and when your ego is seeing an opportunity and running with it. Again, the way we do that is to check in with ourselves. To take a moment and be honest with yourself and ask a few hard questions.

So if the ego is a saboteur, how do we let go of the big ego? How do we set it aside to welcome bigger opportunities? I gave you an example of an entrepreneur in the workplace who feels that they have to do it all. Sometimes that can also show up in your family or with your children, or perhaps in your financial life. Are you a person who's always reluctant to accept help? Are you the man or woman who's afraid to ask for directions? Are you the person who takes the job away from someone else and completes it rather than helping them learn how to do it? These are all examples of your big ego. Sometimes ego doesn't work for our benefit. Ego can be the restrictor of our own growth. Defining where ego interferes is a critical step if you really want to move to your next level.

Letting Go Of The Need To "Do It All"

The Buddhist philosophy of radical acceptance challenges us to set aside ego in all cases. The challenge is also to set aside pride in all cases. Pride and ego are set aside so that opportunity can come in whatever form it is meant to, so that God's blessing can fall on you without interference from your own belief that you can do it better. Ultimately we're talking about a very simple truth here: do we believe in the spiritual being, or God, or universal presence that works for our benefit? If we do, then we simply accept what shows up and do the best we can with what were given. We are rational. We look at things objectively and are willing to set our ego aside. We are willing to ask for help, to delegate and share responsibility. We must be willing to teach others rather than take the job from others, willing to share ideas and to hire help. We must be willing to take criticism and critique and improve ourselves. All of these are challenging because it really takes a step of faith. Here is the limiting concept that holds all of us back:

KEY:
You can't really do anything wrong!

You have to accept that things may go one way or another way and that both ways are going to be for your benefit. *Then* you're in a position to have the critical negotiation with the big ego. However, that can only happen once we understand the big ego's role.

This is a really hard concept for people to grasp. Sometimes it's really hard for people to let go of the idea that "I have to do it all. I'm the only one who can do it." And I absolutely know that this can be one of the biggest bottlenecks to your business growth, your financial growth, your personal growth. Because it means your big ego is demanding that every single thing has to go through you. If you're in that situation and you notice that every single thing that you're doing in your business, your office, your financial life, or personal life, has to be done by you and go through you, then *you* are the problem. You are being controlled by the big ego. You are the restriction that is keeping your business from growing, your wealth from growing, and keeping love and success from coming to you in a bigger way. Ask yourself right now: "Does everything have to go through me?" What's the answer? What just showed up? If it's yes, and you wish it didn't have to go through you, then let's go back to a couple other chapters where we talked about free choice.

Everything we do and everything we are at this moment is a result of the choices we have made up to now. If that's not where you want to be, then change! Let go of some things. Notice where you are the bottleneck and let go of the need to do it all. Expand yourself by letting go. Be bigger by doing less.

Grow by shrinking, shrinking the things that you do. Delegate, educate, and inspire others. Learn to negotiate with your ego about the things you're holding on to and you'll find that your life is simpler and easier.

The challenge of this chapter is to learn to live with, negotiate with, and let go of your egos, both large and small, when necessary.

Ultimately one of our biggest challenges is to balance the need for challenge and growth, with acceptance. Acceptance of what is, and the challenge of what could be, are both moving you toward your personal growth and development, business growth, financial growth and growth in all other areas. We really have to listen and get the ego out of the way in order to create that fine balance between challenge and acceptance.

Creating The Quick Response List

Being able to ask for help quickly and easily is important, because otherwise the ego will move past that process in order to hang on to the belief that "only I can do it." So when we need to ask for help, who do we turn to? When we are consciously aware that we don't know everything and move to a point of being willing to call other people, who do we call? We need to look at other people as a resource, as a real tool for us to use. What I'm talking about is keeping a *resource list*. The resource list will include people, but it will also include other resources such as books, internet sites, and information sources that you can have at your fingertips. It could even include tools and equipment. It could include past experiences that we can draw upon to help us get clarity about some issue we're working on, or a challenge that we have in this moment.

If we look at it from a "people" perspective alone, which is probably the biggest and easiest category of resources that we might want, who should we consider? As a coach, I encourage people to create a resource list containing the contact information of every person that they know or have an acquaintance with, or that they've met and would be willing to contact for help. Maybe you already have a resource list. It's called your business card file. Or, maybe you already have a resource list and it's called your telephone directory, or your smart phone contacts list. What I'm asking you to do is to narrow that list to the people that you would we be willing and able to call for assistance. Create a resource list of people that you could delegate to, that you could hire, that are specialists in specific fields.

For many people that resource list may be dozens of names. For you it may be hundreds of names. I encourage you to put them in a list. If the list is extensive you may want to break it down by categories. There other ways to break it down as well. Here is how you can break down resource lists: everybody on your list is considered a resource, but not everybody on the list is considered an ally or is necessarily a part of your team. What I'm encouraging you to do is to create departments within your resource list. Some people will be accessible for specific things and can be organized by topic. Others will be general resource people to brainstorm with and to use for resourcing ideas. All of these people would be in a general broad resource group, but within that group you're going to have a second, more intimate level. The second level is people that you can turn to that you have a close relationship with. They're people such as personal friends that you have in business, or from school, or that you may have a lot in common with. These people would qualify as a higher level of resource, in the *inner circle* if you will.

The first general resource list is very broad and includes people that you have an acquaintance with, but they're not necessarily your close friends or people that you relate to daily. The second inner circle list consists of people you see on a regular basis and that you can turn to with a problem. Perhaps you can take them to lunch and brainstorm ideas. Within that list there may be an even tighter list, what many people call their *personal team.* Their team might be, for instance, their spouse, their business partner, their attorney, their CPA and/or financial planner. This inner team might be defined as the people that you trust completely and are willing to share numbers with. You might go as far as to say "here is my tax return and I'm trying to get some clarity about this or that." You're willing to go to them for answers to questions that relate to you personally. They're people with whom you have built a high degree of trust. It may be family members. Not even just your spouse, but it could be uncles, aunts, fathers, children—anybody that you fully trust to share numbers and intimate details of your life with, knowing that it won't go beyond them. Furthermore, you can trust the advice they give you as being in your best interest.

To summarize: the first level is your **resource list**. The second level contains the people within that resource list that you have a more intimate relationship with, your **inner circle**, and the third level is your **personal team**.

There's one other group that I'd like you to add to your resource list, and that is your **alliances and affiliates**. Your alliances and affiliates are people that you either do business with or that you have a working relationship with in some way. A working relationship is defined as people you do business with for mutual benefit. These are people who want to help you because when they help you and you prosper, they prosper also. If in your business, you have vendors that you buy from you, those vendors have a large interest in helping you be successful. If you buy something from them and your business is successful and you sell more, then you'll continue to buy more from them. Those are people whose interests are aligned with yours, and you have an *alliance*. It may be a business alliance or a personal alliance, but you have an alliance with them.

Now, start using your resources. This is a critical piece! If you can bring yourself to say, "Yes, I am willing to move my big ego out of the way," the next part of the challenge is to identify who you will turn to for help. Having that resource list to turn to and having it available to you quickly and easily, whether it is on your computer or on a piece of paper in your pocket, is a critical piece of getting your big ego out of the way.

EXAMPLE:

Imagine yourself trying to operate your computer but you have no software or programs. Yes, you may be able to turn it on but in order to use it effectively, you must use a variety of programs or computer resources to get the maximum results. What happens when you lose power or your computer crashes? That would be very much like loosing your resources in business or life.

EXAMPLE 2:

When writing this book I had to reach out to many people and ask for their support to help edit, review, publish, create art, and market for me. I turned to my resource list and instantly had the help of dozens of people with expertise in areas where I knew very little. I couldn't have done it without them. What a shortcut!

When you want better or faster results, you need to turn to your resource system and say, "Who can help me?" **You have to negotiate with your big ego and be willing to go down that list and give people a call**. That's where the big ego must step aside. And you know what? People love it! People love to help. If people were to call you and say "I need your help," what would you do? First of all, you'd start smiling, and secondly, you'd be willing to help them. It's amazing the resources that we have available to us through our friends and acquaintances. We have a world of potential assistance just through that stack of business cards that we have in a box, or the names in our telephone contact list.

Learn To Ask For Help

People want to help each other; it's human nature. When you set aside ego and genuinely ask for somebody's help, what you are really saying is, "I trust that you know something I don't know, and would you please share it with me?" Maybe those are the exact words you use. Being willing to turn to a resource list and use those resources can propel you forward. You can quickly solve problems that might take you a long time otherwise. You can move from an education process that you would have to go through and step right into an observation and implementation process with somebody else's help. That person from your resource list will help you be stronger, better, and quicker. having a current resource list becomes your readily available tool. You can get that information and you can move your business or personal life forward using your resources instead of trying to do everything yourself. Please be willing to do that. **I need your help in this!** Did you hear that?

So great, you now have a resource list, and you're going to use it. You're going to turn to people for help, you're going to start noticing when you need to let go and negotiate with your ego to allow you to use your resources. You're going to find the balance between accepting what is and the challenge to want more. These are all pieces of understanding the ego and letting go of the ego. Pieces of accepting what is, and asking for the help we need to move through our current situation. We can be our own worst enemy. We can sabotage ourselves if we don't do these simple steps. Now I want to add a simple request: I want to request that you make an intention to ask people for help even if you don't need it, just to demonstrate to yourself how easy it is and just to practice the skill of asking for help. That may seem ridiculous, but it's something you may need to practice.

Resource exercise:

Here's a quick exercise. Each day for the next seven days I want you to identify one area that you will delegate or in which you need help. I want you to ask for help from three people in that area, and notice how they respond. The request is for the next seven days, one problem each day, three people on each problem. Please do not use the same people for every problem, every day. Expand your resource list. Don't go only to those people that you are most comfortable with. Stretch yourself! Yes, I'm really saying you need to talk to 21 different people this week. Ask 21 people for help on seven different problems, seven different days. Be genuine, don't make something up but use real issues, and real questions or problems that you have. I want you to practice asking for help. It's as simple as saying "I need your help with…" It's easy! By now you have your resource list and you know how to negotiate with your ego, so start using your resource list and asking for help tomorrow.

Do this exercise for at least a few days before you go to the next chapter. The next chapter will appear to go in an opposite direction, so you need to be experienced in asking for help before you move on.

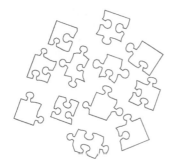

Chapter 8

YOU ARE YOUR OWN EXPERT

The challenge or principle that we are working with in this chapter is **"You are your own expert."** Trust yourself, trust your inner knowledge.

Let's start like this: how many of us challenge authority? How many of us question authority and think that we have a solution that's better than whatever's being proposed or imposed on us by somebody else, whether that person is our boss, our parents, our society, or our government? How many of us believe that we have a better answer, a better solution. What do we do with that better answer or solution? How many of us find ourselves basically not employee material, but only boss material, and find ourselves at the same time feeling like a victim of other people's choices, without control over our own destiny? Are you experiencing a smaller life that comes out of experiencing situations created by poor solutions to problems and actions lead by others? Maybe you experience this at work or at home or in your personal life because you don't get to make your own choices about what you do and what you get? This is another of those areas where you get to find the right balance as *you work on you*!

Learning To Trust Yourself And Your Inner Knowledge

As I work with people, I find that they have their own answers. This is an important key, so let me say it again. **People *do* have their own answers!** People know what they need to do. People, if you ask them the right questions, have the right answers to direct their lives in the best possible way for themselves. You, too, have your own right answers—if only you would ask the right questions! It is important to remember that we are spirit, mind, and body. Very often we act from our bodies instead of accessing our spirit or mind. Our intellect and our spiritual core have the answers if our physical bodies ask the right questions. This is the entire principle I'm presenting in this chapter: that our spirit and soul have the right answers if we will in our physical bodies ask the right questions. Those questions are generated from our physical body and from our physical involvement in the world, typically in response to some physical situation. Again, our spirit and soul have the right answers if our body will ask the right questions!

What I'm saying is, **"We are our own experts"**. We should be our own experts and we should rely on that expertise. One of the big problems with this is that when we are our own expert we have a natural tendency to try to impose that expertise on the world around us. At the same time, those around us are trying to be their own expert and impose their ideas on the world around them. So, as I've said before, you must work on yourself and try not to direct those around you. Those around you will be affected and directed as a natural result of you making your right choices and of you asking your soul and spirit what you need, what you want, what is the right thing to do for you. Those basic, powerful questions will allow your spirit and soul to respond to your intellect with information that is true for you.

So, if you are able to accept that this is the case, that this is really true, then it seems fairly simple: all you have to do is ask yourself the right questions and be willing to listen for the right answers. You may be reading this and thinking "I never get an answer. I never can tell what the responses I get actually mean. I have a lot of questions, but I don't have any answers". Or you may be saying, "I don't even know what the questions *are!* I don't know how to access my inner knowledge, what is in my spirit and soul, because I don't know how to ask.. If you accept that you are your own expert, then what's the first question? If you don't know the answer to that question, simply ask yourself "What is the first question I need to ask myself? What is the question I have right now that will help me understand what I should do in the next moment, in the next hour, today, this week, or this month, or with my life? What is that next question?" The questions may be as simple as "What should I do? What is best for me? What do I want? Or what will I do?" Or in dealing with a specific issue you may ask, "What can I accomplish in this situation? Or what's the best way for me to handle this?" Questions that begin with the word "what" are most likely to elicit clear answers.

Wait On The Answers

Let me add one more piece... Often, in my experience, you may ask a question and not wait for the answer, and therefore believe you're not getting an answer. So if you are saying you have lots of questions, but don't ever get any answers, it may be that you are not leaving space and listening for the answers. The truth is that you have all the answers immediately but you may not be able to hear them immediately if they are coming from your spirit and soul. You may have no practice in listening on that level so you may think you are not receiving answers. Do you get quick answers on the physical level or to questions that have little consequence attached to them? Let me give you an example.

If I ask you to think of a number between one and ten, by the time I've made that request you thought of a number. Probably a few numbers ran through your mind and you settled on one. If I ask you what your favorite food is, probably three or four foods came to mind and you settle on chocolate, or pistachio nuts, or something else. Where do those answers come from? They come mostly from your physical body (if it's a physical question). You know what your answers are. There are certain things you know you do or do not want for dinner tonight as soon as you ask yourself the question, "What do I feel like eating?" We ask ourselves questions all the time that relate to the physical world. But we rarely ask ourselves big, basic questions that require our Spirit and Soul to respond like "What do I want? What's important to me? What can I do to attract the love to my life that I want? What do I want to do in my life to make money or as a career? What are the things that I truly love doing? What can I do to attract those things to me?" All those questions are bigger, deeper questions. Often we want to stay with the easier, superficial questions, the questions at a physical level, because were afraid of the bigger answers.

The process of how to attract what you want is answered in the first chapter of this book.

Learning The Truth May Require Change

The reason we're sometimes afraid of receiving direct answers is that the answer may require us to change something about the way we're living. Remember, as we talked about earlier, we resist change. Our ego is trying to keep everything the same, to protect us. It's a natural tendency of the human situation for us to want to stay where we are, stay with what we know, even if it's uncomfortable or not the best thing for us. So we avoid asking ourselves the bigger questions that may lead to change or require some movement or a different choice on our part.

When you look at your own situation in light of this principle: "you are your own expert," If you ask yourself the right questions you'll get the right answers. It's pretty simple. It's important to respond to those answers for yourself and not impose them on other people around you. Imposing the answers on yourself is where you'll find resistance. That's where this simple principle requires some work to execute. But the principle itself is simple. All we have to do is know what the right questions are, ask them, and wait for the answers. Oh Yes, and then take *action* on what shows up!

Let's talk about waiting for the right answer for a moment. We often need to create space for things to show up in our lives. Sometimes as we ask ourselves questions, we don't allow space because we really don't want to leave room for the answer. So we ask the question in a way that allows no time or space for that answer to show up.

EXAMPLE:

When a question is asked of us, by ourselves or someone else, we may or may not immediately have an answer show up. It is often beneficial to wait for the answer, for example; not long ago I was trying to take apart a lock on a door knob to replace it but there seemed to be no way to get it apart. I kept asking myself for and looking for a solution. Eventually I quit working on it and a few hours later a thought came to mind and I went and reexamined the underneath side of the knob and found a very small covered plate imbedded in the handle which revealed a screw to take the mechanism apart. I had never seen that design before but by waiting, my mind and spirit came into play, and the possibility of a secret opening came to me. If you want to experience this first-hand, simply write down the question that you don't seem to have an an answer to on a piece of paper next to your bed before going to sleep. Very often in the morning you will have a new approach to that question, or a new thought, or idea that will lead to your answer. Try it, it works!

So, the challenge I have for you is the challenge of creating space for answers to show up, and then being true to those answers. Trust your inner voice, your own inner knowledge, and that you can access your own answers.

Often in life we see people who seem to go their own direction, seem to walk their own path on a different course than many other people in the world. Sometimes those people who take such a different course seem strange or odd or out of step with society. But those people are simply accessing their own answers and being true to themselves.

Remember in chapter 3 of this book we talked about finding your true life purpose. Finding your true life purpose is often a matter of asking yourself questions and listening for the answers. "What am I looking for? What do I want? What's important to me?" Sometimes those answers seem to be canned answers because they're not your answers, they're society's answers. If you truly want to find out what your own answers are, let me give you a very simple process. Many of you already know the process or have heard of the process of automatic writing and automatic response. It is a form of journaling and It does work.

THE AUTOMATIC WRITING EXERCISE

Automatic writing works like this: you sit at a table with a blank sheet of paper before you and at the top of the paper you write down a question for which you'd like to have an answer. And, in response, you start writing. You do not direct the writing or try to edit what your inner voice is saying. Let me give you an example: imagine a situation where you had a fight with your spouse. You'd like to resolve the issue with them and get things cleared up, but you both believe you're right and neither one is willing say "I was wrong." Going to the other person and saying "I'm sorry we had this fight, but I was right" doesn't clear the air, and doesn't make the negative energy go away. So a simple way to get an answer from your inner self that you can really trust is to simply sit for a few moments at your desk with a blank sheet of paper. Write across the top of the paper this question: "What can I do to clear the air with my spouse and resolve the conflict?" Or it could be as simple as, "What can I do?" or "What's the right thing to do?" Write one of those questions at the top of the page, and then sit and begin writing. Maybe the first things you start writing down are things like "I hate it when they do that," or "I'm sure they're wrong. I'm sure I'm right". Maybe you will reinforce your position. But as you continue to write, just let whatever is coming to your mind flow to the paper without editing it, and let it just lay there in black and white. Don't even read it as you write it, just get those thoughts out, remembering to re-ask yourself the question at the top of the page anytime you get stuck. "What can I do to clear the air with my spouse and resolve the conflict?" or whatever the question was that you wrote at the top of the paper. If you continue to go back to that question as you write, you will eventually come to the answer from your higher self, from your soul and spirit. An answer to a larger question may not happen on one sheet of paper. It may happen on five sheets of paper. It may not happen in a five minute session; it may require a five minute session every morning for two weeks. But what you will see emerge is a response that processes through the anger, processes through the emotion and gets past the negative energy and down to your central core self, your spirit and soul, and that answer will float to the surface.

I introduced the journaling and automatic writing concept in an earlier chapter and it could probably be used with almost every chapter in this book. It is an effective way to gain clarity, resolve conflicting issues, and access the power within you.

You can use this process on a daily basis. Every morning, asking yourself some larger question like "What do I want from life?" Or, as we talked about in earlier chapters, "What's my true life purpose?" Or you may ask yourself basic questions like "What do I want to do for a career?" or "Where do I want to live?" Start with basic questions and you will slowly get answers. You will, over time, have those answers reveal themselves to you and you will also over time learn to trust those answers.

Begin by asking yourself small questions. A small question might be, "What can I do today to enjoy this day?" Another small question might be, "Who can I turn to for help today?" You will see that with the small questions, answers come quickly and very clearly for you. The more questions you ask, the quicker the answers will come, and you'll learn to trust the process and start asking yourself bigger questions. Work up to those bigger questions in life. Don't begin with, "What is my life purpose and what am I supposed to be doing on this planet?" Wait and ask yourself those questions once you have become confident with the process.

If you develop a habit of automatic writing, asking yourself questions daily, not editing as you go, but going back later and reading through one or two weeks worth of writing focused on a single question. You will notice that patterns will show up and long-awaited answers will reveal themselves. The more you do this, the more you will trust the process. The more you will trust that inner voice, your higher self. And the more you will be willing to change based on the responses you get.

Eventually, you'll be able to communicate very clearly with yourself. You will learn to trust the response from your spirit and soul, and as you develop this skill that muscle will become stronger and stronger. You will be able to skip the writing and simply ask yourself the questions directly.

Another challenge with this principle is to grow the muscle of "I am my own expert, so I will trust my own answers and I will make my own decisions." This goes for any situation. You may be an employee, and you are saying to yourself "I can't make my own decisions, I have a boss that makes the decisions for me, and I don't have any choice." Of course you do. One of the biggest mistakes we can make is to believe that we work for somebody else. You work for yourself! If you don't like it, then you can change. Yes, you may have to make decisions and act within certain frameworks and constraints. If you choose to go home at noon every day from your job, you may lose that job. What if going home at noon every day to work on something else is the answer that comes up for you when you ask yourself "What can I do to get this thing done?" or "What's my best work today?" Obviously, you may have to change jobs if you really want to respond to and honor that answer. That's a choice you will have to make. At least you asked yourself the question, accessed your inner knowledge, and tried to find what will work for you. Again, you work for yourself. You make your own choices, and you always have choices!

In traditional coaching, one of the core principles is that no advice is given, because in coaching we believe the client has their own answers. Much of coaching is about asking the right questions to expand possibilities and help clarify the options and possibilities for that client. You, as a client, are then free to make the right choices for yourself based on your own inner knowledge and rely on your own strengths to come up with the answers. Sometimes when you do that it may not seem to fit your situation. You may ask yourself, "What am I supposed to do in this situation?" And the answer may come up, "Quit the job". Or the answer may be "Go apologize," or "Go return the money." It may be something that feels very uncomfortable and it may be something that you really don't want to do on a physical level.

One of the challenges in accessing your own answers is that the answers are spiritually and soulfully based.

They may conflict with your physical wants and desires. Because you live in the physical world, because of pride, risk, fear, or other emotions, you may not want to act on the answer that shows itself. That's where the challenge lies in this principle. Listening to your higher self, and knowing that you are your own expert can be very challenging. This is the muscle I want you to grow. I want you to start with such small and simple questions as "What do I want for lunch?" and listen for the answer. Don't go get a hamburger at Burger King just because everybody else in your office is going there. Don't automatically say "I'll have a cup of coffee this morning." Instead, ask yourself "What do I want to drink this morning?" Maybe what you really want is an orange juice, but you're in the habit of drinking coffee. Or maybe it's the other way around. Maybe you're in the habit of doing things because your friends and peers do something, but it is not the right thing for you.

Start asking yourself easy questions at first and develop the habit of listening to those answers and responding to them. Sometimes it will be right for you to quit your job, and sometimes it will be right for you to go apologize, or sometimes it might be right for you to pay somebody back money that you got from them in an inappropriate way. Something may have happened that means you need to take a humbling step forward to clear it up. When you act on those things and when you listen to your own answers, they are always, absolutely *always* right for you.

The Role Of Confusion And Doubt

Now let's talk about confusion and doubt. When you access your own answers, you may run into confusion. Sometimes you may seem to receive conflicting answers. You may receive many answers that don't seem to fit together. You may get a response that is very weak because you have not developed that muscle. It's much like going to the gym and working out with weights. Sometimes when you try to lift a weight it turns out to be too heavy, and your arms simply cannot lift it. It may be very much the same for you at first, when you ask yourself powerful questions about life. If you're not ready for the answers, the answer you get may be too heavy to carry or lift. You're literally unable to carry that answer. You may need to develop and build that muscle, the muscle of trusting your own answers and *being willing to act on them*. The muscle will become stronger and stronger over time.

When confusion, struggle, or doubt show up, you will need to get more clarity before you can take action. Maybe you are getting a lot of internal resistance. That internal voice that is constantly giving you answers to questions that you haven't even asked yet. Let's talk about that inner critic, the part of our ego that is trying to keep us safe. Let's say we accept the premise that we are our own expert and we do have our own inner knowledge that we can access by asking ourselves the right questions and listening for the right answers. Then we get to the question: do we or don't we trust the answers to come up? That inner critic or resistance, our small ego, is giving us answers and confusing us in order to play safe, to keep us small, and keep us from changing. The mind is a complicated thing. The Spirit speaks through it, and the soul speaks through it, and even our body speaks through it. Yes, even our body speaks through our mind and voice. For instance, this morning you may have still been sleepy but you chose to get up, you set the alarm, but your body may have been saying I'd really like to sleep a little longer. "It's okay, it'll be all right." Your mind tells the body to hit the snooze button. But then your spirit speaks to your mind. You get in touch with your higher self through your spiritual core, which has it's own clear voice. Tapping into that voice will give you clear answers to act on.

The question becomes, how do we distinguish the true answer from our own mind and ego games? How do we know? We know through practice. We know through habit.

We gain certainty through testing over time which voices are which. It's been said that we should judge any act by the fruit it bears. What's the fruit that your negative voice bears for you? It keeps you small, and keeps you stuck in one place-. Does that negative voice keep you from moving to your next level or living a purposeful life? If that's the case, then it's not the voice you want to trust and listen to.

Over time you will learn to use powerful questions and learn to know your spiritual self. You will be able to listen to that spiritual powerful voice and that voice alone, without confusion from your inner critics and the negative voice of your small ego. Remember the small ego is trying to keep you safe but without change, and without growth you are not living a life of purpose.

There are entire books and entire fields of study that are dedicated to dealing with that inner critic, that negative small ego, and the internal dialogue that it generates. The field of psychology is full of literature about it. Please notice If there's an ongoing resistance in your inner dialogue or a true block when you want to make meaningful change, then I encourage you to seek help from a professional in this field. For the purpose of this book and this specific principle, I'm going to assume that is not the case with you today so that you can continue to move forward with this idea and try this principle on for size.

Inner Voice Or Inner Critic?

Next I want you to pretend that the voice you hear when you ask yourself a powerful question is the true voice that you want to listen to. Again, I want you to start asking small questions to begin with, so that we can move forward and start to discern those voices and act on the true voice from your spirit and soul. I want you to learn to identify those voices and where they come from, and then begin to act on them in a trusting way, believing that they are the voice of your inner self coming through strongly. Many books have also been written on the subject of your higher self, or your inner child. These are different pieces of ourselves that we can access and that we can ask questions of in order to access wisdom or knowledge. If it's true that we are made in God's image, and he has his knowing and being in us, then we really do have our answers. We just need to ask ourselves the right questions. In order to ask and get a clear answer we need to identify which answers are from our Higher Self which is God speaking to us as opposed to that internal critic, or ego, trying to get us to play small.

This may seem very difficult at first. This principle challenges us to trust that we are our own expert, and that we have our own answers. It's a difficult challenge. But you will be able to develop it through practice and patience.

Many times you may want to give away responsibility by asking other people what to do or for the answer. In many cases this is an entirely proper use of your resources. It's an excellent way to gain support, get other perspectives and broaden your options. But, if you want the knowledge that is unique to you, that's capable of strengthening and lifting you up and putting you on your course regardless of all the different answers you're hearing from the world and other people, then access your inner self. Ask yourself. Be your own expert. Ask yourself to confirm answers you were getting from your resources. But if there is a conflict, trust your inner voice and go back to your resources with better questions.

CHECK YOUR ANSWERS EXERCISE:

Let's stop right here for a moment and ask yourself a simple question: "What is the most powerful question I need to ask myself right now?" What is the answer that just came to you? What thought flashed through your mind? Automatic writing or journaling, as we talked about, sometimes reveals those answers, but sometimes just listening and trusting reveals those answers.

I want you to ask your own questions and access your own answers. Challenge yourself to trust those answers, and take action as you discern the true answers from your soul and spirit. I want you to learn to trust yourself in small things first, with small questions and small answers. I want you to recognize the pattern of how *you respond to you*.

KEY:
You cannot choose wrong!

Yes, the choice you make may take you through some challenging times but those times may be necessary to your future success. Remember that there are lots of paths to your success and that God's resources are unlimited. Every choice you make CAN lead to your successful future!

Over time you will learn to trust that inner voice coming from God in you. You'll learn to discern that voice from the challenging inner critic coming from your ego. You may be able to access old issues from your childhood and deal with issues that have been blocking you for years and have kept you from moving forward. But that's just one small part of accessing the knowledge of God in you. That perfect, unique "you" knowledge is available to you right now. It's what will help you maintain your critical path.

Knowledge Is Power Is Responsibility

In his book *Critical Path*, Buckminster Fuller told us that we're on a path leading to a certain point, and that if we don't watch out we're going to wind up where we were headed. He warned us that if we weren't happy with where that path is leading, we need to make changes. For some of you that is your situation. You may be on a critical path, and you may need to make changes or you'll end up where you're headed. If that's the case, I want to encourage you once more to access your inner wisdom. Ask yourself the right questions and listen for your own answers.

Trust what shows up and start acting in small ways based on those answers. And yes, you *do* know the critical questions, and with practice you will be able to listen and discern the true answers. I guarantee it!

Challenge yourself to move forward. Sometimes this means stepping away from society and the way everybody else is doing something to find your own way, your own path. Sometimes it makes you a little bit unique. Sometimes you don't seem to fit in as well as you did before you put yourself into motion. And sometimes the result is that you will become a leader. You will have an inner wisdom and strength that people will admire and will be drawn to. Challenge yourself to move forward, live a purposeful life and be exactly who you're supposed to be. Begin to have your own answers and be your own expert. Let your inner self out if you want to meet your potential.

This is a powerful principle. Challenging yourself to be your own expert and to make your own decisions after tapping into your spiritual core will serve you well as you develop the habit of listening to **you-the-expert**!

Chapter 9

GRATITUDE AND STEWARDSHIP

Through this entire first section of **"you work on you"** in **The Future Formula**™ we've been talking about many things that have to do with our attitudes and our belief systems. The challenge I want to offer you right now is probably the culmination of all of the attitudes and beliefs. It comes partly from the work of Wallace Wattles, who in 1910 first published his book *The Science of Getting Rich*. The ideas in that book have been reproduced by Bob Proctor and others.

In Wallace Wattles' book he basically asks, "what if *all* it took was gratitude and having a positive belief about something for it to come true?" In other words, what if all it took was being grateful for what we have, which we've mentioned before when we considered our belief in something bigger and our being spirit first? What if we could couple a grateful attitude with the positive beliefs we talked about in Chapter 1, in the very beginning of this book? If you believe from Chapter 1, that you can create reality with your beliefs, then the only thing that may be standing in your way is your attitude.

If all it took was gratitude and a positive belief, what would you create? What would be possible for you? Pretty simple really. You may instantly have very big plans, really big dreams and big ideas as I pose the question to you. Maybe the answer is, "gosh, I'd have lots of money. I'd have wealth, I'd have power and I'd do this and I'd have that. The world would have peace, the world would have no more hunger." All kinds of things come to mind, but let's bring this back to **you working on you**.

KEY:

What would you do if all you had to do was be *grateful* and to have a *positive attitude* and *think positively*?

QUICK CREATION EXERCISE:

I want you to take a piece of paper right now to list five things you would do if being grateful and having a positive attitude was all that was required.

It really is that simple! But, I know as you're reading this you may be thinking, "Well, yes, I can list those things, but I don't really believe it yet." And therein lies the challenge. The challenge with thinking positively is that it has to be 100 percent. If there's doubt, then things don't show up for us in the same way. If we say we believe one thing but then act differently, things don't show up for us and we wonder why. You may be doing everything positively, but if your attitude is not positive it can block your positive beliefs and results. We may need to have an attitude adjustment in order to be able to have an attitude of gratitude to support our positive beliefs. We have to be aligned in our thinking and our beliefs, our actions, and our attitudes and grateful for what we have. If you need a quick attitude adjustment, simply go back and read Chapter One again and **choose to believe it!**

Some of you may be reading this and thinking, "You know, it's hard for me to be grateful for what I have because I don't have anything." Or, "What I have isn't any good," or "The things that happened to me aren't fair." And that's what this challenge looks like—overcoming this type of argument. That is the challenge.

Winning Or Learning, No Losing!

It's sometimes hard for us to accept, that **even when a bad event happens, we should be grateful**. It is been said by many people that as you look at any event in your life there are only two results that will come from that experience or event: there is either winning or learning. *There is no losing...* unless you choose not to learn.

If that's true, that means that everything that happens to us is positive. And if everything is positive, then it should be easy for us to have an attitude of gratitude and be grateful for what shows up. If everything that happens to me is positive, I'm grateful for that. What about you? It may be just the particular way that you look at something that keeps you from seeing something as positive in your life and has you seeing it as negative instead. I now look at things that I used to see as negative as "interesting," and watch and wait for the positive to unfold. Let me tell you a quick personal story that illustrates my point.

EXAMPLE:

One of the strongest and most powerful events in my personal life and the life of my family was the death of my mother. She was killed suddenly in a car accident and as a result, my family drew together in a way that they never had before, in a way they never needed to before, and I noticed change happening from this event. I can now look back on this event with gratitude for the effect it had on our family, even though I still miss my mother. I am grateful for the effect it had on my father. He became a warm, caring, and loving man, a huge change from the very reserved man he had been before. My family, my brothers and sisters, all drew together. We had experienced what the world would perceive as a terrible, negative event and yet it bore positive fruit in many, many ways. Sure, we don't have my mother in that family relationship and that's sad, and I still miss her very much. But I'm also very grateful for the results that came from her death.

It's a *hard* lesson! It's hard to get our head around an event like that and look at it as a positive. But choosing the attitude of being grateful for what we are given has to include *everything*, the easy and the difficult.

Gratitude, Positive Attitude, And Stewardship

The ability to be grateful for *everything* is an expression of *stewardship*. Being good stewards of what we are given allows even the worst experiences to bear positive results and we are then given more. That principle applies to money, friends, and opportunities in life. It is our *attitude of gratitude* that allows us to be good stewards, to approach life with the right mindset, and puts you in a position to receive a positive result. It will make your move to the next level much easier. We will learn that until we master one level we won't be ready to move to the next. Being grateful for all the things at that level is as important as any other aspect of mastery.

You Choose Your Attitudes

Before we go any farther, I want to be absolutely clear about one basic idea. That idea, simply stated, is that at any given moment we are free to choose our attitudes. Attitudes are *not* based on circumstance, although in many cases we pretend they are. Many people will say to me, "I'll be happy when I'm making more money," or "I'll be able to think more positively when I get a new job," or "I can't be happy until I find the right person to share my life with." These are all statements that tie our attitude of gratitude or happiness to a particular circumstance of our life, when in fact our attitudes are something we choose independent of what's going on around us. The Dalai Lama has said in his book, *The Art of Happiness,* that **all humans *only* want to be happy**. and that most of us define happiness as the state of being that is achieved through circumstance. He states that the attitude of happiness is available to us at every moment. It doesn't depend on money, relationships, or any physical circumstance or even how you *feel*. Happiness, gratefulness, and even contentment, are attitudes that are available for us to adopt at any moment simply by our choice. Again, let me say that **your attitudes have nothing to do with your circumstance**. If you could understand this simple principle it would help you understand why some people who seem to have everything are still very unhappy and ungrateful, while other people with very little are both grateful and happy. It's all in the attitudes they're choosing. Remember in the early chapters of this book, we spoke about you having free will and always being in a position of choice. One of the best things you can do for yourself is to develop the habit of choosing attitudes of happiness and gratitude.

EXAMPLE:

I recently had a client who called me to say that his company was having the worst month in it's 12 year history and he was completely distraught and depressed. When I asked him what had happened, he told me that he did not know but that all of his 15 man sales team in the office were also depressed and nobody was even picking up the phone to get sales. Everyone was completely down and there was a general attitude of defeat and depression. He said it was horrible because he did not know how to change it. He told me that even he was coming into work late and leaving early and couldn't bear to talk to his sales team because they were so depressed. My client telling me this was the founder, owner, and CEO of this company, and even he was pulled into the total company funk. The overall attitude was one of depression and accepting defeat. I challenged my client to choose a positive attitude for the next two weeks until we were scheduled to talk next. I challenged him to be the first to work, the last to leave, and to be upbeat and positive regardless of circumstances. I asked him to be engaged with his entire team and share that positive attitude and excitement about work, regardless of what seemed to be happening. Ten days later he called me with exciting news: the company had reversed the negative sales month and they were on track to have their best month ever! (this is a true story). When I asked him what had happened he said "I don't know". He still couldn't link his choice of attitude to the amazing results he was seeing until I pointed out to him that he hadn't changed anything except his attitude. His positive attitude and acting optimistic, even in the face of defeat, allowed everyone around him to also become optimistic and business boomed!

You get to choose your attitudes: Optimism, Gratitude, Happiness... Your choice!

Now, I want to challenge you to think really, really big and positively. What would you do if all you had to do was be grateful for what you're given right now, and have a positive thought about what you want for the future? Go back to your list of the seven areas of your life from previous chapters and check your attitudes in each area. There are no limits! If you think there are limits, then *that* is your limit. There are no limits, period. Dare to think big, bold, positive, and outrageous thoughts, knowing there is no limit to what you can accomplish if you are grateful for what you have been given and think positively about your future and what you want. What is the limit of your beliefs?

The challenge of this chapter is to train yourself to think positively and to be grateful. it is important to change your *default* setting to an *automatic attitude* that is without exception positive, grateful, and happy. The goal is to train yourself to think positively in situations, and to do it automatically, without having to think about it consciously. I want to challenge you to start training yourself. The way you do this is to simply notice and catch yourself in negative thoughts or attitudes, and then to reprogram yourself. Train yourself so that when you notice a negative attitude showing up or getting in the way, you can simply reprogram it, and *consciously* change it. Consciously put that new thought in place as your default programming.

When you notice a limiting belief showing up which keeps you from thinking positively, change your attitude and shift the negative belief to a positive belief. "Poor me. Why me? I can't help it. It's never worked for me." All those are attitudes that you can change, if you only first notice them. You can begin to be grateful by simply saying "thank you" for what you have. Gratitude is expressed in that simple expression. Thank you, God; thank you, ma'am;

thank you, sir; thank you, mom or dad; thank you, son; thank you, business partner; or even thank you to yourself. Be grateful for the position you're in and for what you have.

Over time and with practice, you will create a new default attitude that is automatically grateful and positive leading to more happiness!

KEY:
Being grateful for what you have is not the same as settling for what you have.

I am grateful for what I have, *and* I want more. I am grateful for what I have, *and* I know there is more for me. So when I say that I am grateful to be in this position today, to be able to be here, to have the wealth that I have, however much it is at this moment, to have the car I'm driving, or the wife I have, or the job I have, or the children or family or all the other things I'm grateful for— saying that doesn't mean that I'm going to settle for having just those things. I constantly want more for myself and from myself. I also constantly expect more from the people around me. As I work on myself, I encourage you to work on yourself. It will amaze you how much the world around you changes as you work on you. Being grateful is not the same thing as settling for life as it is today. If you were settling for what you have, you would not be seeking your next level and moving forward. I am absolutely grateful for the position that I'm in at this moment because it allows me to move forward to the position that I will be in tomorrow. I am not going to settle for where I am today.

I'm challenging you not to *just think* of being grateful and thinking positively, but to train yourself to *be* grateful and *be* positive automatically, and to catch yourself when you're settling. If you seem to be settling it may be that you are on a plateau and integrating and incorporating and mastering all the change you have recently gone through. That's not settling. That's developing, that's incorporating and assimilating. That is you taking in what you've been given and making it your own, so that you can act naturally from that position.

But, when you find yourself stuck and not moving, not having a positive attitude, not being able to be thankful for what you have, it may be that you are settling. Maybe you have just settled down. Nobody ever settles "up" unless it is at the end of a poker game! Settling down means slowing down, settling into a lifestyle that's less active and without movement. In a family sense, settling down can be a good thing. But, in most of the other ways, settling down is not a good thing. Settling is about you quitting on you.

Be Grateful For What You Have And Expect More.

Have a positive attitude about what's possible. **Anything is possible!** Anything is possible if you believe it's possible and if you're grateful for what you've been given so far. Train yourself to *believe* that way. Train yourself to *think* that way.

Start being thankful for little things, and *notice* when you're not. Notice when something disturbs you or when you have negative thoughts and are not grateful for something. Then simply change that behavior. **Remember, you get to choose your attitude**. Train yourself to be grateful. This is a huge, huge piece of the puzzle. And it's a huge challenge. Some people may find it very difficult because it requires noticing and being vigilant. Be aware at all times of your actions, your speech, your behaviors, and your emotions. Notice the energy that you put out in the world.

KEY:

When you are positive, happy, and grateful for your position in life, you will be attractive to other people. People will want to be closer to you and partner with you. They'll want to *be* like you. You will attract tremendous opportunity. So, I encourage you to be positive, be grateful, and don't settle.

GRATITUDE JOURNAL EXERCISE:

The only exercise I'm asking you to take on for this chapter is to start a *gratitude journal*, simply notice and acknowledge what you have to be grateful for. Start a daily habit of writing down at least three things that you are grateful for in your day. Do this in the evening before going to bed. Don't make it work, keep it simple. Read back through your journal once a week. Over time you will shift your habit of thinking to automatically notice and be grateful for the positives in your life. That good stewardship will bring you more positives!

Section One Summary

YOU WORK ON YOU

Let's go back and review a little bit of what we've talked about in this first section of this book. We looked almost exclusively at issues and principles that are about *you working on you*. In the second section of the book we're going to be looking at the impact that you have on the world. But, still *you working on you!*

In the introduction to this book I talked about building your own puzzle. This idea will tie into every chapter in this book, and in this first section I've introduced you to some simple principles that may add a piece to your puzzle. There are a certain number of principles and ideas and thoughts floating out there in the world, and through relationship and experience you will wind up coming in contact with many of those and have a chance to try them on (more about this in chapter 12). It's almost like you're trying on clothes. You're looking to see which colors look good on you, and which sizes fit you best. Are the shoes too small? Or, are the shoes just right? You may feel a little bit like Goldilocks testing the porridge and trying the beds. Sometimes a puzzle piece doesn't fit. It's way too big, or way too small. Other times it's just right. You may have picked up a puzzle piece as you read the earlier chapters in this book. You may have introduced to a new thought or a new belief that builds on what you already believe and that fits in neatly with the life puzzle that you're already building. The puzzle that you're building, when it's complete, will be a puzzle of infinite knowledge, infinite knowing, infinite happiness, and infinite success. That complete puzzle will put you in a pure, *complete* state. You may thinking, "that must mean that we never really complete our puzzle." That may or may not be true. If I disappear from this Earth, it may be that I just completed my puzzle. Or, it may be that I've just left this Earth and I need to complete more of my puzzle later. I don't know, but whichever of those alternatives happens to be true, I will continue to work on my puzzle and I encourage you to work on yours.

KEY:

It's always about *you work on you*. It's never about *you work on them.*

If you're doing a good job of working on yourself, then you will automatically always be influencing and impacting others and allowing them to work on themselves. We can't change other people, but we can influence other people by how we change ourselves. I don't have the power to change you. I can barely change myself. But through this book and the relationship we're building, I may be influencing you and others. There's a lot to be said for the example that Gandhi set. He said, "My life is my message," meaning that your life behaviors and choices are sending a message to all those around you. Your life is sending a message every day, and people are modeling your behavior. Know that you are an influencer and example to those around you, both good and bad. As you change and grow, you inspire, support, and challenge everyone around you.

In the first section of this book we looked at how your thoughts can create your reality simply by envisioning and creating your mental pictures and expecting that reality to show up for you. **The human mind makes very little**

distinction between what we dream or imagine and physical reality. That's why what we create in our mind is so powerful. It's a very simple process, a simple idea, and sometimes very challenging to execute.

We also discussed in the second chapter that we all have free will. You have free will and are responsible for the choices you make. Each of us is, at this moment, a result of the choices we've made up until this time in our lives, and in the future we will be a result of the choices we make from now on. We do have free will and we do attract and create our own mistakes as well as our own successes. We get to choose. By now you have started to notice the responsibility you have to make good choices and the power you have as you choose.

The third chapter in this book talked about living a life of purpose and not getting caught up in the process of making money or striving and struggling your entire life. We talked about finding your passion and purpose in life and the true reason you're on this planet. It's not all about just getting more toys. Life isn't like the bumper sticker that says "He who dies with the most toys wins." It's really about identifying your purpose in this life, because that's where true fulfillment comes from.

In chapter four we talked about each of us being *spirit, mind, and body*—in that order, not the reverse order. You are just housed in your physical body temporarily, and so your priority needs to be identifying who you are spiritually. Who are you in your spirit, and your mind, and finally who are you physically? If you look first to your spirit and ask yourself what is the right thing to do, what is your spirit telling you? What is God's Spirit saying to you? God lives within you, and you are a reflection of God. You are made in his image. And because that's true, you have God's knowledge and God's spirit in you. That spirit is an awesome resource that you should turn to first. Remember, you're spirit, mind, and then body.

In the next chapters we talked about you working on you first! That wasn't meant in a greedy way. It meant that if you take care of yourself first, then you have the energy and power to take care of others and support others—to *effectively* care about other people. After you get the energy flowing to your oxygen mask you'll be able to help your children put on their oxygen masks. If you don't, you may not be able to help anyone. We are often caught up in a dilemma of making a decision that is good for us and possibly hard on somebody around us. I urge you to do the right thing for yourself, knowing that it will ultimately always be good for the people around you as well. It may be challenging and difficult, but it will be good for them.

Later, we talked about maximizing your strengths. This is a very basic principle that should be fairly easy to understand: we all have gifts, strengths and natural talents. If we want to be successful, we must maximize our strengths. We focus our energy on them. We look to our strengths first. Ask yourself, why were you given these strengths and talents, if not to maximize them and to make good use of them on this Earth? You've been given stewardship of those talents and gifts. Stewardship is about doing good with what you've been given, knowing that it's your responsibility, and that you will also be blessed with more.

In chapters seven and eight we talked about how the ego interferes and that you need to be able set yourself aside. You may have thought "Well, this looks like the opposite of putting yourself first." Putting yourself first is not an ego thing, it is a balance thing. Setting the ego aside is not an ego thing, it is a balance thing. I'm asking you to find that balance. If you can set aside ego and look at things objectively, as if you're outside the situation, you get a totally different perspective. You can let go of some of the emotional and energetic charges that may be altering your view of the situation, and you will then be able to have a really clear answer as to what is the right thing to do. When you ask yourself what is the right thing to do, if ego is in the way the answer you get is often very blurred or distorted. Setting aside ego is a very important piece of the puzzle.

We talked about being your own expert. You are the expert for yourself. Don't give away that responsibility to other people. As we mentioned a little while ago, you are responsible for your choices. **You do have free will so don't give away your choices**. Take responsibility for yourself. You are your own expert, and nobody knows more about your situation than you do. Nobody has your unique spirit that lives inside of you except you, so begin to trust your expertise and develop that sense of trust in yourself so that you'll be able to move to your next level. And after reaching your next level, don't be satisfied to stay on the plateau. Use the plateau time to assimilate and settle into the new you, but when the next obstacle or challenge faces you, step up. Start climbing to the next plateau. Identify your next level and watch for it. Start asking yourself, "Am I on the plateau, or am I in a growth phase?" Be ready to step up to your next level, because life is a continual growth process.

BONUS CHAPTER: *Identify Your Next Level* Available on the website for a free download at www.coachingservices.com/books/bonus

When we stop learning and growing with God, we start to die. If we don't die physically, we die spiritually and mentally. Don't be satisfied with a five day a week job that only lets you come alive on the weekend. Life has more for you! Don't become complacent and settle for the plateau you're on today, because eventually you will be challenged to move to your next level. Go back to chapter one if necessary, and look again at **The Future Formula**™ to create the life you *really* want.

Finally, the last chapter in this first section taught us to be grateful for what we have. I challenged you to adopt the attitude of gratitude and a positive attitude about your future and what's possible for you. It's such a simple concept. It seems to be such an easy choice. Be grateful for what you have, even the negatives in your life. Be thankful for what you have and always be ready to be given more. **Expect more**. Be a good steward of what you have. **Be the optimist who sees opportunity in every calamity. Don't be the pessimist who sees calamity in every opportunity.**

So, as I've said many times, this first section of the book was all about "you work on you." It's all about you, isn't it? It's all about working on yourself so that you have a greater impact on the people around you. You're here for a purpose and you have choices. Please take responsibility for your actions and be thankful for the results. If you're still reading this book, you have probably experienced tremendous changes already. Maybe you've experienced tremendous changes in the way people react to you and how they view you. Maybe you've noticed it in yourself—that your energy, your attitudes, and even the actions you're taking are different than they were not long ago. Maybe the phone started ringing with business opportunities, or a family member called you up and you've reconciled old arguments. Or maybe you just noticed that you have a brighter outlook on life.

KEY:

Sometimes when we're stuck we don't realize we're stuck. We don't see ourselves the way others see us. **We don't know what we don't know, and we don't see what we don't see**. We may be on a plateau thinking that we have arrived at the top.

The challenges in this book have been given to you to help you notice where you are and to create opportunity for choices and changes. I'm sure that by now if you've really been reading these principles and challenging yourself with them, there's been an impact. There's been some meaningful fruit, some positive energy, some change that's come out of this. Before you go to the next section of this book I want you to take few moments, identify the change that's been happening in your life. Acknowledge what you're doing. Notice how far you've come since the beginning of this book.

AUTHORS CHALLENGE:
Maybe you're only skimming this book. If you're doing that, I really encourage you to go back to the beginning and use this as a *workbook*. Do the exercises in each chapter or portion of a chapter each day, or each week. **Identify the changes that you can make in yourself and do the work**. That's why I call this a workbook. Do the work!

Yes, it's possible to resist this suggestion and read this as an educational book. But I caution you: reading it that way may have no impact. It may add to what you know, but if it doesn't change what you do and how you show up or how you influence others, then what's the point? **Unless you do the work and challenge yourself with these principles you will remain the same**. I love the old saying that says "If you don't change directions, you're liable to end up where you were headed". If you don't like where you're headed, then go back and begin this book again. Embrace the principles and ideas, try them on and use them as a catalyst for change. Acknowledge the changes that you've made. Congratulate yourself. Treat yourself with a celebration when you reach a milestone. When you do something really good, especially if it's been difficult, reward yourself. Celebrate!

Now, Let's get to other principles about how *you* interact with the world... still YOU!

Chapter 10

EXPONENTIAL GROWTH/ COMPOUND EFFECT

E instein said that compound interest is the eighth wonder of the world. He said that because it's almost magical. Compound interest is an example of the principle of exponential growth. Simply put, it means that the growth is being multiplied by the previous growth. If you think of linear growth as 2+2= 4, 4+2=6, 6+2=8, etc., then exponential growth could be referred to as 2x2=4, 4x2=8, 8x2=16. And what you'll find if you continue that process is that very quickly the multiplied number outpaces the simply added number because it is building on itself. This is the principle of exponential growth.

Exponential Business Growth

As a coach, I work with my business clients to get them off of a linear growth pattern that is frustrating, and ultimately puts them behind their competition. We find that by using the principle of exponential growth we will eventually reach a point of critical mass where the business is building on its own. You may have had this happen in your own business.

Linear growth can be represented by a straight line that goes up at a steady, shallow angle from left to right. Exponential growth, on the other hand, will start in the same position, appear to be flat, but then becomes a curved line growing steeper and steeper until it goes almost straight up. Which would you rather have for your business? Which would you rather have for other areas of your life? Most of us would choose exponential growth. Most of us want to see results that are bigger, better, and faster as we go forward. It's the way we make more money, and the way we move ahead, not only in business, but in many other areas of our lives. **Exponential growth is the simple process of multiplication of efforts as opposed to simple addition**. It is also what makes *compound interest* work. For any given amount of money, no matter what the interest rate is, the money will grow faster and faster even though the interest rate does not change, because you're gaining interest on your original money plus the interest that you have accrued. We've all experienced this in our bank accounts, and we all know that the higher the interest, the steeper that curve will get in a shorter amount of time as the account balance grows.

This principle has direct application for you in any area of your life that you want. In chapter 6, we spoke briefly about the multiplication of your talents or gifts. We said that when we take one personal attribute and use it in combination with another personal skill or attribute the result is not the same as using them individually, but instead is magnified or enhanced. You achieve a greater result faster, it's just that simple, whether it's applied to money, business, or personal development, the idea is the same and the principle doesn't change.

Let me ask you a simple question. Do you have your money in a simple savings account or a checking account that bears no interest? Or, do you instead look for places that you can put your money that gives you the highest interest rate possible? I suspect it's the latter. I suspect you have used this principle of exponential growth in some of the most obvious places. What I'm asking you to do now is to apply the same principle in other areas. Where are you not getting interest on your efforts? Where are you not getting any interest on your talents and skills? Where are you not seeing exponential growth in your business? The interest that I'm talking about is the multiplying factor that I mentioned a few paragraphs ago.

EXAMPLE:

Let's assume you have a business creating a product that you designed yourself. You're very talented and the product is very unique because of your creative approach to design. However, you have focused your energies on the design and construction of the product, because they exercised your creativity, and this was rewarding for you. However, the product is not selling very well because you have not multiplied what you're doing with other skills or talents that you may have or the people on your resource list have. Imagine applying your creative skills to designing a unique marketing program to promote your product. Imagine using your creative approach to engage people to work with you. That would be an example of you multiplying your unique talent of creativity. If you stopped with the design and construction of the product and believed that that was the limit of your ability or skills, then the product sales might follow a linear path based on how many sales outlets you could get them into. But in the second example, when we multiply your creative skills and focus them on marketing there is no end to the speed of growth. And the real beauty of it is that **you don't have to have all the multiplying skills yourself**, you can get those from people on your resource list by hiring, affiliations, and partnering.

EXAMPLE:

Here is how it worked for a recent client: I was hired because my new client was not seeing the growth in her company that she had in the previous 5 years. She had reached a plateau because she had reached the limits of her knowledge and beliefs and could go no further. I recommended looking for affiliates to broaden her markets through the affiliates knowledge and connections. She called me a few months later, very excited, to tell me that her business had grown 300% in just the last quarter due to a connection she made and the opportunities that opened up as a result. In other words, she took all her experience and multiplied it times the person she affiliated with and got an exponential benefit. In her case, she actually worked less and made more! You can do the same.

Like many of the ideas in this book, this principle is very simple, and the benefit to you can be achieved very easily by doing little more than you are doing now. Also, like many of the other principles, it starts with you noticing those areas of your life that are on a linear growth pattern as opposed to exponential growth. As you begin to understand how you might apply this principle, I encourage you to take a piece of paper and write down those areas where you believe this principle can be applied. There are areas of your life or business where you want to see faster growth and bigger results, where you want to see things move forward faster. Exponential growth accelerates your progress with very little additional work on your part.

EXAMPLE:
Here's another example: let's assume that you want to invest in single-family homes. However, you don't know anything about it and you would have to learn a tremendous amount before you could get started. Your growth would be very linear in that case; it would depend on how fast you could learn and implement what you're learning. It would also be potentially very risky for you because you had not done that before. What if, on the other hand, you chose to partner with someone who had a lot of experience in the specific real estate area that you want to invest. Maybe they are looking for partners with money to invest with them. If you partner with them you will be using the *principle of leverage* that we will talk about in chapter 20 of this book. You will be multiplying your efforts through them for your benefit. Partnerships are a quick way to multiply your efforts in areas that are outside of your highest and best use to achieve exponential growth. If you are trying to do everything yourself, then you are not taking advantage of this principle.

Consider using other people as a shortcut, because they can accelerate your growth by bringing their skills and abilities, and multiplying them by yours. Go to the resource list that you created in chapter seven and ask yourself whether there's somebody that can act as a shortcut and multiply your efforts. You may bring them in as an employee, or an affiliate, or a full partner. That will be determined by what you want from them and what they want from you. All of your efforts will be multiplied through them and it will accelerate your growth. This is not limited to one person. As your business grows you may bring many people in to multiply your efforts.

Another application of this principle of exponential growth would be to simply take two or three of the principles we've talked about previously and use them in conjunction with each other. If you've been employing these principles in your life as you read through this book, then you are already multiplying the benefits of each of these ideas. It happens automatically. If you grow in one area, that will automatically support your growth in every other area. Whatever you learn winds up having application in many areas of your life for the rest of your life.

KEY:

You can't unlearn something. Yes, you may forget it for a while, but that concept you previously learned will come back to you when you need it.

Your continued education is the greatest multiplier there is. As you learn one new thing and implement it in your life, your growth in that area will accelerate. Every time, no exceptions! That is the purpose of this book.

Benefit Of Continued Learning

People are always telling me that they are lifelong learners, and I guess I would put myself in that category as well. The benefits are huge, because whatever you learn will be automatically applied as needed. It is the *interest* that you are getting on your investment in yourself. You want that interest to be paid to you at the highest possible rate, and I therefore encourage you to be a sponge. Soak up all the knowledge and education you can and ask yourself, "Where can I apply this?"

As you read through and implement the other principles in this book, I want you to consider each one and ask yourself which other principles this one can work with. How can you multiply them and get maximum benefit?

More Growth With Less Work

You may be thinking that I'm asking you to do more or work harder. In fact it is exactly the opposite! I know that through the multiplication of your efforts you will achieve more while doing less. In the example that I gave you at the beginning of this chapter we put in the same four sets of two, but in one example we wound up with 8 and in one example we wound up with 16. We didn't have to add more twos to get to 16. It was only that we were multiplying instead of adding that allowed us to achieve twice as large a result. That's what's available to you as well. You won't have to put any more in, or work any harder. It will feel like working smarter, but in fact it's simply multiplying your efforts so that you get a higher, more efficient result.

The fact is, many people don't grow at all and never achieve even linear growth, because they are not focused on addition all the time and therefore sometimes have subtraction. It's the old idea of two steps forward, and one step back. So if they're adding the same four twos into the equation, they may wind up with less than eight. Lots of people operate in that pattern and don't know how to break out of that cycle.

KEY:

Compounding interest only works when we're multiplying, so it becomes critically important to make sure that you are multiplying your efforts and not just adding them, and certainly not subtracting them

EXAMPLE;

Let me give you one final example, and maybe this is the most obvious: When your business starts to make money, it is tempting to take that money out and spend it for bills, or necessities of life, or even toys. But, if you choose to reinvest that money in your successful business you get a greater return and see accelerated growth. You also have the added benefit of total control over your investment. **Reinvesting in your business is the most obvious example of compounding the returns on your money.**

Exponential growth exercise:

I'm only going to ask you to do one thing as you complete this chapter. I want you to take a piece of paper and on the left-hand side make a list of all the areas in your life that you would like to see grow. On the right-hand side of the paper identify how you will multiply your efforts to achieve that growth. In previous chapters we've talked about how to access your own answers. You may not immediately think of how to multiply your efforts to achieve growth in the area that you identified. That does not mean that you do not know how. It only means that you have not accessed that information yet. Start that list right now by writing down the areas in which you'd like to see growth on the left-hand side of the paper. It may work best for you to write at the top of the right-hand side of the paper this simple question: *how will I multiply my efforts*? I want you to take the paper, identify your own areas for growth, and ask the question; how will I multiply my efforts? I know that by doing this you will access the answers, and then be able to multiply your efforts so that you can achieve an exponential growth as opposed to linear growth.

> ## KEY:
>
> The reason I'm asking you to write down this question, *how will I multiply my efforts*, is because **it's impossible for you to ask a question that does not have an answer. Every question has an answer, or the question could not be asked.** That doesn't mean that we have the answer immediately or easily. We often have to be patient and continue to ask the question. You will attract the answer when you ask the question,very much like you attract opportunity when you're ready for it.

Einstein had it right. Compound interest or exponential growth may be the eighth wonder of the world. If nothing else, it's a least a shortcut to help you achieve your goals faster and easier.

Chapter 11

WITH FREEDOM
COMES
RESPONSIBILITY

The principle for this chapter is focused on the simple idea of freedom. Simply stated, it is this: when we accept freedom, we take on responsibility. The reverse is also true: **when we take on more responsibility we are given additional freedoms**. We hear a lot of talk about freedom. People have always wanted to be *free* to make their own choices, *free* to express themselves fully. They've wanted freedom of speech, freedom from slavery, freedom from tyranny and oppression, freedom from government, freedom from taxes and much, much more. Smokers want to be able to smoke where they want. Non-smokers want freedom from that smoke. People want to choose their personal partners, and they want to choose their own business partners. They want to choose where and how they live, and they want freedom from others imposing their decisions on them.

This is an old, old concept that probably goes back to caveman days. There was probably one caveman who said "By golly, I want to be free to choose to hunt quail instead of musk ox." That caveman may have starved, but the principle goes that far back.

What Do We Pay For Freedom?

What do we have to pay to get that freedom? Throughout history we've seen examples, and historians chronicle all the different sacrifices that people have had to make in order to achieve and acquire the things that we call freedoms— freedom to make our own choices, the ability to choose to be individuals, the ability to be responsible for our own lives. And that's exactly what it is: it's a responsibility!

Responsibility comes with freedom, or I could say freedom comes with responsibility. **Responsibility is the price we have to pay for freedom**. It's always been true, always! If we want freedom from slavery we have to be responsible for making our own way, making our own choices, and being successful on our own.

With every freedom that we're given there is a price of responsibility. Responsibility to carry ourselves forward in a different way. Responsibility to let other people make their own decisions. Responsibility to pay attention to ourselves and our actions and not dwell on everybody else and their actions.

Again, remember we're focusing on generalized principles. The principle I want you to see here, look at, and examine from all sides, is the simple principle: with responsibility comes freedom. With freedom comes responsibility. There's no getting around it and there's no getting away from it.

EXAMPLE:

Remember when you were a teenager and you wanted to stay out late? You really wanted that freedom—the freedom to make your own decisions about when you came home, who you hung out with, and what you did. You know, the freedom to get in trouble or the freedom to not get in trouble. What was the responsibility that was associated with those freedoms? The responsibility was that if we were given that freedom our parents said, "Sure, you can stay out late, as long as you don't get in trouble." Right? Isn't that still the price of freedom? We have a responsibility not to get in trouble with our freedom. We have a responsibility not to abuse it. We have a responsibility to share it with other people, to speak it, to live it, to use our freedom wisely and have that be the example we set. We have a responsibility not to get in trouble with our freedom.

Through a lot of this book we've been talking about freedom of choice and that freedom of choice carries a heavy responsibility. With Freedom, all of a sudden it's nobody's fault but yours. **Nobody else is responsible for your choices but you.** If you take the freedom of choice, you take the responsibility, you pay the consequences, and you take the heat.

It's a little bit like the example with the federal government. You may turn the responsibility for preparing your income taxes over to somebody else, a professional CPA, but if you get audited who has to take the final responsibility? Who will get fined, or sent to prison, if you don't have enough money to pay your taxes, or if you deliberately under report your income? You will be the one responsible. Ultimately, you are responsible for all those things associated with you. Harry Truman said "the buck stops here." That means that there's no one to pass responsibility to. If you have infinite freedom to make decisions, decisions that affect you and maybe even other people, then along with that freedom comes responsibility.

I've had many employees in my various businesses, and there was always a responsibility that came with having people work for me. I loved having people work for me, supporting my energy and my ideas. But along with it came responsibility for those people that I hired. I made some of their decisions and took a little bit of their freedom for myself. But I took not only their freedom, I also took some of the responsibility for them that went with the freedom I was taking.

As you read this book you may be saying "Well, that's not me" because you don't have employees. Perhaps you are the employee. But even if you are an employee, make no mistake, **you still work for yourself.** We've talked about that principle in earlier chapters. You don't get to blame your employer. It doesn't really work to blame the company or say things like "My company doesn't have a savings plan, or an IRA, or some sort of pension plan. We don't have profit-sharing, so I'll never get wealthy." If you give up taking responsibility, then you are also giving up freedom. You are giving up the freedom to control your life and to be responsible for your own finances and your own decisions.

Sometimes it feels good to get rid of responsibility for your own financial success. It may feel good to get rid of the responsibility for your own relationship with your spouse husband or wife, or for the responsibility of raising your children. It may feel better to give those responsibilities to other people and have the schools be responsible for raising your children. It may feel lighter or easier, and yet when you give away that responsibility you also give away the freedom to create a life for yourself and your family, or you give away the freedom to make your own choices in other areas of your life. You may be giving away the freedom to become who you are *destined* to be—the freedom to fulfill the dream that we've been talking about in earlier chapters. When you had those personal dreams for yourself and a vision of what was possible, you set goals to meet those dreams and visions. You put steps in place. And if you give away the responsibility you won't be able to take some of those steps. You need to be able to grasp your freedom and to take the responsibility that comes with both success and failure. We need to be ultimately responsible.

Dare To Be Big! Dare To Live! Dare To Be *Great!*

There is a huge world out there that many of you want to give away. By that I mean you want to give away your power to other people. And rest assured, there are other people out there who will gladly take it. And what do you do? You pay them. You pay them big time! You pay them lots of money! They're people like your financial advisors, your stockbroker, your real estate investor, or your boss. These are just some of the people who will take some of your responsibility in return for money. They're leveraging their time and energy and using your money. In many cases that's okay because it may be buying *you* freedom to do other, more meaningful things with your time. But recognize that you are still ultimately responsible for the performance of those people to whom you delegate work on your behalf. Be discerning and hire carefully, knowing that you are still responsible.

In some cases, you may need to take responsibility back. You may have given responsibility to someone else and lost the freedom to direct your own life. Remember, **you are responsible for you**. Be willing to make your own choices. Be willing to stand on your own two feet and suffer the consequences or reap the rewards and benefits. It feels so good to take back responsibility and celebrate the victories for the positive choices you've made.

I know some of you reading this book are saying "But I'm not ready. Not smart enough. Nobody in my family is successful like that. I wouldn't even know where to begin." And if that's really the dialogue that's running through your head at this moment, if that's really what's your inner critic, the small ego, is saying to you, then I have a simple, one-word solution for you. *Education!* Simply know more. Remember, we talked about it earlier: fear goes away as we get our questions answered. That's the benefit of education. Educate yourself. Do it strategically in very specific areas so that you'll be able to take responsibility in those areas with confidence.

KEY:
As you know more your confidence level grows.

Learn, study, and read. Earlier in this book we talked about the fact that you are a reflection of the last five books you've read and the five closest people around you. You may be in a position where you need to shift that paradigm. Shift those things that surround you. Trade up! Continue to educate and challenge yourself, learn, and grow. Become confident, and when you're ready, opportunities will show up for you to launch you into more freedom, more responsibility, more abundance, and much more reward.

No Responsibility = No Freedom

Do you see the pattern here? There are people on this planet who live a very, *very* small life. They have given away responsibility all around them and they lose freedom. Where do the ones who give up the most responsibility wind up? They wind up in jail. They wind up in state and federal prisons all across this country. They're doing it strategically, intentionally, and why is that? Because they cannot handle the responsibility of freedom and taking care of themselves. Being responsible for every decision they make. For some, it is an overwhelming prospect, and through their own devices they put themselves in a situation where they have no responsibility and all decisions are made for them, and in turn, have no freedom.

On the other end of the scale, we have major national business leaders, politicians, corporate leaders, religious leaders and many others who step out in front and take a bold stance for what they believe. They're willing to take the responsibility that comes with that risk of putting themselves out there. They are willing to take the responsibility that comes with that freedom. And as a result, they have the freedom to shape lives, to influence people, to benefit people, and to offer their ideas for other people to expand on.

You and I are somewhere between these people that have ultimate freedom and responsibility and the people who have no freedom and responsibility like those in prison. Somewhere on that vast scale, you're at a point right now where you're probably reading this and saying to yourself "I want more freedom." And I'm here to tell you a simple way to get it. Simply take on more responsibility. If, however, you're not ready to take on more responsibility or you're not comfortable with that idea, then simply learn more.

CHOOSE FREEDOM EXERCISE:

The challenge for you right now, in this chapter, is to pick an area of your life in which you would like to see more freedom and are willing to take on more responsibility. Possibly, this will be an area in which you are learning to take responsibility in order to get more freedom. What area of your life would that be for you right now? Would it be relationships? Would it be financial? Would it be personal health? What about business? Or, something else entirely? In what area would you be willing to take more responsibility so that you could have more freedom? Maybe it's all these areas. But for the sake of this specific chapter, start with just one area. Choose one area in which you are willing to ask for more freedom and take on more responsibility. Or, maybe you're willing to start increasing your knowledge and confidence level through strategic education. You will become more comfortable and confident because you will know more. Identify that specific area for you and challenge yourself to make those changes.

At the end of this chapter, like other chapters in this book, there will be a list of questions to help you start this process. They will be provoking, challenging, and sometimes very personal inquiries. Take the time to answer these questions. Don't go to the next chapter until you're ready.

This does not have to be difficult. I am not talking about a radical change of your entire life, but only asking that you start with a small change, taking on responsibility in one small area of your life. You can take on any area of your life if you're willing to take the responsibility that goes with it. You can grow that area of your life and be given tremendous freedoms to make choices that will really serve you and move you forward.

KEY:

I don't care what area of your life you choose to look at, I will tell you now that **if you can consider it, it's available to you.** I don't know if you caught that? Let me say it one more time: I don't care what area of your life you choose, more freedom is available to you in that area if you can imagine it. I also don't care what level of freedom you believe you've already achieved, there is always another level of freedom available to you— if you're willing to go to the next level of responsibility as well.

Responsibility Of Entrepreneurship

I'm not advocating that everybody reading this book go quit their jobs. Now, you may be thinking "But, that would mean that I would gain a lot of freedom. I'd be taking responsibility for making my own livelihood. I'd be free of the tyranny of having to conform to a 9-to-5 workday, going to the office every day, taking the direction and orders for my boss. I'd be free to do whatever I want during the day, making my own living the way I want to. And I would be willing to take on the responsibility for my own income in order to do that." Great! If that's what you're led to do. I'm not advocating that for everybody. Not everybody's ready. Not everybody has the confidence level, the knowledge, and the abilities that are needed to be their own boss. If you feel led to quit your job and take that freedom and responsibility for yourself, then I would encourage you to be very strategic about how you did that. Create a plan based on a strategy to achieve your goals.

MY EXAMPLE:

I haven't worked for anybody since I was 17 years old. It's not that I couldn't, but at a very early age I made the decision to take on responsibility for making my own income. I was very independent, and I was very willing to take on responsibility to get those freedoms. In order to get them, I took on what was a relatively small responsibility at the age of 17, and I grew that responsibility through my entire life. We'll talk more about growing responsibility in a minute. My entire adult life I have worked for myself and at times it's been extremely challenging. I've had about seven different businesses, all of which have been successful, but they were all challenging in the beginning. I have made a lot of money, and I have lost a lot of money.

I'm telling you this so that you understand that **there is a learning curve in business.** Almost all business requires hard work and good decision-making in the beginning. I know many people who are self-employed, including most of my friends. Most of those friends are now becoming business owners as opposed to being self-employed. They are starting to work *on* their business and not *in* their business. This allows them to take on more freedom and more responsibilities and start second or third businesses. Taking on responsibility and moving from a position of being an employee to being self-employed in your own business is not for everybody. I'm not advocating that for everybody because there is a tremendous responsibility that goes with it. As you are reading this book you may know that you're not ready for that yet. Let's assume for a moment that it's something that you want, that you may be ready for it at some point. You will need to continue your education and learn more so that you will be prepared to take on the responsibility of business ownership and working for yourself. As you continue to embrace this idea, learn more, and create a strategy, you will gain the confidence and expertise to take that step and begin working for yourself as opposed to working for somebody.

This is one of the first areas that people typically look at, so maybe you are examining your work situation right now, and maybe you're ready to make a change and take on responsibility for yourself, but I want to throw in a word of caution here. I've seen many people go work for themselves who were not prepared, and in some cases they have gone back to being an employee because they found that the employee model gives them more freedom in *other areas of their lives*. Not everybody is cut out to be self-employed or to be a business owner. Thank goodness, because many people need employees.

Let me remind you yet again that you need to listen to your own heart, listen to yourself and **listen to your higher spiritual self**. Ask yourself what's appropriate and right for you to do next, and trust your own answers as they show up. Don't do something because you "should," or even because I am suggesting something in this book. I'll be frank with you, I am unwilling to take responsibility for any decisions you make based on reading this book. I am not advocating that you do any specific thing. I'm putting your responsibility and freedom right back on you just as I would want you to put it right back on me. It's my responsibility to take care of me. I work on me. And you work on you! **We are all responsible for our own decisions, period.**

Please don't get this wrong. If you're ready and willing, and able, and your spiritual and soulful self, and even your physical self, are telling you that "Yes, in this area I am ready to take responsibility for myself. I want to start my own business and I want to move ahead in that way," then I applaud you and support you. More power to you! Congratulations! I wish you great success. Please also consider all seven areas of your life because for you, it may not be about business.

I know for a fact that if you are reading this book and embracing the ideas and principles I've set forth in it, then you are absolutely capable of making the decisions about which areas you need to take on responsibility for yourself. If however, you are not ready to make big decisions, then start with small decisions. I encourage you to identify small areas in which you can take responsibility, and gain freedom, and build that muscle as you continue to work on yourself.

A moment ago, I talked about growing responsibility. Being responsible is an *attribute*, a quality that you cannot just be given. We *become* responsible, we *grow* in responsibility, we *develop* responsibility. We develop the attribute of responsibility over time. We do not receive it as an automatic gift at some point in our lives when we have a certain birthday, or reach a certain milestone. Sure, we get doses of it. Most of us got a big one when we left home for the first time. Maybe for you that was when you graduated from high school. Maybe it was when you went to college, or when you got your first job. All of a sudden you had to be responsible for yourself. And if you were successful in taking on responsibility for yourself, it was probably because you developed responsibility over time. You had lots of little doses of responsibility leading up to your leaving home.

KEY:
Responsibility is an attribute that you gain over time. Over time are the key words.

What was your first dose of responsibility? For me, like many of you, I was responsible for doing a few small things around the house at a very young age. I think I may have been about five years old when I was given responsibility for making my own bed. And the freedom I got along with that was the ability to not be micromanaged by my mother. I was given more freedom around the house. I was able to begin to choose things for myself. It was part of my growing up process. I was later given an allowance and rewarded for taking responsibility, and when I took on that responsibility successfully, what happened? Of course, I was given more responsibility.

One of the biggest challenges in life we can face is to suddenly have responsibility thrust upon us when we've never had to be responsible before. We suddenly find ourselves with greater responsibilities as life changes. That occasionally happens when young couples marry, or young single women have children, either intentionally or accidentally. Life changes abruptly, and you are suddenly thrust into a position of responsibility. Sometimes it happens when a parent dies, or when we lose a job. It may be very difficult to suddenly become responsible because we have not had time to grow into it or develop it. Responsibility was held by our parents, our employer, or someone else. Suddenly we have to become responsible for our own future, and at the same time we are suddenly given freedoms.

For you it may be reading this book that is challenging you to be more responsible. Were you ready to take on more responsibilities, or was there resistance? Again, remember these are generalized principles. I am talking about the coupling of responsibility with freedom which is a very generalized principle. But that generalized principle can have very specific applications for you. This principle may have hit you in a very specific area of your life.

EXAMPLES:
Let me share some real-life examples with you of how my wife and I taught our children responsibility by giving them more and more freedom and asking more and more of them. These examples may ring true for you as well. Maybe this is how you learned responsibility?

When our children were very small, about four or five years old, we asked them to start unloading the dishwasher and setting the table for dinner. It was a lot of responsibility and there was a lot of resistance. They didn't want to be responsible. They wanted us to continue to do the job for them and for us to be responsible for them. When they were seven or eight years old we asked them to do their own laundry. Lots and lots of resistance, because they weren't ready, and they didn't know how to run the washing machine, they couldn't figure out how to do it, and on and on and on. We showed them all those things and they took responsibility for doing their own laundry and they gained the next level of freedom with responsibility.

As our kids started middle school, we gave them a large allowance at the beginning of the school year and said "Here's your money for the entire year for clothes. You can buy whatever kind of clothes you want." This was incredible freedom for a child that age, and an awesome responsibility. Freedom and responsibility go hand in hand. One of my daughters bought a pair of $150 Nike shoes and that used up most of her money. She had to wear last year's clothes the entire school year as she learned responsibility for her choices. No, we didn't bail her out and give her more money because she would not have learned responsibility that way. When she wanted to buy more clothes she didn't have any more money, unless she found a way to earn it. However, she did have some amazing shoes and learned valuable lessons about responsibility!

When my children started high school we sent a note to the high school with them the first day of class. The note simply said "Keep this note on file. This is to acknowledge that our children have our permission and the right to leave school at any time for any reason they deem necessary." We got a telephone call immediately. The school said "We can't possibly give that responsibility to children." Our response was that our children can handle the responsibility. They have always been responsible. The teachers left that note on file for four years and all of our kids graduated at the top of their classes or very nearly. They were excellent students. They knew what they needed to do and they took responsibility for their own grades. We never got called in to deal with our children for scholastic issues because we gave them and taught them to be responsible for themselves.

Each of our children had cars when they were 16 years old, bought with money that they had earned on their own. They had taken on that responsibility because they knew if they wanted their own car, and the freedoms that that would bring them, they would have to earn the money themselves. And they did! As a reward, we offered to pay their insurance as long as their grades were good.

I tell you all this to show you how responsibility and freedom come hand-in-hand. My children got incredible freedom, one step at a time. They got freedom to leave school in high school if they wanted to. They rarely did, but they had that freedom. They had the freedom to buy their own car, even if it might be the wrong kind of car, when they were 16 years old. Actually that process started when they were 15 so they'd be ready when they turned 16. They had the freedom to dress how they wanted, wear their hair the way they wanted, and much, much more. Why? Because they had been good stewards of responsibility, so more responsibility was given to them.

Are You Developing Responsibility?

We make our own choices, and we take responsibility for ourselves as we grow up. We continue that process the rest of our lives. It is not something that someone else can give us, we have to develop it in ourselves. Successful people in this life are people who learn to take responsibility and can handle responsibility themselves. When I keep saying "You work on you," one aspect I'm talking about is your developing responsibility in order to gain freedom.

This is an integral part of that "you work on you" process. If you work on becoming a more responsible adult in society, and more responsible in your own household and with your family, you will automatically gain more freedom. It will happen as a result or byproduct, as a payment or reward for being more responsible. It is also important to know that it is up to you to *take* it.

Again, I am not advocating a specific action. I am advocating that you listen to your own heart, look at your own situation, notice your own responsibilities, and determine the next area for you to take on more responsibility and freedom. Create a strategic plan to do that and get into action. Whether it's a small step or large step is not important. What is important is taking steps, any steps.

Enjoy working on this principal. It can be an easy one, and we should all be doing it anyway. It's a generalized principle with very broad application that can have profound affect. Take more responsibility and be given more freedom! Pretty easy. Or the reverse… take more freedom and be given more responsibility! Still easy.

FREEDOM AND RESPONSIBILITY EXERCISE:

Please look over some of the following questions to help you identify the next area or level of responsibility that you are ready to take on. Know that you will also receive new freedoms as your take on those responsibilities. New freedoms around choice of lifestyle. New freedoms around developing that dream of yours and moving closer to your goals. New freedoms with relationship and business, business partners, friends, abundance and wealth, and personal health. You can develop responsibilities and freedoms in any area of your life. Now a few questions:

1. What is the largest responsibility you have today?
2. What is the freedom that comes with that responsibility?
3. What is the largest freedom you have today?
4. What is the responsibility that comes with that freedom?
5. In what area of your life do you want more freedom?
6. What responsibility are you willing to take on?
7. Who in your life do you need to give responsibility or freedom to?
8. How important is freedom in your life?
9. What will you commit to do, starting today?

In the next chapter we will introduce you to the concept that two of life's most important aspects are *Experiences* and *Relationships* because it is only through them that you are challenged to make choices. It is through your experiences and relationships that you are given the opportunity to lead your life.

The Authors Encouragement

By now you've come to the end of chapter 11, about halfway through this book. We have covered some incredibly large challenges, some life-changing principles. Some of these may seem like details, and not that significant, and yet they're also extremely important. They relate back to some of the key principles that we started this book with. Those principles were based on the idea that you work on you, and that nobody else can do your work for you. The first section gave you principles that allowed you to work on yourself. Many of the following principles allowed you to work on specific areas of your life. Some principles may seem more or less important to you personally, but I encourage you to not set down this book until you complete it.

It's important to continue to work through this book because the principles in this book encompass most of the principles that you'll need to work on in your entire life. You can continue to work on these principles over and over. You can expand on them. They'll take you to level after level as you grow and move forward. The principles will relate to your relationships, your business, your finances, your personal growth, your spiritual growth, your personal health, and every other aspect of your life. Keep up the good work!

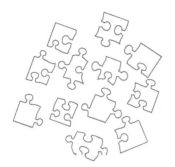

Chapter 12

EXPERIENCES AND RELATIONSHIPS, THE CATALYST FOR CHANGE

S imply stated, this chapter is about the principle of experiences and relationships. This principle tells us that only those two things, experiences and relationships, are important, because they are pivotal points for us that challenge us to change or continue without changing. They are the *catalysts to change!*

We All Live A Life Of Experiences

About three years ago I met a man in his mid-70s. When he was 17 or 18 years old he made a list of 100 experiences that he wanted to have in his lifetime. It was his bucket list and he filled most of his bucket early in life. He was speaking to a group of young people about what he thought life was all about. Having started with 100 experiences on his list, he had accomplished about 70 when I saw him speak. There were a few that he hadn't done yet. And, a few that were on his list from when he was young that had changed as technology changed and more things became possible.

Generally his list of 100 things remained the same with very little change throughout his life. After speaking to him I found that he was concerned about the number of years he had left and his physical ability to do some of the things that were remaining on his list. For instance, in his mid-70s he didn't know if he would ever be able to take a trip to space. He had already accomplished many similar things: in the mid-50s or 60s he flew an F-4 fighter jet across the desert floor only 50 feet above the ground. He had also been one of the first people to canoe the Amazon River from its headwaters to the ocean. He had in fact, canoed all the major rivers of the world. He had been to both polar caps, and places where no white man had ever been.

This man had lived a full life of rich experience and created a lifestyle from it. He would take film crews from National Geographic or the Discovery channel and other organizations along with him. They would provide for his trip and his supplies, and pay for him to have that experience. For the last 20 years, his adventures have been chronicled on PBS, Discovery, OPB, National Geographic specials, and more. If I told you his name you might recognize him.

He believed that life was largely about what we experience. He believed having the goal of wanting to experience as wide a variety of things as possible allowed you to experience much, much more than if you had no goals. His list was being accomplished largely because he had a list. The few things that hadn't been accomplished were his major regret in life. Many of the experiences he had were very difficult and they were life-changing. Because of the nature of his challenges he had seen friends eaten by alligators right before his eyes. Not a pleasant experience, but certainly a life experience. He has seen people drown in tidal waves, he's been at earthquake epicenters, he's been in remote parts of the world, on safaris, and filmed animals in every type of natural surrounding. He's been charged by bull elephants and lived through every possible imaginable situation. He had experiences that most of us will never ever have, and frankly, most of us would never want to have.

But if we accept the principle that life is about experiences and what they can teach us, then experience is a very valuable tool.

What are the experiences that you hope to have in life? What experiences have the power to change you? What is the most profound experience you've had so far and what was the impact it had? I think most of us will agree that experience can be a profound teacher.

Would you believe me if I told you that you are changed, at least slightly, by every event or experience you have in life? Even the most insignificant, small experience will cause some small irreversible change in you. That's how important experiences are.

How We Change, Repetition And Impact

It is said that we create big changes as a result of one of two processes. The first process is repetition. If we repeat an action long enough, soon it becomes our natural action. I will speak all through this book about how we can affect change, both physical change, and change of habits. through choosing *and continuing to choose* a new course of action. That involves repetition. The second process that brings about change is a highly emotional, impactful event—in other words, a powerful experience. If you have a highly emotional or dramatic experience, it has the power to change your life forever. You will be changed from the moment you have that experience. From that experience you may decide consciously or unconsciously to do something different than what you've always done before.

Change Is Inevitable And Constant

The truth is we change from every minor experience as well as the major experiences. If we identify a large experience that we want to have, that's wonderful, but we also need to notice that the small experiences we have are impacting our lives as well. Every experience is an event that causes us to make decisions and choices. Those choices will affect our lives from that moment forward. As we discussed in the beginning of this book, we are constantly making those choices and putting ourselves on a slightly different path.

Experience has the power to change our behavior. Have you noticed what happens as you have an experience? When you experience something you get to choose, to make life choices based on what has happened. Now, not all life experiences are good, are they? Sometimes experiences can be very negative and very destructive, and other experiences can be wonderful. A death in the family, for instance, or a birth in the same family, are very different experiences in some ways, and yet as we look at each of those experiences, it's clear that they're both experiences which cause us to make both behavioral and intellectual decisions about how we view life and what we will do. We instantly label them good or bad. We label the death a bad thing and birth a good thing, unless the death was welcomed to end suffering and the birth wasn't wanted. Events or experiences are simply that, they are an event or experience from which we go away a little bit changed.

> # KEY:
> Most events and experiences are neither good or bad until we label them, then we attract the result we expect. Good or bad, you choose!

Our life experiences allow us to make choices. They allow us to look at what happened and ask ourselves "Do I want to do that again?" You may not be able to change the experience you have gone through, but you do have the power to affect the experience the next time. There may be things you choose to do that will change the experience when it comes around again. Or, there may be things you do that change the effect of the experience on you. Years ago I had severe back problems. I found that regular exercise helped me avoid the back pain by staying in better physical condition. That was the choice I made to avoid the experience of back pain. That was 25 years ago, and I'm still exercising to maintain my physical condition to avoid the back pain. If I stopped exercising tomorrow the pain may or may not come back, but the physical habit of working out and maintaining myself physically will be with me the rest of my life. One major experience shaped the course of my life. I'm sure if you look back you will see similar experiences and events that have shaped your life because of the decisions you've made following those experiences.

Repeating A Negative Experience, For What?
How many times do we have to experience something to learn the lesson it contains or to make the choice it presents? This could be an entire book by itself. How many times do we have to experience something to learn the lesson

that is there for us, that the universe or God is trying to teach us? As you read this book you probably know exactly what I'm talking about. How many times have you been married? How many different jobs have you had in your life? I'm not saying it's wrong to have more than one marriage or more than one job, but we are often in the same situation that we've been through before because we didn't learn the lessons the first time. Remember the definition of stupidity: doing the same thing and expecting a different result! If you notice yourself in the same situation or circumstance, there may be a lesson for you to learn. Maybe your experience didn't teach you anything or didn't change your behavior last time around. Maybe it didn't have an impact on you and therefore you didn't choose to do anything different as a result.

I want you to start noticing the experiences that you have in your life. Every day you have dozens and dozens, probably hundreds, or possibly thousands of different experiences. Some are very small, or almost inconsequential, and others are very large. Whether large or small, all experiences and events have the ability to have a profound effect if you use them as points of decision. Do you want to experience that again? If so, make very little change. If, on the other hand, you don't want to experience that again, then make immediate changes. This requires you to be conscious of the experience! The best experiences are the ones we become aware of the moment they happen. When we notice how we react and what the effect is we then have the power to change our reaction. I want you to start to notice and be more conscious of experiences as you're going through them, so that you can consciously choose the path you want to be on. Notice the impact those small changes are having on your life.

I want to share a story with you to demonstrate how our lives can change as a result of experiences. Many years ago one of my employees won a free bungee jumping experience. This was when bungee jumping was very popular. The bungee jump she won was way too scary for her and she had no interest in pushing herself to that extreme. I, on the other hand, thought it would be a great experience and an opportunity to test my limits and see if I had the courage to push beyond my innate fear of falling and trust something to be fun and safe. I knew the experience was obviously going to be both thrilling and very emotionally challenging to push through. My employee gave me the bungee jumping tickets and a week later I went with my twin 14-year-old daughters about 100 miles north to the jump site. It was a gorge over a dry creek bed out in the middle of nowhere. A one lane bridge stretched across a deep gorge. The bungee actually went into a canyon about 400 feet deep. I could see immediately that this was not going to be an easy experience. It really seemed to be the ultimate bungee jumping challenge because you really have the feeling that you're jumping off a bridge into oblivion. Except for the bungee cord there was absolutely no way that you could possibly live through it.

When we arrived there were about 30 people on the bridge taking turns bungee jumping with one bungee jumping cord. The event managers were very diligent about training people prior to letting them go through the process. They talk you through the process as they buckle you into a harness. They had people sign a release holding them harmless and then one at a time took them to the point where you stepped over the railing of the bridge and stood on a little platform on the outside edge. At that point you were hooked to the bungee, standing out there on the edge of the bridge with all the other people watching, and at times there were 30 or 40 people there. All the people watching would start counting backwards from ten. Ten, nine, eight,… The intention was that everybody's energy would help support the person in overcoming their fears so they could jump off the bridge when the countdown got to zero. Many people jumped—forwards, backwards, with their eyes closed, their eyes open, whatever. I was able to witness many jumps before it was my turn. I was also able to witness many people not jump. Many people were unable to step over the railing of the bridge and stand on the platform on the outside. Some made it onto the small platform, but after repeated counts by the audience were still unable to jump. That instinctive fear of heights, and fear of falling, and fear of trusting the bungee cord made it impossible for them to let go and have that experience. So, the experience they had was not jumping, and from that experience of not jumping, decisions and choices were made. They experienced the "What if I don't jump?" question. "What's the effect of all these other people thinking that I don't have the nerve? How do I feel about myself not taking the risk? How do I feel about protecting myself and playing it safe?" Jumping or not jumping was not the issue. It was an experience for them either way. Interestingly, as I was being connected to the bungee and going though the training, both of my 14-year-old daughters came to me and said "Dad, I want to jump, I want to jump!" They had been watching other people jump and thought they had the nerve to do it. I honestly didn't think they did, because it was taking every bit of my nerve to consider stepping over that wall and making the jump. One of my daughters would never even dive into a swimming pool from the edge, and now she was telling me she wanted to dive off a 400 foot bridge into a 400 foot gorge. I said to them, "Well, let me jump first and I'll tell you what my experience is and then we'll decide if you want to jump or not". As they hooked me up to the bungee I remember thinking I'm going to do a big swan dive, and I was absolutely okay until the moment I stepped over the railing and stood on the outside little platform. Instantly, and I mean *immediately*, my entire mind and body were screaming at me "Don't jump!!! Get off the bridge! Don't be stupid! Save yourself! Don't jump!" And meanwhile my logical mind that wanted me to jump was saying "Nobody else has died, the bungee is secure. They do this all the time, and it's absolutely safe. You're not going to die."

It was much more than an internal dialogue, it was a shouting match. Finally, the only question was: would I jump when the people counted me down? Did I have the nerve? Absolutely, I did! But, did I remember the experience? No! I don't! My mind was so occupied with the battle, the battle that the experience had created within me, that I remembered only glimpses, brief moments, of that first jump. I did remember it taking a long, *long* time to reach the bottom. I did remember the mental battle going on even as I was dropping, and it seemed like a long, long drop, with lots of time for more mental sparring. It was a few seconds that seemed like a few minutes before the bungee cord snapped and caught me. As I started rebounding the first time I immediately thought "Oh my gosh, it's over, and I don't even remember." At that point they lower a little hoist to you and to pull you back to the top of the bridge again. After it has pulled you up, they said "Would you like to jump again?" And because I was unable to remember the jump, I told them yes, I would jump again. That's what I was there for. I wanted the experience. So, as they finished hoisting me back up I remember thinking "That was great. Now this time I'm going to pay attention, and I'm going to enjoy the experience, and I'm going to be totally focused and aware of what's happening. This time I'm going to jump off backwards into a backwards swan dive and notice the scenery falling away from me and enjoy the experience of the free-fall." Once again, I stood on the platform and they started to count and once again my mind started screaming… "You were lucky the first time! Get off the bridge! Save yourself! Don't be stupid! Don't jump!" And yet I knew the bungee jump cord was strong enough to hold me because I had just had the experience. I knew I would live. I knew I would be okay, and yet the internal battle raged. I did dive off backwards when they counted down to zero and I do remember slightly more of that experience. As I came back to the top the second time my daughters were both demanding that they go next. I was totally amazed that my daughters were willing to experience the jump and were as excited to have that experience as I had been. Even the daughter who was afraid to dive into a swimming pool was willing to dive into a 400 foot gorge with no water and only a cord to hold her.

An experience like that challenges our thinking and challenges our behavior. But what it also does is change our beliefs and our behaviors from that point forward. The girls both had the courage to make the jump and loved it. The daughter who was afraid to dive in the swimming pool never had a problem diving into the pool again. All three of us came away from the experience saying "If I can do that, bring myself to a 400 foot cliff and dive off a bridge with only a cord separating me from death—if I have the nerve to do that, then I can do anything." Even my daughters had the experience of believing they could challenge themselves and achieve anything. It was an incredible boost to their confidence in every area of their lives. "If I can bungee jump, I can do anything!"

Have you ever had a similar experience like that instill great confidence in you? An experience that changed you profoundly from that moment on, based on that one experience? Think about it right now.

CAPTURE YOUR GREATNESS EXERCISE:

What was the experience that had that kind of profound effect on your life? Take a moment and write it down. Remember and notice how different you were after that experience. Notice your behavior before the experience and your behavior after the experience. What changed? What was the choice you made? What was the impact that it had? Now take that farther and ask yourself what impact that experience had on your business, or the people around you like your family, and your spouse? Write it down so you capture what you learned about yourself.

> # KEY:
> **You cannot change someone else, when you change, the world around you will also be effected and change**. All experiences have the power to change your life forever, because life is only about experiences and relationships.

Relationships also have the ability to have a profound effect on us. From our relationships we get to fine tune our emotions and develop behavior about how we will react to others. We get to notice our language. We get to notice our impact on other people and how they react to us. From those relationships we get to make a lot of choices, don't we? If you're reading this book and you are married, you know the huge impact that your spouse has on you. You may be constantly feeling that you need to modify your behavior or choose something different to satisfy someone else. Maybe you have changed to simply get along with someone that you work with. We are constantly changing our behavior based on relationships.

Relationships; Brief Encounter Or Life-Long?

Sometimes relationships are long-term and can have an ongoing effect. Other times ,they are as brief as a momentary encounter. Yet it's still a relationship. Every encounter we have with another person causes us to come away slightly changed or to be on a slightly different path, and arrive at a slightly different destination. Whether it's a simple introduction on the street to somebody new that you will never see again, or a relationship with a family member that lasts for decades, that encounter has the potential to change you forever.

I've listened to many personal growth speakers, religious speakers, and financial speakers over the years. These people often have one or two points in their presentation that really have an impact on me—that really land, I guess you'd say. It may be a piece of my life puzzle that I've searched for. They showed me a piece for just the right place and I was ready to use it at the time they delivered their presentation. The effect might be so profound that it changes my life from that moment on. The relationship I have through conversation, listening to a presentation, or reading a book presents me with choices that can alter who I am. The same is true for you, and it's time for you to start noticing the choices that are presented to you through the relationships you have with others. Many times those relationships will raise questions about yourself and you will have to ask yourself "Is this what I want to continue to do, or do I want to have something different?" So, relationships present another opportunity for us to change.

As you read this book you may remember noticing that you have had relationships that you seem to repeat with different people over and over. Maybe you've been bullied and continue to be bullied. Or, maybe you are a bully and continue to bully. Have you been taken advantage of financially? Has it happened repeatedly? Have you had a tyrant for a boss and even though you've gotten different jobs the same type of person seemed to wind up as your boss again? Have you had relationship with boyfriends or girlfriends and continue to choose the wrong type of person over and over?

Relationships are an opportunity for us to create change in our lives. Many people believe relationships are a mirror of our own life and our own issues, so that what we see in the other person is a mirror reflection of our own issues. Often the issues that we have no problems dealing with in other people are not *our* issues, but the ones we have problems with *are* our own issues. The reason we have trouble dealing with them is because we don't know how to deal with them in ourselves. These people and their issues confront us with with our own challenges. Other issues we may be able to easily dismiss since we've already learned how to deal with them and they trigger nothing in us. So, when you see an issue or a problem in somebody else, start to notice that it may be your issue as well. It only shows up as a point of contention because you don't know how to deal with it in yourself. Relationships have the power to have us notice what we need to change in ourselves. If we don't make those changes, we will almost always repeat a relationship with similar issues.

THE MIRROR EXERCISE:

I want to challenge you right now to create a list of the people in your life with whom you have had problems. Make a list right now! Make a list of the people that you've argued with and with whom you don't get along, and include on that list the people that you least want to be around. Then ask yourself, "How do they mirror who I am? What could I change so that I don't have to repeat a relationship with them again? Do I have multiple relationships with the same type of people? Do I run away from one relationship and run right into another relationship that's identical?" If you're running from negative relationships, start to notice what it is about you that puts you in those situations, and change who you are so that the relationship shows up differently the next time and won't have a negative effect or impact on you.

At the same time, make another list of the people that you love and most want to be around, and start noticing what it is about those people that attracts you. Why do you want to be around them? What is it that you like about them? How do they mirror who you are? Remember from our very first chapters in this book: you work on you! It's not about you trying to change somebody else's behavior to make a relationship better.

It's about you changing your behavior to make the relationship better. The relationships you attract are to show you what you need to change in yourself. It becomes very important to notice who you are choosing to be with because they are there to show you something about yourself. If you don't notice and change, then you're doomed to repeat the same relationships over and over.

Do you know that you attracted and chose the people that you are in a relationship with? You chose your parents. You chose your children. You chose your spouse. You chose all those people and attracted them into your life because each of them is there to challenge you to change in a specific area. I know you may want to believe that it is some cosmic or divine mistake that brought "so and so" into your life, but believe me, you brought them into your life for a purpose. If you look at all the people around you from that perspective you'll quickly realize there are lessons for you to learn and changes for you to make in your beliefs and behaviors. It's not about you changing them, *it is about you changing you.* They are there to help you and they are there only at your invitation.

Only experiences and relationships cause us to choose a different path.

Imagine the profound change that took place in the 70-year-old man that I told you about earlier who had the list of 70 experiences he had accomplished in his lifetime. Almost every one of the experiences he had was as challenging as my bungee jump. He had a full and daring life exploring his own list of experiences. And I'm sure the changes he made as he went through those experiences and relationships changed the course of his life many, many times.

Don't misunderstand me, I'm not recommending that lifestyle for you. You may have wild and daring experiences or you may have very safe and calm experiences. One is not better than the other. I am, however, recommending that you become aware of your experiences and the opportunities that they have created for you to use as decision points for how you want to go forward in your life.

BUCKET LIST EXERCISE:

I also want to challenge you to **make your own bucket list**. Identify experiences in your life that you still want to have at least one time. take a piece of paper and write them down. Add to them as you are inspired or prompted to and scratch off those that you have completed. Keep this list nearby and let it be a reminder of all the experiences that life still has to offer you.

I remember that when I was growing up my father used to say "There are many things in life worth doing one time." One of the things on his list was to swim in the Great Salt Lake. If you've not had that experience, it is a unique experience and not like swimming in any other lake. Because of the amount of salt in the water of the Great Salt Lake the human body is much more buoyant than it is swimming in fresh water, or even in the ocean. You can actually float with one third of your body out of the water. You can float with your arms and hands completely out of the water above your head. You don't have to tread water. It's a totally different experience and it doesn't stop there! If you don't take a shower immediately when you come out of the water, you'll absolutely regret it, because you will dry with a white crusty surface. It's one of those things that's worth doing once in your life. I did it with my family when I was about 12, and my father finally was able to scratch it off his bucket list. It's not something I necessarily care to repeat, but it's an experience I'm glad I had. Did I make a profound change as a result of having done it? No, probably not. But I did learn from it and it has stayed with me all these years. There are many experiences in life like swimming in the Great Salt Lake that teach us something. Some are much more profound like bungee jumping was for my daughters and me. There are also many relationships that have the potential for life-changing impetus in our lives.

Notice What You Choose

The challenge of this chapter is to simply notice. Be aware and notice the experiences that you're having, and the relationships you are having, so that you are able to make positive changes as you move forward based on what you've experienced. Experiences and relationships change your life. They are what life is about. They are the catalyst for change on this planet, *when you notice and are aware* of what's happening to you and around you. Remember, change happens through repetitive action or profound events. Please notice your experiences! Become aware of the relationships you're having and which ones you are repeating. Make a list and detail the experiences that you still want to have in your life, and start moving toward them. Set a goal to have an intentional experience.

In the next chapter we will be talking about a specific application of some of these relationship principles and how to get more without doing more.

Chapter 13

RADICAL ACCEPTANCE ALLOWS THE IDEAL OUTCOME

T his chapter is about radical acceptance. It's about letting go. It's about allowing things to happen that were not necessarily "supposed" to happen, but that are in your best interest. When we notice that we're struggling and we want to make a change, the simple principle of letting go, or radical acceptance means that we accept whatever is showing up. We then choose to work with whatever's there. It's a simple principle that would seem to be easy to implement, and yet it's very difficult for most of us to do, because it goes against how we are trained. Almost everyone is brought up to believe that they can make things better if they *work* at them. We are taught that good things come to those who go after them or struggle to achieve them and who work hard to get them.

Notice The Hard Part And The Challenge

You may have believed that: "You have to fight through a bunch of stuff to get to the success…" Yes, it's true, sometimes you do. But often letting go of the struggle accomplishes more than trying to push your way through when something is seemingly going against you. Sometimes radical acceptance allows things to come to you that wouldn't be able to reach you otherwise. Sometimes your lack of acceptance is the very thing that is causing the challenges. *You may be your biggest problem.*

When you notice that you're in the middle of a struggle and that things are difficult, please consider radical acceptance. Consider letting go of your attachment to a specific path or outcome. Have you ever noticed how easy it is to give somebody else advice? How easy it is to have a solution for what they should or should not do? "Oh, they just don't get it. They ought to just stop talking to their kids like that. They ought to just show up for work on time. They ought to do this, they ought to do that." It's sometimes very easy for you to see the solution to someone else's problems but very difficult to find a solution to your own problems. Why is that? That is because when you look at somebody else's problems you step outside their situation. You're not part of that situation. You're not emotionally entangled in the outcome or results. You have no interest in the outcome, because it won't affect you directly. And therefore it's very easy for you to say "Oh, they should just move. He should just quit his job and he should start working for the company that made him a better offer, and he'd be a lot happier," or "She should leave her husband," or "They should take a vacation once in a while, but they just never make it a priority to get away." Whatever you see as their solution is easy for you to see because you're not in the situation and don't have the emotional attachment to the outcome.

It's possible for you to be able to step outside your own life situations, for you to remove yourself emotionally and be able to step back from the challenging and difficult situation you're involved in, and say: "Hmmm, I see what's happening. I accept what's happening. Now, this is very interesting. How are we going to work this out?" And as soon as you let go of the struggle and create a little mental and emotional distance, you will gain a little objectivity in your mind and you will be able to see yourself as you saw those other people for whom you have the answers. You'll start having answers for yourself. You'll be able to distance yourself and find creative solutions.

Radical acceptance is just saying "Okay, this is what it is," or stepping outside of it and saying "This is interesting—now what can I do?" You can deflect negativity almost like judo or other martial arts when they teach you that you don't resist the blow, but instead, step aside and accept the blow, and use your opponents energy to throw him to the ground. Isn't that exactly what I'm asking you to do with radical acceptance? I'm asking you to quit fighting and pushing against any negative energy that's coming at you. Accept the energy, step aside and use it's force by letting it flow past you and redirecting, instead of trying to stand firm and resist.

It's a very simple concept that's very difficult to employ because it means such a change from how we are trained to think. Aren't we trained in school that we need to struggle with things? Haven't we been told over and over again that it's hard to pass your exams and get A's without doing hard work? And weren't you taught that you have to stand up to anybody who pushes you around? And so, as adults, we grow up to believe the same thing—that being successful is hard work. Life is hard! It's a struggle! You're going to have problems with your kids when they're teenagers, you know it's hard to make a marriage work, it's hard to get along with your boss, everything takes work! Even if you work for yourself, that's hard, too. Life is hard, and it's because we're in this position of resistance. We've been set up by the world to be in a position of perpetual resistance.

I always tell people that it's true... *if you say so*! But there's another choice...

Instead, if we just accept what is showing up, it will be so much easier. Maybe you do have a boss that's difficult to work with. How can you work with him? If you had a friend or relative who had that difficult boss you would have advice for them, wouldn't you? It would be very easy for you to see what the solution is—for them.

PRETEND YOU KNOW EXERCISE:

I have two little exercises for you that will demonstrate what I mean. First of all, think of a time in the recent past when you'd been really really struggling with something or somebody, some specific situation that was a huge challenge. When you've imagined that time, I want you to do two things: first, remember what it was like. Remember the situation in detail, and remember all the ideas and solutions you tried to deal with that situation. Remember how exhausting it was, and how much work it was, and how long it took you to find the right solution—that is, if you ever found the right solution. Maybe you never did find the right solution and you're still in the ongoing struggle right now. Maybe the problem's been going on for a long, long time.

I want you to notice how it feels to be in the middle of that situation, in the middle of that challenge. I want you to notice the struggle, the heaviness of it and how difficult it is and how exhausted it makes you. it just drains your energy. I want you to notice how it wears you down and it keeps you awake at night thinking about it, and how you dread seeing that person or getting back in that situation again the next day or the next week or the next month. Notice how it affects you, knowing that the struggle will be ongoing and that you don't have a solution, and what it does to the rest of your life. Put yourself in that situation right this moment and ask yourself: "What is it doing to the quality of my life? What is it doing to my relationships with other people? How do I feel emotionally or energetically?" How much of your attention and energy is it taking?

Now I want you to continue pretending with me. But now, pretend that it isn't you in this situation and struggle. I want you to get a mental image of somebody else in that place where you are or were, and please choose a real person. Choose somebody that you don't know very closely, and put them in that same situation. Picture them dealing with that person or situation. When you can clearly see them there, and see that it's not you, I want you to imagine them coming to you and asking you, "What should I do?" And it's absolutely not okay for you to say "I have no idea, because I'm in that same situation myself." If that's your response, then you haven't truly put them in the situation *in place of you*. I want you to pretend that it's someone else, and pretend that you have good advice for them. I want you to be very creative. What would that advice be? If you pretend, it doesn't really matter, and you can say anything, so pretend that they're in a situation instead of you and pretend that you are giving them really good advice. What is the advice? Think a moment and write it down. What would you say to them about that situation and the struggle they're going through? Write it down! Remember, it's for somebody else and it's just pretend, so write whatever shows up for you. Don't try to edit it, don't try to make it perfect.

Learn To Let Go

When it's for somebody else and just pretend, what you're doing is stepping outside of yourself and accepting the situation because it's not about you, it's about them. You're finding creative solutions because you're not emotionally attached to the outcome. Another principle we've talked about in this book is creativity rather than competition. Don't feel that you have to compete. There are not a finite amount of opportunities that we all have to contend or struggle for. Many people stay in the struggle because they believe if they don't they're going to lose out on an opportunity to move ahead. I will tell you right now, there will always be another opportunity, because you now know how to attract opportunity. We talked about that in the very first chapter of this book.

> # KEY:
> **If there will always be another opportunity,**
> there's really no need to struggle.

Find The Creative Solution

Rather than competing with other people or with the situation, rather than struggling and striving, and contending, I'm asking you to step out and **find a creative solution**. One simple way to do that is to pretend as we just did. When we say "I pretend," it means what we're thinking is just for fun, and it doesn't matter. We're not really talking about reality. This allows our brain to switch open and allows things to come in that are not necessarily based on our experience or what we know works or doesn't work. It opens up to new ideas because, after all, "It's just pretend, so I can say anything!"

Sometimes our pretend ideas come up with solutions that we are blocking because we are too close to the situation. We haven't accepted what's showing up and we haven't been able to step outside of our situation. We haven't said "Hmmm, this is interesting. Now, I wonder what I should do?" We haven't imagined somebody else in our situation. How many of us think we have great ideas for other people? Do you have great ideas for others but have trouble coming up with the right ideas for yourself? How hard is it for you to be able to apply those same ideas to yourself? It's very easy to give other people advice because we have no attachment to the outcome. Who cares? You don't care because it's not going to affect you, so it's easy to give advice. In reality what you're doing is pretending, because it's not your situation or struggle. And again, because you're pretending, you can say anything.

NOTICE THE CHALLENGES EXERCISE:

I want you to start noticing how many situations you are struggling with, that are contentious, and that you're having to strive and work at, and that are very difficult and exhausting and taking your energy. Notice the situations that are robbing your enjoyment of life. I want you to systematically, one by one, write down those situations. Identify a list of those situations, and those people and relationships, and identify where they are, because I want you to be able to let go of them. The way to let go of them is to simply accept them. Let the force of the judo blow that's coming at you simply pass you by and redirect it for your benefit.

This principle is called **radical acceptance** and this is how you can use it: Radical means that no matter what, you will just accept what happens. Have a radical approach! Just radically accept what shows up and believe it's in your best interest and is the best thing for you at this moment. Because as soon as you do, you're letting go of the attachment to a specific result. You can then accept whatever results show up and say "This is interesting, now how does this serve me? How can I use this? How can I look at this creatively, or just pretend, so that I can find what I'm not seeing right now and understand what I don't understand? How can I do this so that I can do what needs to be done to move forward and go through my life and learn what I need to learn without it being a struggle?"

This idea of radical acceptance is not new. This idea has been around for thousands and thousands of years, and yet we still find it very challenging. Our society resists this idea. Our society says "Be all that you can be! Fight for what you want. You've got to watch out for number one!" And this principle of radical acceptance goes against a lot of societies ways of looking at the world. It goes against a lot of the belief systems that I'm asking you to examine in this book to believe. You may find it very difficult to accept things that you don't want to accept. I'm suggesting in this chapter, with this principle, that when you employ radical acceptance you're accepting things in a very deliberate way, in order to find solutions and move yourself forward.

Learn To Live In The Present

Another way to look at this issue of radical acceptance is the idea of living in the present. The benefit of living in the moment is that it allows you to not bring your baggage to the situation. We all have baggage from our past experiences in life. Because something happened a certain way one time, or even many times, doesn't mean that it will necessarily happen that way again. But if you bring your memory of how something always worked before, and the emotions that go with that knowledge, you will expect it to work out that way again and be caught up in the struggle again. If, however, you can bring your knowledge, rather than your emotional attachment, negative memories, ego, and your need to have things work out a certain way, you are actually much more powerful in that situation. If you accept what is happening in the moment for what it is alone, and not what it is because of all the other things that it triggers in your memory, then you have much more power to deal with it. You still have all that you learned from past experiences, and you can use that knowledge for the current particular situation. What you don't have to deal with is all the things that you have felt or all the outcomes where you failed in the past, or even where you succeeded in the past.

Also, I want to ask you not to project implications from this present moment onto your future. I'm not saying you shouldn't consider those things, but I'm asking you to let go of the emotional attachment to a specific outcome. If you can step away from and accept what is happening in the present, you will have much more power to deal with that situation and many more options will be opened for you.

If we live in the moment, we also get to be our highest and best self. Our highest self is one that is enlightened and free of painful emotions, free of our painful past, and free of our painful small ego-driven self. When we come from that place, we can accept situations for what they are: neither good nor bad, neither right nor wrong, neither black nor white, but simply for what they are. In that objective moment you may say "Here's the situation. This is where I am right now. This is the moment. So what should I do? What do I want to do? What are all my options?"

Some people confuse this with trying not to bring past experiences into the situation at all. All I'm asking you to do is to let go of the emotional attachment to specific outcomes and radically accept what is showing up in the moment. Your intellect and knowledge will always be with you, and I'm not asking you to set that aside. Knowledge is cumulative. You will continue to learn, and all those bits of knowledge pile up on top of each other and reinforce each other. Bring all that knowledge to the situation you're in. But what I want you to be careful of is that you don't bring to the situation a belief in a certain specific outcome that is based on past negative experiences. Please don't bring the emotional baggage of 7,000 incidents that somehow seem to relate. Those 7,000 incidents happened in your past. Bring only the learning and the knowledge you gained from the 7,000 incidents, because that will help you be creative in attracting and recognizing the best solution for your current situation.

Now I know as you read this you're thinking "How do I know the difference?" The way you will know is by the level of emotion that shows up. In any situation there is an appropriate response and level of emotion to that situation. The challenge many people have is that they bring a lot of past emotions from similar situations to pile onto their current situation. I want you to notice whether your emotional response is appropriate to your current situation. I want you to notice how you're feeling in the situation and be able to accept the appropriate emotions and feelings without taking on the emotions of the past. I'm not trying to train you to be unemotional. I'm asking you to let the emotion for this moment be sufficient for that moment and don't bring with it all the history and baggage from other emotional moments that may be similar. Let those go. What's important is *this* moment, and I'm asking you to radically accept what's happening in the moment. This approach will allow you to be more powerful!

Have you ever had an encounter with someone close to you and once again they said something that reminded you of what you disliked about them? Or, have you ever made a slightly challenging comment to someone else and they say "You always do that, just like when you said..... 15 years ago". Challenge yourself to let go of the past negative emotions so you can be in the moment and act in the here and now.

There is another principle I will be talking about in chapter 17, in which we will look at how time can work for us and it can work against us. We will talk more about it later, but it's also important here when dealing with this principle of radical acceptance. The point of time that I'm asking you to focus on is now! Now is what's important, right this moment! In fact, there are many who would say that this moment is all there is: 'right this moment." We're past the past and that's why we call it past. The future hasn't arrived yet and we don't know exactly what it will bring. However, the present is with us right this minute, moment to moment, so let's live in that moment. Whatever you are experiencing in this moment is not tied to the past or future. Let's observe our own lives and let's not bring our past emotional baggage to our life in the moment. I'm asking you to be an observer of your life so that you can make rational decisions based on your knowledge and what you have learned.

If you do this you'll find yourself to be much more powerful, much more present, much more alive and much more engaged in life. That's why it is so important to be able to let go of the past and of the future, and to live in the now!

I know that as you're reading this many of you are thinking "Well, that's easy to say, but it's very hard to do." And I have to agree with you, most of us have years of accumulated opinions, emotions, and habits. That's what makes this a challenging principle. So how do we embrace it? Like many of the principles in this book, we must first learn the principle.

> # KEY:
> The way we are able to learn radical acceptance is with practice.

Start with small things. Notice small moments when you're fully present. Focus on extending those moments. Also practice accepting small things like experiences and events. It's easy to accept small, positive things, isn't it? But the problem with accepting small, positive things is that we project them into the future and create an entire set of beliefs and emotional attachment to a result that hasn't been determined yet. We may even say "Gosh, if this continues to happen, I will be wealthy," or "Now that she loves me, my life will be okay." And so sometimes with small positive experiences we create a future vision based around one specific result, rather than focusing on the moment and accepting it for what it is.

Negative experiences, in contrast, cause us to focus on the past. They bring us back to all the bad experiences and all the past negatives we ever had. Have you ever been in an argument over a very minor issue but the person you're arguing with starts bringing up everything you've ever done wrong? They do that because it triggers other negative events from their emotional memory. When that happens we all need to notice that we're not being in the present, we're not accepting what is and dealing with it, but instead we're bringing a lot of baggage to the situation. You can stop that habit when you notice and practice radical acceptance.

The way to practice this radical acceptance idea is to practice with small events that occur naturally. Notice when you get hooked. Getting hooked is you remembering all the events and emotions that relate to your current experience. Your emotions come into play and poison the present situation.

This idea of living in the present is being taken over by your memory of all of your past events, and suddenly your anger toward the person that you were in a small argument with escalates because you remember all the times you've been wronged in the past. Relating your current situation back to a similar negative past result takes away your power. Let me give you an example...

EXAMPLE:

Sharon is a very successful business leader and was recently sued by the IRS for tax evasion and failure to pay the proper tax from a federal filing two years ago. When she hired me to help her accelerate the growth of her business, she had been aggressively fighting the IRS claims for those two years and was spending lots of money, time, and energy trying to prove her point and avoid tens of thousands of dollars in back tax, penalties, and interest. Her business was stagnant because of all the time and energy being devoted to the struggle. With my support, she stopped fighting and struggling, and allowed the process to continue to move forward without taking all her attention and time away from her business. Her business started to grow again as we focused on the future and growth she wanted. Meanwhile, I encouraged her to simply focus on the outcome that she wanted with the IRS. Gentle resistance over time caused the IRS claim to not only be reversed to her favor, but an additional overpayment was found in the process returning over $10,000 to her. All of this came about when she let go of the fight and the emotion attached to winning and simply accepted her situation giving it minimal energy focused on the outcome she wanted.

We have all been trained by society and experience to bring our emotional baggage to every situation. And believe me, you do bring it to every situation, both good and bad, and it's very destructive. It doesn't allow you to live in the moment. It causes you to live in the past and project into the future. The way to get over this and to live in the present is to radically accept what is happening right this moment. The reason I say "radically" is because this is a radical choice. To radically accept is very challenging and difficult because you will have to act in opposition to lifelong habits of thinking. When you're in an argument with somebody, it's tough to tell yourself that you are going to look at it and deal with it in the present, and you are not going to bring all of your past issues and grievances to the argument, because those are past. It is equally important to not project the outcome of this argument into the future, effecting your ability to get along in the next five years, or even five days. The truth is, you don't know what the effect of this argument is going to be. Accept that what you are having is a disagreement right now, so let's be creative *right now* and find a win-win solution.

Unlock Your Natural Power

When we are able to radically accept what is, our acceptance opens the door for other possibilities and solutions as it did with Sharon. It opens the doors for creativity and love to show up, because you won't be held back by the old situation with it's old emotions and solutions. You won't be bound to a specific solution or outcome that may be tied in your mind to a future projection of what's going to happen. Instead, you will be able to operate in the present, and say "What do I want right now, in this moment?" This is one of the most powerful questions you can ask yourself. If you're able to answer this question in the present, without bringing past baggage or future projection to that question, you will come up with very specific directions an goals for yourself. Focus on what you want and not how you're going to get it.

Start radically accepting small events, both positive and negative. Don't project from the positive and don't reach back from the negative. Accept everything that shows up. Be an observer of your own life. Label things "interesting" Instead of "good" or "bad." Don't get caught up in the emotion. Ask yourself "What should I do? What do I want?" Then listen to your internal voice from your higher self. If past emotional baggage shows up, clear that emotion by simply letting go of those thoughts. Simply acknowledge the emotion by telling yourself "Yes, thank you, I remember what happened before," and move past that old thought to the present. When you acknowledge that an *old memory* is showing up, that will defeat it. It will not have power over you. You can then choose to use the information from that past event or not, and you can choose to use the emotion or you can choose to let go of the emotion. Our small ego wants to keep all those emotions alive and bring them back to every situation, believing that they are very important. But it takes you away from the present moment so that you cannot act creatively and with love, and you cannot act impartially, as an observer of your life, and make powerful decisions.

SUMMARY:
1. **Notice what is happening in the moment it is happening**
2. **Accept it for what it is, neither good or bad, until you label it**
3. **Let go of the solutions and negativity that come from your past**
4. **Be creative in finding solution**
5. **Stay present and don't be pulled back into old thinking and emotions**
6. **Don't project into the future based on the past or present event**

This process will allow you to stay powerful and not have to force the outcome. Power is easy, force is a struggle and challenge!

Let go of the old baggage. Become an observer. Get your strength back. Live the life you were meant to live, live who you are at your core. Your spiritual self wants to be free of all this baggage, and wants you to be able to be flexible and creative and resourceful. You'll find yourself having more success in life and things will go more smoothly. You will be happier, less focused on anger and fear and negative emotion, and more focused on what's happening around you at this moment in your life.

Start noticing life. Start noticing things happening in the present. Focus on little things at first. Make progress on the little things that impact you that are happening around you every day. Start being fully aware, and as you do that, it will leave less room for the old stuff to show up. Radically accept the moment and embrace the present!

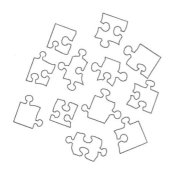

Chapter 14

You Have to Create Space

Albert Einstein said that the human mind is like an attic in your house. If you want to put more stuff in, you have to take some of the old stuff out. Isn't it true? Our human nature wants to fill up all the available space. Most of us can't even imagine moving to a different house because of all the stuff we have accumulated over the years. We've filled up almost every space we have. Every weekend you see hundreds and hundreds of garage sales. And if you drive around on a Saturday, people are trading their stuff for other people's stuff and paying money for the exchange. People have yard sales and at the same time they go next door and buy stuff at the neighbor's yard sale. Maybe it's just human nature?

Creating Space In Your Physical World

That brings us to the principle for this chapter. The principle simply says that if you want more to show up in your life **you have to create space** for it to show up. You have to provide the space for opportunity, people, resources, ideas, etc or they cannot come to you.

This principle seems pretty simple! In reality, it's hard for people to get a grasp on exactly what that means sometimes. Let me give you an example…

EXAMPLE:

About five years ago I was at large conference. As conferences go, this one was very interesting, but I found myself in one of the sessions wanting to be anywhere but in a room with 500 other people listening to a speaker. So I grabbed a book and I left the room for a few minutes. The convention was held at a beautiful resort, and I went to sit at one of the tables by the pool. There were hundreds of tables, each with about four chairs, and there was nobody out there but me. Everybody was in the convention listening to the speaker. I sat down and started reading my book just for a little five minute getaway, and immediately I felt guilty. I should be in there at the convention because after all I had flown all this way, spent a lot of money, and was committed to learning what was going on and yet I wasn't taking part in it. The thought crossed my mind, "I wonder why I'm out here then? Maybe there's some purpose for me being out here? Maybe I'm supposed to be meeting somebody? Maybe I'm supposed to be seeing something out here that I haven't seen yet? Or, maybe I'm supposed to be reading something in this book? I don't know." But I decided if I was going to meet somebody out there I needed to create space for them and I consciously reached over to the chair beside me and pulled it out away from the table. Remember, there are probably 500 chairs on the patio and not one of them is occupied. I sat at the table by myself on the patio reading my book and it wasn't even 60 seconds before somebody was standing by the empty chair that I pulled out. They asked if they could sit down. It was an amazing process and I was stunned! This was a person that I had never met, a beautiful woman, and I said "Sure." She sat down and we started talking. The person later became a client and became a teacher to me as well. She and I later created a referral relationship that lasted many years.

One of the first questions that come up is: what should I let go of to create the space for something new? The answer is simply to ask yourself "what is not productive, or no longer necessary." In the example above, I was not getting anything from the speaker and therefore decided to do something different, make a change, and push out the chair.

I'm convinced that would not have happened, had I not created the space, had I not pulled out the chair and made room for the first overture. Sometimes creating space is only about creating space in our mind, and sometimes it means creating physical space. Sometimes it means emotional space. We've all heard the phrase: "Give them some space. Give him some room."

The Ten Drawer Syndrome

Creating space must be done intentionally because it goes against our natural instinct of wanting to fill everything up. I have often heard the expression that nature abhors a vacuum, but I never really understood what it meant until someone explained it to me like this: they called it the ten drawer syndrome. And went on to explain that if you have one drawer you will fill it up, and, if you have ten drawers you will fill them all up. Think of your closet. It's almost like a natural law. And if that's the case, then our usual state of being is all filled up—our houses, our time, our lives in general, everything is filled up. Most of us have little or no empty space. So it makes sense that if we want to have something new show up, we have to create space.

Let's talk about creating space in our mind for just a moment. Remember the principle. If we want something to show up we have to first create space for it, make a home for it, and welcome it. Creating space in our mind is no different. That's what we were talking about in earlier chapters when we talked about belief systems. In the very first chapter in this book, we talked about the simple principle that whatever you really believe you can have, you can have.

> # KEY:
> Everything is created first in your mind. All man's inventions were an idea first!

But sometimes our minds don't have any room. Sometimes our minds are full. Have you ever felt it was hard to focus, or hard to concentrate? Have you ever noticed your thoughts jumping all over the place? Have you ever noticed that it was hard to hold one idea in your mind at a time because your mind is so full that all the ideas are vying for attention and crowding to the forefront? How does it feel to consider putting one more thought or idea in there? The possibility of exploring a new idea may seem overwhelming because you simply don't have space.

You may need to be the Einstein of your mind and let go of some of the ideas that you're holding on to in order to create space. How do we create mental space? The answer to that question seems like a contradiction, so please stay with me for another page or two.

RELATED FACT:

First of all, our minds are an infinite resource for mental storage. There may or may not be a limit to it, but if there is, it's not a limit that you have reached. I recently read that every cell in the human body contains a strand of DNA which tells the character and the makeup of that individual. That's why they can now take a single cell and clone a complete new animal from it—because each cell has the DNA blueprint or pattern inside it. Some cells are only 1/1000th of an inch across, much smaller than the head of a pin. And yet, each cell contains an entire strand of DNA coding for who you are. I read that if the DNA coding were written out in books they would fill 1,000 books with 600 pages each. That's 600,000 pages of information in every single cell of the human body. Imagine the immense capacity for storage that the human brain must have if a single cell can contain that much information.

Now, back to this idea of creating space in our mind. I've basically just said that we don't really need to create space. What do we need, then? What we need is *better organization*. All we need is focus. What we need is the ability to look at things and categorize them by importance. It's very much like our computer systems. Engineers are finding they can store more and more information in smaller and smaller spaces by organizing better and using better materials and processes. We need to learn to be able to do the same thing with our minds.

The human mind sometimes needs to create space for new ideas to show up, but it's generally because an old idea hasn't been put away. The old idea is hanging onto the space within our thoughts and it does not want to let go. Changing our habits of thinking creates space for new ideas and new thoughts to show up. As a coach I work with my clients to identify old thinking that needs to be changed so there is room for new thinking. If you can't have a new thought or a new idea and implement it and believe it, it will never come to pass for you. It will never become a part of who you are and have impact in your life. The human mind is very much like your desktop. It can't work when the papers are piled too high. You can't be productive in that situation. If you bring new ideas into your office and put them on your desk they get lost because of lack of organization. It's a combination of capacity and organization. Your thoughts can be organized with the same process as your desk. You must look at each thought and decide where it fits and mentally file it with the associated thoughts. If it doesn't fit anymore then we choose to let it go and replace it with new thinking or leave space for new ideas to show up. This is that puzzle building process that I talked about in the introduction of this book.

How To Create Space In Time

Let's consider the idea of making space for time. Obviously, we can't make time, can we? But we can organize our time. We can schedule our time. We can manage our time. And that's what we're talking about when we talk about making space in our schedule. If you use a tool like a calendar to organize your day, you will be much more likely to be productive and still have time available.

You hear people talk about making time for their kids. We know that if we don't make quality time that we can spend with our children, it lessens their chance to grow up into successful, happy, and healthy adults. It's important for us to spend time with our children and we have to create the space in our schedule. Again, it's very much like clearing our desk and filing the papers where they belong so our office and desk become functional again and there's a space for us to work.

Sometimes we don't make time for ourselves. I work with dozens of people who make time for others, time for work, and for lots of busy stuff, but won't create space to be able to take care of themselves. They don't create time to work out and be healthy, or relax, or read, or refresh and renew themselves. They make time for others but not for themselves.

> # KEY:
> **It is very important to be *productive* and not just *busy*!**

EXAMPLE:

It is important to manage and schedule and organize your time. It's important to create space in your life if you want things to show up. The other night we wanted to try out a restaurant that was brand-new. When we walked in the door and asked the hostess how long it would be to get the table, she told us it would be an hour and 45 minute wait. Almost two hours! I would almost be ready for my next meal by then. Did we feel welcome? Were we encouraged to come on in? No. There was no room for us in that restaurant, and so we went someplace else to eat. We are like the restaurant, we need to keep some space available.

Thoughts, ideas, relationships, people, experiences, are all the same. If your mind is like that restaurant——too full, with a waiting list—all those things will go find a home someplace else and you will be stuck where you are. If the same people never leave the restaurant, nobody else can ever come in. The people that are sitting there are all full, they stop eating and ordering, and the restaurant dies. The restaurant doesn't have any room for new energy, new people, new money. Hungry people cannot come in because the existing customers won't leave. What does the restaurant do? The restaurant trains its waiters and waitresses to present customers with their bill in order to encourage them to leave. In some parts of the world that is considered rude, but in the US most restaurants train their serving people to present the bill when the people are done with their meal or sometimes even before. That's to create space! The servers in the restaurant and the management know that if they want another customer, then they have to make space to get more people to come in. They intentionally create a constant turnover, always making space so the restaurant is not stagnant, but is always in a renewal process.

You are very much like the restaurant. There are probably some thoughts and ideas in your mind that need to be presented the bill. They've been fed for a long time, but now it's time for you to bring in some new thoughts and ideas. There may be some people in your life that need to be shown the door and given the bill. There are probably many things in your life that you need to create space for. It may be time to make space for renewal!

EXAMPLE:
I own a mini-storage business. I recognized many years ago that this type of business is a transition business, meaning that it's a high turnover business. On average, every day at the mini-storage facility, one to two units are rented and one to two units are vacated. It's a high turnover business, and yet there are some people who don't want to leave. Some people stop paying their bill but still don't vacate. They're like people sitting in the restaurant talking long after they've finished their big meal: even though there's a waiting line for people to come into the restaurant, they don't get up and leave. In

the mini-storage business, we eventually serve them with eviction papers and a notice to seize their property if they don't pay their rent. We need that space or we need them to pay their rent. 90 days later, if they still haven't paid, we auction their property to create space. We cannot rent that space until somebody vacates, So we have to force the space to open up!

The restaurant, the mini-storage, and you and I are all the same. We all have to have a process that we can go through to create space. Sometimes we have to serve ourselves with the bill. Sometimes we have to give ourselves notice. We have to bring ourselves the check and say "Hey! I realize I'm in the way. I need to create space for relationships, space for experiences, or I need to create space for time. I need to create room in my mind for new ideas by letting go of the old ideas." There is a process for you to go through with this idea of creating space, and I want you to start that process right now.

CREATING SPACE EXERCISE:

Ask yourself the following questions and write down your answers:

Where am I overcrowded?

Where am I not creating space?

What area of my life needs to be presented with the bill?

Where do I need to start serving eviction papers?

Which thoughts ideas or beliefs need to be let go?

Continue with this process, because I will absolutely guarantee you that if you don't, at some point you will become stuck. If you don't have room for new ideas, new relationships, new events and experiences, or new thinking to show up, it's inevitable that you become stuck. If you notice that right now you're not growing in some part of your life, the problem may be that you need to create space in that area to begin to grow again.

Creating Space In Relationships

Let's talk now about how you create space for more relationships or more time or more wealth to show up. I want you to consider the concept of *devoting time*. You've no doubt heard the expression: "I'm going to devote some time to this." First of all, what does the word devotion mean? Devotion is very much like dedication except it has a spiritual quality. It's a deeper commitment. It's a commitment that you will hold regardless of circumstance and things going on around you.

One tool that I often use in coaching is identifying that thing which will *compel* my client to follow through. So if you devote yourself to something and identify what will compel you to follow through, you will almost always be successful. If you truly want to devote time to something, you must first create space in your time calendar before you can devote that time. When something is compelling, it means that you cannot change it.

EXAMPLE:

Not long ago a client hired me to help him get his life organized and in order. I discovered that even his house was in total chaos and he had not invited anyone to visit for over two years. He was embarrassed and ashamed, and yet nothing compelled him to make a change and organize and clean up. I had him commit to a party at his house and asked him to send out invitations. That was the thing that compelled him to clean and organize and after that evening he was able to maintain that organization.

You may have something that you are committed to doing right now, but there's no time available in your calendar. If you are truly devoted, an opportunity will show up for you to create space. Every time! Identify those things that you're devoted to finding time for, and as the time shows up, write it on your calendar in ink so it cannot be changed. Do this especially in the cases where these items are for yourself, such as vacations or relaxation time, or exercise time, or family time. Be sure that you put those times on your calendars in ink so they cannot be erased, or given to some other task or job or person.

It is really important to devote time to yourself. Remember that devotion has a spiritual quality to it, that once given it is a sacred thing, a bond you have with yourself. You have devoted your time and you have devoted space, and you have devoted your energies. And once you have devoted yourself, don't let life and all its little issues rob that from you.

If you will do this, you'll find that the things that show up are things that you long for on a spiritual level. If you devote time to your friends on a regular basis, for instance, and you follow through with that, then great things will show up for you in terms of friendships. If you devote money by deciding to pay yourself 10% first of the money you earn, and it goes into an investment account to pay for your own future, then you will be rewarded with more money and security.

I'm sure you can see now that we are blending this principle of creating space with other principles that I have introduced. None of these principles stand alone. They are intended to work together for your benefit. These principles all require your input. It's not possible for somebody else to do your work for you. Remember, *it's all about you working on yourself.* In this particular case, as with many of the other principles, you are the center of the universe! You are the center, at least, of your own universe, right? And whatever you decide to do has more impact on you than anything anyone else can do. But also be aware that what you do will affect the people around you because, again, you are the center of the universe as it's known to you. You are at the very core and very point of where things can be changed. This simple principle of creating space can be a major point of change for you.

SPACE AND DEVOTION EXERCISE:

I want you to look at seven areas of your life:

Physical Health
Relationships and Family
Environment and home
Business or Job

Investments and Finance

Recreation and Fun

Your Spiritual Life

Look at the very core of yourself and answer as honestly as possible two simple questions with regard to each of these areas of your life: "Where do I need to create space, and what do I want to devote this new space to?" Write down your responses. I'm going to ask you right now to focus your attention on what you have chosen to devote that newly created space to in each of those areas so that you begin to attract those things that will truly benefit you.

Isn't it true that the things we devote our attention to get done, and the things that we don't devote our attention to don't get done? That act of devotion starts with creating space for those things to show up and be completed. If we don't create the space, they won't get done. Nothing new can show up if we don't make room for it to come in. Again, regularly examine these core areas of your life and notice where you need to create space.

Pro-active Space Creation

One final caution about creating space: What I am asking you to do is to be *proactive* about creating space in the areas that you want to see change and growth. Don't wait until you are forced to be *reactive*. Often something new will show up and force it's way into your life by pushing something old out of the way. A new idea will force you to let go of an old idea. A new friend will contend for your time and force you to let an old friend go in order to make space. These are all examples of your having to be reactive as something vies for space in your mind, calendar, friendships, family, etc. What you will notice is that this can be a disturbing process that takes your energy as they contend for your limited space. It is much easier for you to be proactive and consciously choose to let go of some things and intentionally create the space for the new ideas, friends, activities that you want in your life for your happiness and growth.

Maybe it is like Einstein said; your attic is full. Ask yourself. You know the answers! Ask yourself, "Is my attic full? Am I allowing space for a deeper relationship with my spouse? Am I allowing space for more wealth to come to me? Am allowing space for my business to grow? Am I allowing space for new opportunity to show up?"

Sometimes it's as simple as allowing space by being proactive and pushing out a chair and devoting attention to what you want. The space will attract its own occupant based on your devoted attention. You have the power! You are at the center of your universe!

Chapter 15

COMMUNICATION HAPPENS AT THREE LEVELS

L et's talk for a minute about the power of personal clarity. In this chapter the principle we want to look at relates back to another principle that states that we are body, mind, and spirit—in fact, we are spirit, mind, and body, in that order. Because we are spirit, mind, and body, we also communicate at three levels. We communicate on the verbal, emotional, and energetic levels. These levels could also be called the body, mind, and spirit levels of communication.

Integrated Communication

If you want to appear clear and powerful in the world, one of the ways you can do that is to align and integrate all of your communications. Alignment of your body, mind, and spirit creates an integrated wholeness in you which is heard by the listener as integrity in your communication. In fact, the word integrate means to make whole. And if we take that a step further, we realize that the word integrate is the root for the word integrity. Therefore, it's a simple principle to understand that if you want to be perceived as having integrity you need to communicate wholly, you need to integrate your communication so

167

that it comes from all levels, body, mind, and spirit, with one clear message. People who are able to speak with integrity are very often charismatic. We are attracted to them because it's both powerful and refreshing to see somebody speak with integrity from their spirit, mind, and body.

EXAMPLE:

Have you ever been waiting for an elevator and as the doors open there's young couple standing at the back of the elevator? They're both looking forward, not touching each other, and not saying anything. When you ask them how their day is going, they both say "fine". You may even ask them what's going on, and they may say "Oh, nothing". But you immediately can tell, even though they have not said so, that they are not "fine" and something is going on. Maybe they were just arguing, or maybe they were just kissing? You can tell before you even step in the elevator, because they are communicating in spite of themselves, and what they are communicating is not lining up with their words. They may be saying they are "fine" but the entire elevator is screaming something else. It's something you can feel. Your senses pick it up immediately. You can read it in the air, it's as tangible as hearing them say the words "We were arguing" or "We were kissing."

Can you tell when somebody is holding a grudge even though their words don't say it? Sure you can. Do you sometimes get a sense that it's a bad time to talk to somebody before you even say a word or they say a word to you? Of course you do. What are you reading from them? What are you sensing? You're sensing the energy and the emotion that are talking just as loudly as, or possibly louder than, any words the other person might be saying.

We primarily communicate verbally, right? We communicate through reading and writing, and through speech on a physical or *body* level. And sometimes we believe that is the only way we communicate. The truth is that speech and the written word are the *poorest* ways to communicate. You often hear people talk about what's written between the lines, or what someone didn't say. You may hear them say "She said this, but what I heard was that." In other words, there was an incongruity. There was no wholeness in their speech. They were not speaking with integrity. Remember, integrity refers to things fitting together to make a whole. Their words and their emotions and energy did not line up and support each other, so the end result was that you got a very mixed message.

KEY:

You have an incredible power that you can tap in to when you align your communication with your body, mind, and spirit speaking from all three levels of your being.

Charismatic Communication

What does it really mean when we say somebody is charismatic? What does a charismatic person speak with? They don't speak with just their words, that's for sure. The charismatic person or speaker is somehow attractive beyond their words because of the energy and emotions that they project that all support a single message. The energy and emotions are in complete alignment with the words, and the message is unmistakable. When this happens the person then appears to have power and integrity. They show up in the world as someone that you would come back to hear over and over again. That person has influence! People with that quality are the world leaders, the policy shapers, the people who attract friends, the people we follow in the news because we want to hear what they have to say. Those are people who get things done, because they have the power of clear communication on their side. Their energy, emotion, and their words all line up. You get a clear picture of what they want, what they're saying, because it comes from every level of their being.

The challenge for you is to be able to develop clarity in your communication. That will require a clarity and integrity in your body, mind, and spirit. It will also require you to be able to identify and recognize when you are speaking with that integrity. When your energy, your emotions, and your words are all saying the same thing, it's a powerful place to be, and people will listen! Suddenly you will have an increased attractiveness that you never had before.

I want you to start to notice when people's spirit, mind, and body don't line up, as reflected in their words, emotions, and energy. I'm asking you to notice when they don't line up because it's very common. Even in professional speaking, it's rare when all three; emotion, energy, and verbal expression, line up all the time. If you start to pay attention and notice when other people have a charismatic quality and you hear a very clear message, then ask yourself, "What am I really hearing? Am I hearing an alignment of words, emotion, and energy?" When this is the case, you get the message 100%. There is no confusion or doubt about their meaning, and there's no misunderstanding of their intention.

Have you ever been in a relationship where you almost didn't need to speak because you understood each other so well? How are you communicating when that's the case? Maybe you're communicating through emotion? Maybe it's a deep love, or maybe anger or hatred. Maybe it's an emotion like that, or maybe you're communicating with your energy. When we are communicating with energy it's basically our spirits speaking through us. It may be your spirit and my spirit in conversation. Have you ever looked somebody in the eye and all of a sudden there was a flash of communication? It's not emotional, but it's just a "knowing." Suddenly you intuitively know something about that person, or perhaps a bond has been created. There is an energetic spiritual communication. That's your energy speaking to their energy, your spirit to their spirit. And when we are able to tap into that we are able to control that alignment of communication. We're able to develop an alignment of purpose and presentation that's coming from an alignment within ourselves, and it's clear to the other person what we're saying. There's no mixed message and there's no confusion. There is no doubt about what we are trying to say.

The challenge in this chapter is simply to learn to speak and communicate clearly. And by clearly, I mean communicate with all three levels of your being in harmony with one message. That's the principle, and it's a very challenging principle because it requires you to pay attention and to change. You are powerful beyond words when your words, your emotions, and your energy are in alignment.

Now, I know you're asking yourself, "Okay, so I understand the principle, I get it. Now how do I change? How do I speak from my energetic self? How do I let my emotions support, and align with, and complement my words?" So let's start with that.

Learn To Speak Boldly

How do we match our words to our feelings or our energy? That may be the simplest and easiest way to change and to create the clarity and alignment of communication we're looking for. If you were to change your words to match your emotions and your energy, what would that mean? That would mean that you would have the boldness to speak what you truly believe, think, and feel. You would have the boldness to speak what you know within your core. You'd have the boldness to come from your spirit and your higher self rather than just from your physical self. Do you know what I mean? In an argument, have you ever caught yourself saying things in a very uncontrolled way? Have you been caught up in the argument and speaking only on a very physical level, from your primal instincts alone? Has that ever been productive or fulfilling? Probably not, because it's not being true to yourself.

KEY:
Speaking boldly with clear integrated communication is not about volume or yelling. It is about speaking with confidence knowing that you are speaking with your whole being.

If you were to reach a little deeper, and communicate from your true feelings and speak what you know to be the truth, the essence of your beliefs, to speak out of that spiritual self that lies inside you and convey those feelings, how much better would it be? You would be both powerful and attractive. But the reality is, it's very scary to speak from your heart and spirit, because it requires you to be vulnerable and take off your outer layers of protection and reveal yourself to other people. That's where the challenge comes in.

Have you ever listened to a powerful speaker and as you listen to them you really get the sense that they are speaking from their core, from their inner self or from a very deep level? And when they do, they're often very, very vulnerable to ridicule and criticism, because they're putting their innermost personal feelings out there on the line and they're speaking from their heart. However, when they speak from their heart their energy lines up with their words —Wow! That's *unbelievably* powerful!

KEY:

The easiest thing for you to shift to create alignment is to shift your words to match your true feelings, emotion, and energy!

How often do you speak your true feelings? How often, instead, do you cover up your true feelings and play it safe? When that's the case you are out of integrity and your words will lack clarity and they will not have power. There will be a conflict that's visible, audible even, to everybody who's listening to you. You must speak from your true feelings first and change your words to match those emotions and that energy. That is both the easiest, and the scariest, way to create alignment.

Clear Your Emotions First, Then Speak

It may be your emotions that are the issue, they may be out of alignment with your energy and your words. You may need to go deal with the emotions, process them or otherwise let them go somehow before you're able to have clear communication. Have you ever noticed that sometimes you can't speak to somebody because you're angry and you know it's better not to speak to them right away? You know that if you speak while you're angry that the message will not come out clearly, and will only cause a reaction in them. You may be saying something verbally that appears calm or neutral, but your emotion is screaming anger and that lack of continuity is very confusing to people. When your emotions are screaming anger they are sending an entirely different message than you intended. If someone hurts your feelings you may want to say "Hey, let's work is out," verbally. But the dominant emotion may be anger and the dominant energy may be a total disconnect from the person you're speaking to. When you try to speak to that person in that moment, as you are sometimes forced to do, it will be very difficult to be understood clearly. That may be why it's so hard to resolve an argument, or to even feel heard until both parties are able to let go of the emotions.

When your emotions are out of whack with everything else, then go and deal with them, go process the emotions and give yourself some time. Then come back to balance before you try to speak to the person, and then your message will be clear to that person. Don't speak when you have an overflow of emotions, because your emotions will be speaking louder than any words you can say. The emotions may be speaking louder than your underlying energy. This is the time for you to notice your behavior and your inability to communicate when you're out of integrity. Sometimes you may have an overflow of words and people think you are just rambling on and on. You may be speaking too much, and it's because there's not an underlying clarity of the emotion and energy that you're trying to convey. You can have an overflow in any area. You can have an overflow of words or emotion, or even an overflow of energy where you are overwhelmed and can't even communicate with your words. Emotion and energy are two different things and represent the mental and spiritual aspects of communication respectively. The critical piece here is to bring a balance, clarity, and integrity to your communication. Otherwise people will read the dominant message, and it may not be the message you want to convey. You may be filling the space with emotion and people can't respond to any words you're saying.

Sometimes a person's energy can overflow, as well. You may have experienced that, maybe as a desire to connect or a spiritual strength coming from your connection to your life purpose and desire to communicate core beliefs. Those things can also dominate, and that's a wonderful thing as long as you can still speak and get your message through. Remember, it's better to shift your words to match your emotion and energy than to shift your energetic core self because in that way you are being true to your core powerful self..

I'm making an assumption here: I'm assuming that you want to be powerful, and charismatic, and be able to communicate clearly. I'm assuming you want to be attractive to other people. I'm assuming you want to move to your next level. If that weren't true, you probably wouldn't still be reading this book. So I want to ask you a few hard questions:

1. Do people want to listen to you when you speak?
2. Are you powerful?
3. Do people "get you" and understand what you're about?
4. Are you able to communicate clearly and precisely?
5. Do you feel heard, or known by those around you?

If the answer is no to some of those questions, then I want you to check yourself. Start noticing when you are coming from integrity and everything is fitting together and also notice when you're not. If you are in alignment, and have integrity of communication, you will be a charismatic person. If you speak first from your energy, then from your emotion, and finally from your words, people will line up to hear you and you will feel known and understood by your audience. You will become a person that attracts other people easily— sometimes, before you ever open your mouth.

As I said when we began this chapter, we are body, mind, and spirit, and we communicate through our words, emotions, and energy. Just as our strongest self is our spiritual self, our strongest mode of communication is the energy we project. It's our essence, the essence of who we are. We have an energy field around us, an aura. So our strongest form of communication is actually the energy that comes from our spirit, the energy we project. To prove this, practice giving people messages by sending your energy, beliefs, thoughts, and ideas without opening your mouth or even using facial expressions. The trick is that the message you are sending has to be your pure true energy, undistorted by emotions like anger or desire. Let someone see your spirit without talking.

How Can You Communicate Energetically?

How do we communicate energetically? That is probably the essence of this chapter. The truth is, you are always communicating your energy at some level. You may or may not be the brightest bulb in the room, but believe me your light can be seen. Some people say volumes before they ever open their mouths, like we talked about a moment ago. It's because they communicate with their energy first, then their emotions, and finally in their words. Some people have the ability to project their energy to fill a large room and connect with a large audience. They have developed that ability over time, but it started with their noticing when they were connecting and when they weren't. You can tell when you're not connecting, because your audience will be bored or not interested with your message. What that really means is that you have not brought alignment and integrity to your communication. Your listeners may be getting a double meaning from what you are saying. So your first step is to simply notice what impact you are having. When people are attracted to you, they are getting clear communication on all three levels. They're getting a single message that is clear, and therefore powerful. If, on the other hand, you are not being understood and people are not attracted to your message, it's important for you to notice that and make changes. It may be that you are playing safe and holding back, not letting people see the essence of who you are. It's up to you to create the alignment that allows your words to reflect who you truly are. Stop playing it safe! Identify your true message and put it out there. When people see who you are at your spiritual core, you will be more powerful!

Occasionally, you will be communicating with integrity, with an aligned message that most people will respond to very positively, but there may be some in your audience who don't get a clear message, and in some cases it may not be about you. It may be that you're speaking clearly but they are not hearing clearly. Or, that they are simply not ready for the message you are sharing and unable to hear.

Become A Powerful Listener And Learn To Hear

It is just as important to have an alignment in how we hear and listen as how we speak. How do you hear? Are you listening with energy, emotion, and words or are you just hearing? If you are just hearing you may be taking in the words alone, and not connecting with the emotion or energy. Have you ever read a book and not remembered a single word from what you read? You read word by word down the page, and yet you didn't remember a single bit of it. It's because you were reading the words only and you weren't connecting with the emotion of what you were reading and you weren't connecting with the energy of it. The same is true in conversation. Have you ever had a conversation with someone and walked away unable to remember anything they said? Were they not communicating clearly, or were you not listening clearly? You were not connecting for some reason. If you want to connect in a conversation, connect with the message, connect with the emotion, and connect with the speaker's energy. Otherwise you're just filling space and time. Employ that same process when reading and you'll find yourself able to connect with the author and you will get more from what they are sharing with you. Learn to connect by listening at all levels, whether you're dealing with the written word or with verbal communication face-to-face, or on the phone. It's your listening muscle that I'm asking you to develop.

KEY:

What we're talking about is two-way communication and connection, which includes both speaking and listening. **The ability to connect with others through energy, emotion, and words will act as a catalyst and propel you to your next level.** Your ability to connect at a deeper level, beyond words, will expand your understanding, capacity, and potential.

It's true that in today's busy world you will not hear messages that are in alignment from most people. Most of the time you'll be hearing their words, but their emotions and energy won't even be on the same page. The classic example of this is the used-car salesman who will say anything to get the sale and because he's not speaking from his heart and his energy and doesn't even believe his own words. You can't wait to get away from him. We see that all the time in advertising, in the media, and from politicians, and more. The challenge for you is to notice how people communicate and what you are willing to listen to. Notice when you connect with somebody else and their message. Why did you connect with them? Was it you, or was it them? Was it both? As you start to notice how people communicate and connect with other people, this will help you become better at connecting and communicating. You'll be able to tap into that alignment and integrity of body, mind, and spirit, and communicate with your words, your emotions, and your energy. You'll notice people respond to you differently.

Be brave and take a risk. Speak from your heart and spirit. Be powerful! Say what you mean. Say what you feel. Connect with people at a deeper level. Be charismatic and be a leader. Become attractive by how you communicate. All that power is available to you when you communicate at that deeper level, integrating your body, mind, and spirit.

This principle of communication is very much like most of the principles in this book. It will cost you no money and take very little time. You don't need to hire somebody or get anybody to help you. You need only spend a few minutes with yourself and start noticing how you communicate.

KEY:

Notice your behavior, notice your speech, notice your language, and most of all, notice the effect or impact it has on others.

I know you have a powerful message to share. Are you conveying and communicating that message to somebody else? Are you connecting with groups of people, or crowds, or your community, or even your nation? Very, very few people manage this, because they don't know how. But now you could be one of those powerful, charismatic people and bring your message to the world.

YOUR ALIGNED MESSAGE EXERCISE:

Before you move on, ask yourself these few follow-up questions:

1. What is the message I have to share with the world?
2. What words are needed to be in alignment with that message?
3. When will I start being true to myself?
4. What first steps will I take today?

OK, now just start!

Chapter 16

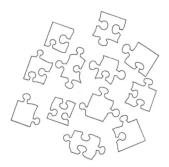

UNDERSTAND
FAILURE,
EMBRACE THE
POSITIVE

H ave you ever wondered what it would be like if everything in your life was perfect? Have you ever wondered what you would do, how you would react, how you would handle it? Have you ever thought about what that perfect life would bring out in you?

For most of us, I think the answer would be, **if life was perfect, we would *do* nothing**. We would not want to change what we had. We would certainly not want to lose what we have. We would not even want to jeopardize what we had. Perfect means it doesn't get any better than this, right? If life was perfect, our inclination would be to be very careful and not do anything that's going to change our situation or diminish that perfection. Life on Earth would actually be heaven! Our lives would be ideal and we would be exactly the same all the time because there would be nothing that would ever cause us to change. In fact, our circumstance would cause us not to change. When you're at the very top, there's only one direction you can go, right? And so, when things are going very well for us, our human tendency is to not want to change. We don't want to make any different choices or rock the boat by choosing something different, because we don't want to jeopardize what we already have. We talked about this idea a little in chapter 12 related to experiences and relationships.

The Benefits Of Failure

What causes change? If we say that absolute perfection causes us to not want to change at all because we want to stay in that place, then the opposite would be that absolute disaster and negatives would cause us to want to make dramatic change immediately. Is there any situation you would want to move away from more than the very worst situation? The very worst situation you can imagine is the one that you run from the fastest. That super negative situation is the one that causes you to examine where you are and what your options are, and how the heck you can get out of there as fast as possible.

There is huge value in our negative circumstances and negative events. Remember what I said in an earlier chapter: it's not important what happens to you. The important thing is how you react to what happens to you and what you do with it. We've all heard the saying "it's not about if you get knocked down, but how quickly do you get back up." We all know that negative events are a part of this world and that we will have to experience them. But in this chapter, I want to challenge you to do more than just accept it and experience it. I want you to embrace it!

When you experience a negative event or when something bad happens to you, what do you immediately want to do? Think back to a time when some very minor bad event happened in the last couple of days. What happened? And what did you do? What was your immediate impulse? What do you do when something bad happens? You probably turn and run from it. You want to get away from that event, and so you make the choice to immediately move away.

EXAMPLE:
Imagine you're out in the garden for a walk, it's a beautiful day, but a bee comes and stings you and you turn and run. You don't stop to examine the situation. but instead you move away immediately. You don't even consider which direction the bee came from, and whether

you're running toward the hive or away from the hive. You just want to get away!

When something negative happens we all run. There are a lot of other situations in life that we run from as if we were stung by a bee. Sometimes it's a personal situation or a job situation. Maybe it's financial or health or spiritual or relationships. If you've ever gotten yourself into an investment that was was going bad, you wanted to get away from that investment as soon as possible, didn't you? You got stung, you got burned, you can hardly wait to make immediate change.

It's our human nature to want to run from from negative events and sensations, and it's against nature to not run from the bee sting. It's very hard to choose to examine our options when were in those situations.

KEY:

The power of negative is so strong that it will overcome incredible amounts of positive.

EXAMPLE:

You're about to go out for an evening on the town and you spend an hour getting ready to go. You pick out exactly the right clothes. You may lay them out on the bed. You look at them, you may even try them on to make sure that everything is just right. You get dressed, you look in the mirror, totally satisfied with how you look, and you think everything is perfect, you wouldn't change a thing. You walk out into the living room and your husband or wife says, "You look great! Let's go!" You get this positive reinforcement and you don't want to change a thing. You're happy with how you look. Your children come into the room and say, "You look great. Have a good time this evening." You think again: "Boy, do I like how this feels. I wouldn't change a thing. I must look really good." And before you leave, you step in to say goodbye to one other person in the house—a parent or a friend, or maybe another child—and they idly make the comment: "You look great, but are you going to wear those shoes with that dress or slacks?" And what happens? Immediately, for most people, that little bit of negative overwhelms all the positive you've been hearing. It causes you to question, "Am I wearing the right shoes? What other shoes could I wear? What are my options? What are my choices?" For many people, it might cause you to go back and change shoes. Some might even question everything else they are wearing because that small negative just undid all the previous positive. One little bit of negative has the power to overcome huge amounts of positive. **We are conditioned to run from the negative**. We are trained to pull back as if we've been burned, or as if we have been stung by a bee.

So what do we want to do with the negative instead? I'm not saying you shouldn't pull back and I'm not saying you shouldn't change. I'm saying, change is essential and how you change is determined by your attitudes. Your attitude creates the results that you get in your life. For example: you might say "oh, I never do get dressed exactly right. I can't even pick out the right shoes. I'm a horrible dresser. I'm a horrible investor. I'll never go out in the garden again because I always get stung by bees!" What would happen if you were stuck in that negative thinking? Your life would get smaller and smaller. You would pull back and play a smaller and smaller game. We sometimes see this in people that become consumed by the negative events and their own negative attitudes.

Negatives Lead To Change, If...

I'm encouraging you to recognize the negative events, negative feelings and emotions, and negative circumstances in your life, and celebrate those as you would the positives. However, rather than focusing on the negative and believing that life is negative, you appreciate the negative event, because it is the impetus for positive change in you. Change is good because change always has the potential for growth, and forward movement and expansion of who you are. Your life changes for the better as you change.

Like all the other chapters in this book, this is a principal for you to work on *yourself*. It's not something that I or anyone else can do for you. I'm challenging you to notice, and change your attitude as you go through life's events, both positive and negative.

KEY:

There is nothing inherently good or bad. An event is an event, and nothing more.

A circumstance is just a circumstance. It is neither good nor bad. **It has no label until you put one on it**. It is the resulting behavior and the changes you make that produce a positive or negative outcome. If you will start to notice, you'll find it interesting that events that you label "positive" bring about positive results and events that you label "negative" bring about negative results. As you label them you begin to attract the evidence that will prove you right. You get to choose!

But just like the bee sting, your label of that event or circumstance will happen immediately, so you must retrain yourself and stop labeling events as negative because that label will attract a negative result. It's totally up to you!

If you look back you will see that almost all the major changes you have in your life came from negative events. A person loses their job and they think it's a disaster. But what comes from losing your job? Often, what comes is a better job, maybe with a new living environment and other interesting changes in life that keep you stimulated, as well as new and fascinating work. Almost certainly it will bring new people and new friends into your life. **Life moves forward from a negative event, unless—and here's the key—unless you focus only on the negative aspect.** If you see losing your job as a disaster and believe that you will never get a better job, then, you know what? That's exactly what you're going to get. If, on the other hand, you say, "This is interesting. I just lost my job, and I wonder what great new thing is going to come as a result of it. This is an opportunity for me to move forward and change," then that is exactly what you're going to get from it. Remember what we talked about in chapter 1, our thoughts create our reality! That includes our attitudes and the labels we give to events, experiences, relationships, and more. Again, it's up to you!

It's also very important for you to acknowledge the positive things in your life and to celebrate your wins, because that will allow you to attract more positive results. Many people that I've spoken with don't look at the great, positive things that happen in their lives. They brush over them. It's almost as if they don't want to acknowledge a positive event because it was a positive, and they want to stay right where they are to receive more positives. When it's good you want to stay in that good spot. But if you don't acknowledge when positive things happen, what's the result? All the little negatives loom bigger than the positives because you haven't acknowledged the positives.

What I'm challenging you to do is to acknowledge both. I want you to acknowledge that as a result of the great choices you have made, positive things are happening to you. You acknowledge the positive as a result of your attitude, your intention you've created, and of the position you put yourself in. But at the same time, I want you to acknowledge the negative, because the negative has the power to create more positive. Focus on the negative as a catalyst for change, as a trigger. When that trigger gets pulled, it allows you to start to examine your choices, look at options, and stand in different perspectives, until you choose something different. Sometimes that happens in the blink of an eye, like a bee sting we run from. Other times, it's an opportunity for us to move to a different city, or have another child, or get a new job, or to retire, or invest in a property. You have gone through many many life changes that are the result of something that at first appeared to be a negative. In many cases, those life changes have played out over time in very positive ways, out of the deliberate intention that you have created to move forward with your life.

I'm here to say that without some negative impetus, many of those things would not have happened. Many of those changes would never have taken place. Do some people appear to lead perfect lives, with only positive change, without negatives in their lives? Absolutely, it may appear that way. They may have learned to stop labeling events and circumstances as good or bad and therefore allowed a positive result to come from *everything* that happened to them. They are noticing events and circumstances and labeling them "interesting," and by doing that they allow a positive result to come from everything. Wouldn't it be wonderful if you knew that everything that happened to you had the potential to produce positive results? It is possible, as soon as you stop labeling events or circumstances as negative. **Events are just events, whether positive or negative!**

What's the challenge in this? The challenge is to celebrate our negatives as well as our positives, recognizing that they all have the potential to be positive. Easy to say, but not so easy to do, because it requires you to pay attention and notice decisions you make that sometimes happen in an instant, like the response to the bee sting. However, as you start to embrace this idea and implement it in your life you will discover that the earlier chapters about positive attitude become even easier. This process becomes automatic. It will become part of your new belief system. I'm asking you to change your beliefs about negative/positive because I know that as your beliefs and attitudes change, your results in life will change! This will happen automatically.

Acceptance of both negative and positive as having the potential for positive change in you is critical. Is it possible to live life just in the positive? Many people would say no, that's not possible, it's not the nature of the world and we will always have negative things happening. But it's that definition of "negative" that I'm asking you to look at. That is the challenge. While I want you to acknowledge the negative event, I also want you to accept it and celebrate it as part of your bigger positive. There is no negative circumstance unless you label it as such. There is only positive. It doesn't matter what happens to you or what circumstance you find yourself in, it only matters what you do about it. How you react to an event is much, much, more important than the event itself. The results from what we would have labeled negative are much more impactful in our life than the results from what we have previously labeled positive. A positive, again, encourages us to stay where we are and not make any changes. We like it when positive things happen, and we want them to happen again.

> ## KEY:
>
> **I am not advocating denial as a choice**. I am not asking you to ignore the events that take place, but instead, to expect all events and circumstances to benefit you in some way. You almost always have an opportunity to make positive change from all events and circumstances. Don't deny or ignore.

Please start noticing your reactions to events and circumstances quickly, so that you can avoid putting a negative label on any of them. As you tell people about the great things that happened to you today, also tell them about the challenging things that happened to you today and how powerful those events will also be. You have a choice. That choice will happen in the moment you experience an event or circumstance, but it will be reflected in how you act, react, and speak about that event.

The *choice* is yours

It simply comes down to this: you are going to have events and experiences that the world labels negative, and that label would then attract negative results. but I'm asking you to take the choice back. For most people they make choices based on:

- Previous life experiences (these experiences don't count, you're past them)
- What the media tells us (this doesn't count, they have a marketing agenda)
- What your friends say you "should" do (that's ok IF you want to be like them)

It's not up to any of the above reasons, it's your decision if you want a different result!

You get an opportunity to step out into the world differently. Your life will actually move forward and change in a positive way. Sometimes you need to have that bee sting, that finger prick, or that tap on the shoulder. Sometimes you need to get burned a little in order to move forward and get out of the flames.

You may be reading this chapter and saying: "But I don't like that. I don't want that. I want it all to be good! I want it all to be easy! I want everything and everyone in my life to be comfortable and happy. I want to live a life of peace and joy." That's actually what I'm suggesting is available to you right now if you will *celebrate* your negatives and acknowledge the negatives as actually being the biggest potential positives. Then everything is positive. For every negative event that has happened to you in life, there has been some positive result. Sometimes it's hard to find, but look deeper and ask yourself, "How did that experience change me on a spiritual level? How did it change me on an emotional level? Or, did it change how I relate to other people? How did it change me physically?" Maybe you had some physical accident, but your faith in God or your own inner strength, grew tremendously as a result. Studies have been done that show that people who suffer major illnesses earlier in their life will live significantly longer than they would have due to the lifestyle changes they choose. Maybe you have had some other sort of negative circumstance that happened to you, but as result you had to dig a little deeper, look a little harder and rely on your own strength, or rely on friends. Maybe you had to turn to your family, and your family bonds became much stronger.

Often as we go through events and experiences it's important to not only keep a neutral attitude which will allow positive results to show up, but to go one step farther and ask ourselves what opportunity is coming from the circumstance. Some other things to ask yourself are: "What is this event offering me? What are the choices I have before me now? What will I choose? How will I do things differently? What opportunities do I have that I didn't acknowledge before this event? What new awareness do I now have as a result of this event or experience? What will I do now?"

Changes are constantly happening on many levels. On the spiritual, emotional, and physical level, we are immediately and forever changed by every event or circumstance we experience, both large and small. They are neither negative nor positive unless we label them. I choose to label most events and circumstances as "interesting," because that allows me to expect positive results. That is not to say that many experiences and circumstances are not difficult or challenging. None of us were ever guaranteed that everything would be easy. But the same experience or event that may put us in a difficult or challenging circumstance also provides opportunity for positive change.

CHALLENGE TO CHANGE EXERCISE:

I want you to start to notice what you have labeled as negative events in your life. Identify two or three of these big, challenging events that you've gone through and write them down. Beside them, write the positive results that those events created. The positive results that came out of those experiences were circumstances that may not have been available to you otherwise. Write down what it was about that event that served as a catalyst to change. I want you to do this, looking back, so that you can reset your thinking and allow yourself to have a different attitude about events you may be experiencing right now or that you will experience in the future. I also want you to take a moment and think of two or three small negative events that have happened to you in the last week. They can be very small, but I want you to notice what was the result. Write those things down so you lock in the learning. Remember, in chapter 12, we talked about life being primarily about experiences and relationships because of their potential impact on us. That principle will only be true for you if you notice those things happening in your life. Sometimes it's good to write them down in order to acknowledge and learn from them.

If you find a dollar bill on the ground it can change your day. That very small event can make you momentarily happy, but it creates almost no change in you, except that perhaps you start watching the ground more. On the other hand, someone else lost that dollar bill. That person may have lost their last dollar bill or maybe they were counting on that dollar to pay for something important. At some point they realized they had lost it. How did they react, and what change did that experience create for them? If that dollar bill was very important to them, did they go back and search for it? Absolutely! They searched all their pockets carefully, making sure they had no holes in their pockets through which the dollar might have fallen. They will make sure they put their money someplace safe in the future, where it cannot come out of their pocket accidentally.

Now, imagine that same event on a larger scale, with a larger bill. A positive event for you is, in this case a negative event for them. Even if it's as small as one dollar, it will create changes in each of you—small changes for you, but possibly large changes for the person who had the "interesting", more challenging experience. It may cause them to re-examine how or where they keep their money, or what they want to spend it on in the future.

KEY:

Remember that all events and experiences have the potential to bring about change and positive results. That is absolutely true unless you insist on labeling something as bad or negative, because you then attract negative results.

"Negative" is potentially far more positive than "positive." It's up to you! **You're incredibly powerful and your reality turns on the attitudes and beliefs you choose.**

It's totally up to you!

Chapter 17

TIME AND VELOCITY

I n this chapter we're going to talk about the principles of time and speed. The principle of time, speed, and velocity relates very directly to all of us, because our lives are based on accomplishing things and doing things by a certain time. We set a goal, and the goal is to be achieved by a certain time. We often measure our success or failure by whether we met our target date or not. Did we do it by when we had intended to, or did it take us much longer?

Time And Velocity Are Arbitrary!

> ## KEY:
>
> Time is a convenience that we have created to serve our own purpose.

We have collectively created time as a mental construct so that things don't all happen at once in our life—so that everything doesn't happen in an instant or an eternity. We've created a timeline based on physical evidence that allows us to measure in increments of time. The concept that time and velocity are arbitrary and controlled by our thinking like everything else in this world, is one of the harder ones for us to get our heads around.

EXAMPLE:

Have you ever been traveling and you suddenly realized you're at your destination? In other words, maybe were driving on the freeway and you arrived at your destination but you couldn't remember having gone to any of the places in between. Your mind wasn't paying attention. When this happens, it often seems that you can't recall any of things that happened during that time or that you can't even remember that time going by. It was almost as if you'd been asleep when you suddenly woke up and found yourself in another place. If that's ever happened to you, and I'm sure it has, then what you did was suspend time and for a brief moment you didn't measure things using that construct. Instead you allowed time to collapse.

What happens to your mind in those cases and what happens to time? Did time speed up and suddenly and you were there? For you, maybe it did. Most other people would not agree, and for the rest of the world time didn't seem to stop when it stopped for you. For the rest the world, time went on as always. Other people were at work, or playing, or driving their cars, but they were paying attention and it took forever to get where they were going, just like it normally does for you. If you remember everything that happened as you took that trip, then that's an example of your mind creating time and keeping things connected to this world's reality of time. You have the luxury of being aware and vigilant of every moment of activity, or you are able to step outside of it. Your mind steps out of time every night when you go to sleep. It happens for all of us. When we go to sleep, we're not even aware of sounds in the room. Our ears are still open, and yet we don't hear anything. Some people will say, "Well, I do, I'm a light sleeper." That may be true, but you still don't hear much of it. Time seems to pass faster for all of us when we're asleep.

Time may just be a convenience, a creation of our minds. If we believe that we create our reality with our thoughts, as we talked about earlier, than managing time would be a logical part of that. When we believe something is possible, we believe it is going to happen, we *expect* it, and suddenly it's happened and it's past. Have you ever looked forward to something and believed that it was going to be possible for you someday? After a period of time you achieved that goal and moved past it, and when you look back at it, it seems like a dream? For those of you reading this that have grown children, if you look at the day-to-day events of raising a child, you know it takes many years until they leave home. But on the other hand, when you look back at those years, they almost seem to have passed in an instant. We can look at time from both sides and think of that child raising process as having taken many years, or that it took only a few moments. Both are easy to imagine. Looking back, it may have happened so quickly that many of our memories no longer fit into that time space. In our mind we have reduced that space because we're now focusing on other more current spaces of time.

I'm suggesting that time is a creation of our own mind and our own belief systems. We get to shift time to suit our needs, desires and convenience. Think of the possibilities that open up if that's true. Wouldn't it be great to be able to manipulate time and be able to move things forward through time at will? To be able to, with our mind, move ourselves forward to an event? Wouldn't that be convenient? Wouldn't that be faster or easier?

KEY:

While we are talking about saving time, it's important to note that the whole concept of running out of time, saving time, and even wasting time, become irrelevant. **It's impossible to waste time.** Everything you do moves you forward in some way. You may feel as if something was a waste of time, but I'm sure you have either learned something or been changed in some way by every experience you've gone through. Time cannot be wasted any more than you can make a wrong choice. Even a wrong choice moves you forward, and thereby becomes a right choice. Every experience that wastes time brings about some change in you and is therefore not a waste. Stop using that as an excuse, It's impossible to waste time.

Also, if time can be manipulated, then we don't need to worry about *saving time*. There's always more time because we can create it. Time is a convenience of our mind so that things don't all happen at once. We've created time, clocks, and calendars in order to bring about a sense of order and to be able to separate experiences. We can not only avoid things that are boring by passing through them quickly, but also, if we have regrets we can go back and fix them.

EXAMPLE:

Not long ago I was traveling down the interstate highway in the late evening. It was dark and I suddenly realized that I had passed my exit. I also knew that the next exit was many miles ahead and would take me far out of my way. I immediately decided that I wanted my exit to still be ahead and within less than a minute I saw the sign for the exit ahead. I know what you're thinking, that I hadn't passed the exit in the first place, but when I also considered that, I was sure that was not the case. Maybe you have had a similar experience, usually when it effects only you. It changes how you look at events and experiences!

If this principle is true, then if we're traveling down the highway that we talked about earlier and we have a flat tire, then what? Well first of all, what caused the flat tire? The flat tire may have been caused by our thinking, to help us avoid something, or to put us in a position to learn something, or it might be part of our bigger plan or larger agenda to accomplish something much bigger than that single small experience. What if we believe the flat tire is just a flat tire? Let's say that we don't want that flat tire because we don't have "*time*" for it or we don't have the *energy* to deal with it. Let's say it's raining and we don't want to get out in the rain to change the tire. Is it possible to go back in time before we had a flat tire and re-create that situation so that we don't get the flat tire? Logically we would say no, that's not possible. But if time is a creation of our minds like everything else, then *anything's* possible. If we can believe it, it becomes true. In the Bible, Jesus says "if you have faith the size of a grain of mustard seed, you could say to this mountain, be moved and if you believed *without doubt*, then the mountain would move." What is that talking about? It's about belief systems. How strongly and how completely we believe something allows us to shift the reality in the world. And one of the realities in the world that we have created is that things are spread out through time. If we believed it was possible and had the faith without doubt that it would happen, we would then be able to go back in time and fix things, undo things, redo things that we regret. We could actually change past events.

Here's the challenge, the hard part. If we go back and change past events, it changes who we are now in the present. We know that you and I, today, are the sum of all the experiences and relationships we've been through, and the choices that we have made up until now. Therefore, if we go back and change things, it affects who we are in this moment. It affects where we are. It affects who we're in relationships with. Perhaps everything might change if we had the ability to go back and change our past.

Here's a huge caution: we are not God and we don't get to play that role. Life will not be perfect, not on this earth. So we have to balance the concept of time and velocity with the reality of accepting where we are, and what's going on in our lives. Which position creates more good for us? Which has us learn more lessons and move forward. Which allows us to have more positive impact on ourselves and the people around us? **We are here for a purpose.** These are questions we need to be asking ourselves and this is the way we need to look at it. Remember chapter 13 where we talked about radical acceptance?

It's also not a mistake that you got the flat tire. I'm bringing up this idea of time and velocity, and their flexibility, so you know that there is no shortage or lack of time.

I'm challenging you to believe that time and velocity are creations of your mind. Therefore, you need to notice the speed and the time with which things happen, and slowly you'll start noticing that you can control those things. And when you can control those things, you can stop worrying and stressing about the impact of things taking a long time, or a short time, or not enough time, or too much time, or a limited time, or an unlimited time. The ultimate worry is that our life span will not be enough. But guess what? It's *exactly* enough! This is an example of the *radical acceptance* we talked about in chapter 13.

For most people the ultimate concern is death and when it's going to happen. The actions we take with regard to our health, our relationships, our business, our work, our enjoyment and pleasure, are all balancing the ultimate big question of: "how much time do I have left?" How many times have you been in a conversation with somebody and said "I can't believe how much faster things are moving than they used to. Life is going faster and faster." Perhaps it is. Perhaps the collective human mind and psyche has been speeding things up by a belief that time is actually moving faster. **If we believe that things are happening faster, then possibly they are.**

This is a very challenging belief to accept, isn't it? The idea that we create time and we control the abundance or lack of time with our intention and expectation. Time and velocity are relative to our own thinking. We've always heard that time is *relative*. **Time is relative to our beliefs, relative to what we're thinking, relative to us specifically**, as opposed to time in general.

So, if you believe time and velocity are relative to your beliefs, what will you do with it? How you handle this concept or potential belief is what makes it interesting and what makes it a challenge. What will it take for you to adopt this principle and be able to say "Okay, if I assume for a moment that I believe that, then how does it benefit me?" Well, the first thing it does is take away your *excuses*, doesn't it? You will no longer be able to say "I don't have time to do that." Now you do. You can't say "I couldn't possibly finish by then," because now you can. You can't say "It happened too quickly," because now it didn't, and so forth. Many of the things that happen "too quickly" do so because you expect them to happen too quickly. You may expect to run out of time before you accomplish something, and therefore you do. In other words, **if your belief is that you don't have enough time, then you don't have *enough* time**. If instead you believe that you have an infinite amount of time because you get to manufacture it, would there be anything you wouldn't take on because of lack of time? Would there be any limits on what you chose to do and probably could accomplish? No! If you had an infinite amount of time to work on any single thing, or if on the other hand, you could be anywhere in an *infinitely* short amount of time. That would take away your "I can't, and I couldn't." It leaves you with only "Yes, I can." Now you get to fully choose what you want and don't want, without being constrained by a lack of time. There will always be enough time for the things you were *intended* to do, and that you *expect* to do.

EXAMPLE:

I had a client a couple years ago that wanted to write a children's book but there was "never enough time". I asked her to just write an outline for the story but that never happened because she was "so busy". Finally, I asked her to commit to starting the book whenever one of her hourly clients canceled their appointment and she said that she would do exactly that but wasn't sure it would ever happen. When a client cancelled that Friday morning she followed through and started the book. After lunch her entire afternoon of work was moved forward to the next week and she continued on the book. She stayed at her office on Friday evening to work on the book and as she later told me, wound up staying the night writing. By midnight she was nearly complete and remembered that her illustrator was in the Philippines just waking up. She called him and he had the drawings to her by late Saturday. The book was done and off to the publishers! When she understood that there would somehow be time for the book, the time showed up! She slept Sunday and told me this story the following day. Amazing!

You Create Your Own Limits

If we take this theory a little farther, it's not just about time and velocity. It's really about your personal strengths and about every single thing in your life that you believe are limitations. **All of your limitations are thoughts and beliefs** where you created limits to help you play small or safe. What if you had no limits? **You are limited only by your thinking!** Flip back and re-read chapter 1 if necessary, you've got time.

In this chapter, I chose to focus on time and velocity because those are widely accepted as being unchangeable. The speed of light is the ultimate speed. Einstein proved that mathematically. But did you know the speed of gravity is infinite? The attraction of matter goes across this universe in no time whatsoever. If the sun disappeared, we would feel the lack of gravitational pull on the earth immediately. It wouldn't take the several minutes of time that sunlight takes to reach the earth. Long before the blackness came, the earth would be shifting in its orbit, moving away from where the sun had been. The gravitational effect would have reached us instantly. What is the speed of gravity? The ultimate velocity of anything is only what we can measure. It's also only what we can believe.

Today, there are scientists working on the theory of traveling at the speed of gravity, not the speed of light. At the speed of gravity there is no passage of time and we can instantly be anywhere in the universe. How do we do that? First of all, we have to believe it's possible. We have to be able to get our minds around the idea. In other words we have to believe it's possible and have faith in it. Scientists can empirically prove that the speed of gravity is infinitely fast. Other scientists are working on theories of folding space so that time and space have no relationship as we know them now. I mention this to you because I want you to see that there are almost no limits to what might be possible. Ideas about time and space challenge us to our very core because those are the stable elements our lives are built on. Or, is that only what we have created?

Our minds are a powerful tool. I'm asking you to believe that our minds coupled with our spirits and the power of God are capable of changing things, including those things we may have believed were unchangeable. I'm challenging you with this principle, that everything is on the table and everything is changeable, and that you have the power to create things with your mind and your belief systems. I'm using examples from time and space because we can all relate to time moving faster when we are asleep, and we can relate to a memory lapse that allows us to be at a destination and not remember getting there. In this case the time went by *infinitely* quickly. And yet, somebody had to be driving the car down the freeway. You just don't remember it, and so, did it not happen or not? Did that time not take place for you? If you could suspend yourself in time over a longer period of time would you get hungry? Would you get thirsty? Would your hair continue to grow? Would you age? The answer is simple: maybe it depends on what you expect. What do you believe would happen? If you believe that there is no time passing, then you would not get hungry or thirsty and your hair would not grow.

What's the practical application of this principle? Beyond the fact that we have you thinking differently about time, the most basic application is that it allows you to create infinite possibility. Taking away all your excuses is the negative side of that coin. The positive side of that coin is that infinite possibility means no limits, period. **We're limited only by our own thinking**. We talked about this earlier, but now we can see that even bigger things, including time and space and distance and velocity, our entire reality, are all subject to our beliefs. If you challenge yourself to believe these things, do your goals change? Do your desires shift? In many ways they already have, just from being exposed to these ideas. If you want something, why not want it now? If you're clear that you really want something for yourself, or for others, and you believe that something is possible, why not believe that it's possible in this moment? Why wait? Time is an excuse that we have created. Without limits, how big can you think? What's possible for you?

Speed Of Money

Let's talk for a moment about something more practical and relevant to today. Let's use money as an example and talk about the *velocity of money*. Many people believe that they can't make more money because there's only a limited amount of money in the world. Therefore they believe that the amount of money that's available to them is defined by how much money is in the world. Since they think of things from a competitive perspective, they believe that other people are competing with them for that same money.

> # KEY:
> The reality is that there is an infinite amount of money available, and that it's really the speed of money, or velocity of money exchange, that's limiting how much money they can make.

We talked about this before. For instance, if we took the exact amount of money that's available in the world right now, and *everybody* spent their money twice as fast, *everybody* would make twice as much money. No more money is needed for everybody to make twice as much. That's just the velocity of money in action. So it's absolutely possible for you to make twice as much money, because money can now be made and spent infinitely fast. There is no limit to how much money you can make or spend, or how long it takes for you to make or spend it. With the new technologies that allow money to be spent at a simple computer keystroke, or with a phone call, or through the swipe of a credit card in a card reader, you can either make or spend money instantly. This can be done in quantities that are only limited by whoever you are making or spending it with. So, **the velocity of money becomes an important factor for your personal wealth creation,** and since time is only a creation of your own mind, there is no limit to how much money you could make, or how long it would take. What would it take for you to say "There is an infinite amount of money and all I have to do is make it and spend it faster,".

An unlimited income becomes available to you and if you now couple that with an infinite amount of time, then what's possible for you?

Thousands of years ago when money was first used as a barter exchange medium there was very little physical money available, so it was very precious. It was only spent for precious items that you could not make or build or grow yourself, and the money changed hands very slowly. As technology has advanced over the years we started making coins from precious metals, and later we started printing paper money. As we did that, money was exchanged faster, so governments made more money available to meet the supply and demand for money. Now we have money that has moved into the realm of credit and even credit cards. In the early 1900s, we started using credit with the banks instead of exchanging hard currency. The banks allowed you to have a credit line. Money is now earned and spent at the computer, or the ATM, or the click of a transaction at the bank. We don't even have to have our money backed up with gold anymore. **Money is just a creation of everybody's collective mind** working together. We have all agreed that this is how money will work, and therefore that is how it works. But if everybody suddenly decides "I don't believe it, I just don't trust it, I don't think it will work anymore," then suddenly it won't. If that happens, the flow of money stops, currency systems break down, and it becomes true that money has no value because of people's belief systems. The economy just falls apart.

So it is our belief about the value and velocity of money, how quickly we can buy and sell things to make our money, which determines how much money we make. You get to choose. If you couple that idea with the idea that time is a creation of your mind, you get to not only choose how much money you make because of velocity, but how long it takes you to make it because of time.

This is just one example of time and velocity and the effect it can have. When you look at these ideas and take them on as a challenge what will it mean for you? If you take the principle that says time and velocity are creations of your mind, I would first challenge you to change your mind! What would you like to believe? Would you like to believe that there's an infinite amount of money available to you? You would, wouldn't you? You'd like to believe there's an infinite amount of time also—time for fun events, time to be spent with your family, time for personal growth and meditation, time for reading and time for doing things other than just work. Maybe you want more time for work, but even then, wouldn't you rather believe there's enough time? **There's always enough time**. Don't you want to believe that there is no limit to those things? I'm here to tell you that there's not. The limitation is in your beliefs. Change your beliefs and change your reality.

That was the first thing we talked about, back in chapter 1, and it applies to everything!

JUST PRETEND EXERCISE:

This is a very challenging concept because it causes you to question your foundational beliefs. You may be saying "Oh, I don't believe this." If that's the case, and you don't believe it is possible, then you will never experience it. But let me just ask you three simple questions…

1. What would you choose to do if there were no financial limits?
2. What would you say yes to if you knew you would have enough time to complete it?
3. Do you want to choose abundance, or do you want to play safe?

Like many other chapters in this book, I'm going to challenge you to start *noticing* where your beliefs have created limitations. I want to challenge you to expand your mind and believe that it's possible to choose your own timeframe, and choose the speed of money, the speed of relationships, the speed of accomplishment, and even the speed of your personal growth. All these things are limited only by your mind.

You create or limit all your reality with your mind. Your belief systems make it so!

It's time to practice coloring outside the lines!

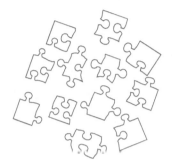

Chapter 18

FULL
ENGAGEMENT
THEORY

T his chapter is about the concept of full engagement. Full engagement is the act of being fully engaged in whatever you're doing. When you're fully engaged, you engage more of yourself than normal and you therefore actually accomplish more and see much better results than you would see from normal engagement and normal activity.

In the first chapter of this book I introduced a process to achieve the future you really want. That process is called The Future Formula™ and I mention it now with the idea of *Full Engagement* because it is important to first define *what* you want to fully engage in. That can be done with The Future Formula, clarifying your life purpose, or other processes in my books, but it is important to note that Full Engagement works on whatever you apply it to, positive or negative.

EXAMPLE:

Let me give you an example of The Future Formula and Full Engagement working together. I was very fortunate to be able to retire the first time at the age of 47 and live on the passive income I had created. I believe that was a direct result of my own belief and declaration that I would retire before I was 50. I told everybody for 20 years leading up to my retirement, and was able to retire, not from something that I'd been planning, but from something that came along as an opportunity to fulfill that expectation. I was able to play a big card in the game of life and retire on passive income. When I stopped working my thought was: "This is a great opportunity. I'm going to be able to catch up on all the reading I've wanted to do, play golf as much as I want to, and do all sorts of retirement things." But in a very short time I was completely bored with the lack of activity, the lack of schedule, lack of demand for action. I realized that in order for me to continue to be excited about life, I needed to step up the pace and re-engage. One of the areas that I was still excited about was having the time to do a lot of reading. Books are, and have always been, a great source of education and inspiration for me, and one of the challenges that I quickly encountered was that I was not a very fast reader. I would start to read and become instantly bored because I couldn't read fast enough to keep up my interest level. My mind would wander to all sorts of other things that were going on. As I was reading, I often wanted to turn on the television, look out the windows, I would notice sounds in the room, listen to conversations. All sorts of other things were going on in my mind because the bulk of my mind was idle because I was only able to read at about 300 words per minute.

I went out and bought a book titled "The Evelyn Woods Book of Speed Reading." I highly recommend it to you, not just because it teaches you how to read faster, but because it proposes a theory very similar to what I am calling "full engagement." The book actually proposes that if you read faster you will retain more because you're using a bigger percentage of your mind on that one specific activity, and therefore that activity makes a stronger impact. It's sort of like when your computer is running and you have a lot of other programs open. The more programs you have open, the more your computer has to divert energy and speed to maintain those programs, and less energy and speed remains to devote to its primary function. If you turn off all the other programs the computer is able to run much faster, and it will also be less likely to crash or make serious computing mistakes.

50,000 Word/Minute Mind In A 300 Word/Minute World

One of the fascinating facts from the Evelyn Woods book was that the human mind thinks and processes information at approximately 50,000 words per minute. That is our average brain capacity for processing. If we accept the 50,000 words per minute processing speed as fact, then my reading 300 words per minute barely kept my brain awake. I could do that in my sleep. In fact, our dreams probably process information much faster than that. The human mind is capable of processing at an incredible rate of speed. When we use it at less than its maximum potential, our brain gets bored, distracted, and wanders off. That is one of the fundamental problems with our education system today.

Engage More To Get More

The principal of full engagement is that if you want to learn faster, retain more, and get more from your experience, then you need to be fully engaged in that experience. Have you ever done anything in your life that took your full involvement? Let me give you a couple examples of what I mean. Because events that are either highly emotional or highly physical require a large portion of our mind to process, they have the potential to engage us fully at a very high level. For instance, when a woman is delivering a child, Lamaze breathing techniques and birthing techniques keep her very, busy and focused. Her mind is fully engaged in several activities to intentionally take her away from the pain. The technique takes her focus away from the painful portion of the process allowing her to go through the process without experiencing as much pain. She's also given special breathing exercises—but not just breathing exercises, she's also told to count along with these breathing exercises. Additionally she's been told to focus on her partner or on a spot on the wall, along with the breathing and counting exercises. The object of all of that is to fully engage her mind someplace other than the pain of childbirth. It's an attempt at full engagement, knowing that if we fill the mental processor with enough other information, the mother will be unable to focus as strongly on the pain of the birthing process itself.

Let me give you one more example. Often people faint from stimulation overload, or from fear. When we're already fully engaged, and then add additional input, our internal mental computer crashes, and that's when we faint. It's very much like your computer needing to reboot and going to a black screen.

> # KEY:
> Our mind wants to fill itself and give it's full attention to something but, like a circuit in your house, when it goes beyond it's capacity, it trips your breaker and shuts down.

Not too long ago I had the opportunity to go skydiving. As a first-time skydiver, I thought that the challenge would be to jump out of the plane. As a friend told me, "To jump out of a perfectly good airplane even with a parachute just seems crazy." I discovered that the training for skydiving is about 20 minutes long and is very intensive. They tell you lots of things to do, and they have you doing a lot of little tasks, many of which I'm convinced are probably unimportant, but the trainers have you focusing on things other than the fact that you are about to jump out of a perfectly good airplane at 13,000 feet above the ground.

Normally, if your mind was not engaged in something else, it would be running lots and lots of rational scenarios and reasons for you to not jump out of the plane. You would be consumed with fear or anxiety, or doubts and worries about what was going to happen. For many people, that battle between rational thinking and taking the literal leap of faith is only overcome by all of the little details that they are telling you to do—to cross your arms in a certain way, to look up and to the right, to swing your legs over the edge, and arch your back, and put your feet together, and point your toes, and so on. All those little details focus your mind away from the fear of jumping out of the plane. They want you to fully engage in the process of jumping so that you don't notice the fear and emotion that are trying to keep you from jumping. Often, first timers actually faint. Their mental computer crashes as they're jumping from the plane. That's why in most areas, they make you do your first jump as a tandem jump with an experienced skydiver to pull the cord and get you safely to the ground.

I'm using this as an example to show you that when you're fully engaged in one activity, it does two things: it has you experience that activity more fully, and it also precludes you being fully engaged or even partially engaged in other activities.

> EXAMPLE:
> Often clients hire me to help launch new businesses and many time they have multiple ideas and want to start multiple businesses. Normally my response is to ask them to pick one to start, because it is impossible for us to focus in two directions at the same time. If they are two businesses that support each other, then we can consider the simultaneous start-up because we can then be *fully engaged in one direction*. Successful new business start-ups always requires full attention. Distraction and overload often are the cause of failure.

Full engagement is a process of you becoming fully involved using your entire 50,000 mental word processor and learning at a very advanced rate. As I read the Evelyn Woods book, it gave me a detailed, step-by-step process to be able to read faster and faster. In fact, it tests you on your reading speed in the beginning, then takes you through a few chapters and tests you again. My reading speed tripled. I went from 350 words a minute to almost 1300 words a minute within about an hour. Well, how can that be? It's because I hadn't known this techniques of reading fast. I assumed that if I wanted to retain information that I actually needed to read slower, not faster. And I found, when I read slower, retention was even more challenging. Have you ever tried to read a passage when you're distracted and then had to go back and read that passage again? Have you ever decided that you were going to read in bed, and after reading two or three pages, you fell asleep. Then the next day when you get into bed again, you can't remember those few pages and you have to read them again! Some people get stuck on the same two or three pages for weeks because their mind is not engaging in what they are doing.

The assumption is that if we read slower we will retain more. However, the reality is that when we read slower we are giving our brain more time to wander off. When we do something, anything, slowly, we give our brain time to try to fill that excess capacity. It's interesting that when we read faster, and engage more of our brain in a single activity, we actually not only complete the task faster, but we have a higher retention, and a better understanding of what we just read. Amazing! I challenge you to test this yourself and measure your own results.

Now, just as there are specific skills and techniques for reading faster, there are specific skills and techniques for doing other things at a faster rate. There are specific techniques to be fully engaged in any activity in which you are participating. Often, it takes time for us to come up to speed on things. How long did it take you to learn how to drive? When you were a child, you probably had no interest in driving and you simply rode in the car. You weren't engaged in the process of driving the car at all. Later, when you became a teenager, you became more involved in the process; you watched from the front seat or over the shoulder of your parent as they drove. At that point you were slightly engaged in the process. But when you turned 16, you probably wanted to get your driver's license so badly that you became fully engaged. The first time or two you actually sat in the driver's seat and drove a car, I would bet that you were almost fully engaged in the process of learning to drive—so much so, that you may have forgotten certain basic things around the periphery of learning how to drive. You were so engaged in trying to steer the car, work the brakes, work the clutch and the gas, shift the gears, and let out the clutch without jerking the car, that you may have forgotten something as simple as putting on your seatbelt. All of this was because your mind was fully engaged in the process of "driving" the car, but what happened after you had been driving for a while? After the first year or so, you probably became somewhat disengaged, didn't you? After a while your driving took place on autopilot. It no longer took a huge portion of your conscious brain and mental processor to drive the car.

Perhaps while you were driving, you started doing other tasks. Have you ever seen a woman putting on her makeup while she's driving to work? Or seen someone eating their breakfast on their way to work? Have you ever seen a person talking on their cell phone while driving, almost fully involved in their conversation with somebody else? If the person that they are talking to gives them some horrible or surprising news, where is the result? Their mind becomes fully engaged in that news, and what mental capacity is left to focus on their driving? Almost none!

How often have you been engaged in something dangerous, or exciting, or something that requires very fast reaction on your part, and someone has actually had to remind you to breathe When we become fully engaged in something we often forget about even the most basic tasks.

When we engage in any one activity, and then give that activity even more of our focused attention, we increase our involvement in that activity and we therefore get more from it. It's also true that wherever we put our attention, that's where we will see growth and development. How much attention are you giving to the important activities in your life? How often do you give them your full attention when you're engaged in them? What is the most important thing in your life right now? Many of us would say our relationships with our family or our spouse. And yet how much time do we give to those relationships? On a scale of one to ten, are we giving them a nine or ten, or simply giving them a two or three? How much time are we spending engaged in those activities that we've already identified as the most important in our lives? If your relationships are being challenged, or are in trouble, it may be because you're not engaged fully in those relationships.

The principle is simple: if we want to get more, we have to give more. One way to do that is to become fully engaged in whatever is most important to you. Have you ever noticed an athlete when they are engaged in a very slow activity. For example, when Tiger Woods is at the top of his golf game, he is absolutely in a zone. That "zone" is full engagement! It is where nothing else is allowed to break through, nothing else is allowed inside the mind except that single activity. It's a hard, tight focus. It's your full engagement in just one activity at a time. Professional golfers don't take interviews while they're walking down the fairway because they are fully engaged, focusing on their next golf shot. When we are fully engaged we don't smile, we don't laugh, and we don't engage in conversation, because we're totally focused on the activity at hand. And what's the result? The result is better performance, increased learning, and increased involvement causing you to outperform the competition, and probably outperform your previous experiences. Maybe it's just about you doing your best at any given activity.

KEY:

Become fully engaged! Use every ounce of what you are and what you have. Commit yourself to an activity. Focus hard on what you are doing and the results will increase almost exponentially. I challenge you to do it today, in one area of your life that's the most important to you. If you notice your mind wandering, continue to refocus on your original activity. Increase the speed or intensity in the activity to hold more of your attention.

Also, pick up a copy of the Evelyn Wood speed reading book. It's a wonderful book!

EXAMPLE:

You're sitting in your living room and trying to watch a movie on the television, and your children are running around the house, your phone is ringing, you smell dinner cooking on the stove, you hear the dog barking outside, and you're still trying to pay attention to the movie. That's normal behavior, typical of how most people behave. Full engagement looks a little different: you're sitting in a darkened theater, there are no distracting sounds, there's nothing but the movie on the screen, and the screen is enormous! You're sitting close enough that you see nothing else in your peripheral vision. You hear nothing else but the movie soundtrack in the theater, because the movie is so engaging that everybody is totally silent. You are fully engaged in the experience of the movie. Now, ask yourself: which of these events, the darkened movie theater or the distracted scene in your own home watching a movie on television, has the greater power to move you? Which of these events has the power to change your emotions or energy, or cause you to want to change your behavior or thinking? Even if the movie at home on your television had some profound effect on you, how much more powerful would it have been in a movie theater where you are able to totally engage?

That's what we're talking about with full engagement: it's taking as close to 100% of your attention as possible for you at that time. That level of engagement has the most power to move you forward, to motivate you to take action, to initiate change that's going to have an impact on your life. If you're going to do something, you owe it to yourself to do it 100%. Now, if you're reading this and saying to yourself, "Well, yes, but I would really rather watch the movie in the comfort of my own home, and I don't mind all those other distractions," then I suggest to you that you're playing life small. You may be avoiding full engagement in order to not leave your comfort zone. To protect yourself from uncertainty and change. (Re-read Chapter 7 about the "small ego" if necessary)

Ask yourself how fully engaged you are in the activities you're participating in today. Ask yourself what you want from each activity. How much are you willing to give to it? Are you willing to play full out, or are you playing and giving only a small portion of yourself to that activity? If you are playing it safe and not fully engaging, what are you getting from that? What's the benefit to you?

Identify Where You Want Bigger Results

The challenge is simply this: identify the things in your life that you want to be fully engaged in, and don't hold back. If you hold back, you're just shortchanging yourself and everyone around you. The opportunities for impact, for learning, for growth and achievement, are being limited by your partial engagement. It's hard to know whether you want or don't want something unless you fully experience it, and that only happens when you choose consciously to fully engage. How many people would settle for half of someone's love? Don't we all want to be fully loved and cared for by at least one other person on this planet, and express our own love to them at its fullest? Don't we also want to experience other things at their fullest? Why would you choose to only halfway experience happiness, affection, family connection, or any of the things that you cherish in life? Engage fully in those things. Experience them! Don't be afraid of them. See what life has to offer you when you fully engage. Play a higher level game! Use all of your 50,000 words per minute capacity. Use your potential! Don't step away from it, step into your potential and see what you're capable of with full engagement.

Engagement exercise:

Step 1

Identify the things in your life that are the most important to you and write them down in a few words each on the left side of a sheet of paper. It may be as many as 20 or more different things in your life. This list may include people, activities, physical things, beliefs and ideas, skills and attributes, and more…

Step 2

Place your list in order by putting a number beside each thing starting with 1 as the most important, and most highly valued by you, and going to the least important. This order would then identify where it is most important for you to fully engage to get the most from that aspect or area of your life.

Step 3

To the right of each thing on the list write the first thing you will commit to doing to more fully engage with that thing. Add a time or date that you will do it. Write it down beside the engagement activity.

Step 4

Share this list with someone close to you or someone that will hold you accountable for following through. Keep it simple, take action!

EXAMPLES:

If your relationship with your partner or spouse is on the list you may simply commit to a simple act of a smile or a hug daily, or some other loving gesture.

If your spiritual growth is on the list it may be as simple as dedicating 15 minutes daily to thank God for the blessings you have received.

Are You Playing Small?

I want to ask you two questions. First question: where in your life are you playing small? Where do you hold back? When you read that question, immediately something popped into your mind. I know that, because that's the way the mind works; it fills the void. Asking a question creates a whitespace that's designed for an answer to show up, and an answer almost always does show up. What was the answer that showed up for you when I asked that question? Maybe it's about relationships, maybe it's business, or about your happiness, or peace or tranquility, or some other area of your life that's just not developed yet. Maybe you're holding back in the area of adventure and excitement. There is no right or wrong answer. I'm only asking you to notice for yourself. The right answer for you is the answer that popped up when I asked the question. Trust yourself. Are you willing to move forward in that area? Wherever you've been holding back, are you willing to step fully into engagement with it? What would that feel like? What would it look like? Whatever popped into your mind wouldn't have come up if you weren't ready to embrace it and engage in it. Again, trust yourself!

What Are You Afraid Of?

Second question: what are you afraid of? That's right, what are you afraid of? Something popped into your mind again. What showed up when I you read that question? Your fears are having you play small in some area of your life, and sometimes you may need to just break through those fears. As we talked about in earlier chapters, most of our fears can be reduced by getting answers to questions associated with those fears. But sometimes we just need to step fully into something. We need to challenge ourselves to read as fast as possible—again, this is the metaphor for every other area of our life. You need to be willing to play big, to go to the dark movie theater and step away from the television. You need to be willing to fully engage in whatever area of your life that's calling you. Life has a lot to offer. It's infinite and it's being offered to you. Don't hold back and don't let your fears keep you from the rewards of life that are waiting for you. Notice the areas in which you are holding back and notice what you're afraid of. Make an effort to fully engage in those areas, and then start noticing. The results will be profound, and the impact will be amazing. Life will change before your very eyes, immediately, as you start to fully engage. Great things will begin to happen for you in those areas where you do fully engage. When you engage at 50,000 words per minute instead of your normal 300 words per minute you will start to unlock your full potential. Step up to the plate! Start swinging! This may be your second or third inning or it may be your eighth or ninth inning. In either case, it's time to start swinging, it's time to move on.

Don't let the time slip by. Fully engage!

Chapter 19

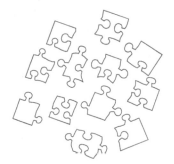

GROWTH IS THE NATURAL ORDER OF THE UNIVERSE

G rowth is the natural order of the universe. All things want to grow. Things get bigger, the universe expands, wealth accumulates, trees get bigger. It's the natural order of all things. **Growth is a natural part of God's plan for the universe**, and what I want you to notice in this chapter is, where you are stopping that process in your life.

Have you ever noticed that even the biggest giant Sequoia trees grow from a seed that you can hold on the end of one of your little fingers? It is a natural process for things to expand and grow. It's part of how everything is designed. The universe itself is expanding at 5,000 miles per second in every direction, so fast that light cannot keep up with the expansion of the universe, and so it's hard for scientists to map the size of the entire universe. The size of the known universe is limited only by how far light can travel and then return to us. So it's only limited by what we know about what we can see of it. And yet it continues to expand because that's the natural order of everything!

This principle of growth as the natural order will be seen everyplace that you look at life. Every spring, after the winter snows melt away, everything starts growing. It continues to grow. We whack it down, we cut it, we trim it, we shape it, and it continues to grow. In the fall it goes dormant and in the spring it starts growing again as vigorously as before. Things naturally want to grow. From the moment a baby is born, he starts to grow. He starts growing not just physically, but he starts growing in terms of his mental capacity, he starts learning immediately. An infant starts growing in terms of his accumulated knowledge, knowing more and more and being more and more active based on what he has learned. He starts developing relationships, and those relationships start growing immediately, and continue to grow all the way through his life. As you're reading this you may be thinking: "Oh, sure, but I don't see so-and-so anymore who used to be my best friend." Does this mean that your relationship has gone backward? Not necessarily. The natural order of things is for things to continue to grow unless you get in the way. Things will naturally continue to grow unless you block them from doing so. We'll talk more about this later in this chapter.

We Live In An Abundant Universe

Let's look at how things grow and what areas of your life should be growing around you. If you accept growth as the natural order of the universe, the natural design of creation, then you have to accept that we are living in an abundant universe. Otherwise things would not have the potential to continue to grow. There are people out there who believe that we do not live in an abundant universe, and that there's not enough to go around. They don't believe that if they share, there will still be enough for them. They come from a model of high *competition* as opposed to *cooperation*. They come from a position of: "If you make more, then I get less." That *scarcity* thinking is naturally opposed to the idea of an abundant, growing universe. In one of the bonus chapters I discuss the win-win possibilities of life. Simply stated here: If we're playing win-win, then everybody can win and succeed and grow, because it's the natural order of things.

That bonus chapter and five others can be downloaded free at:
www.coachingservices.com/books/bonus

If we believe that the universe and everything in it is designed to grow and expand and develop, then we have to believe in abundance. There is more than enough of everything! Our limitations are really created in our minds and not through reality itself. **Scarcity is not the natural order of the universe**. That is a creation of our mind because of failure and learning the wrong lessons from experiences in our past. Therefore we make up a conversation with ourselves that says "The universe doesn't have enough resources. There isn't enough money to go around. There isn't enough love to go around." And so on, and so on. Most of these things are not defined by a finite limit. **Money does not have a finite limit**. We just spoke about that in chapter 17. Because of the velocity of money, the amount of money available to us is infinite. How about love? Is love limited? If you love someone, does it take away from the love available for other people? No! We have an infinite capacity for love. How about knowledge? Is it limited, or is there still an infinite amount of knowledge yet to be uncovered and understood? Obviously, everybody from a child to a scientist is uncovering new knowledge every day. We continue to learn more and more, and as we expanded the edges of what we know, we're given even more insight. That's also the way it is with money, our spiritual growth, our relationship with God and the universe, our personal knowledge, our relationships with people as they grow. Everything expands and grows! That is why 80% of the wealth in the world is held by the oldest 20% of the population. Your finances will naturally grow through your lifetime.

I haven't really aimed this book toward any one subject more than another, but I want you to look at the area of finance, because that's an area where people get stuck all the time. Most people believe that: "Well, my father made $50,000 a year, so I should make $50,000 a year, or maybe a little more." They believe in a scarcity model, that there isn't *enough* for them to go beyond that. They have bought into a common belief system that says there is a limit to their income earning ability. If you have said or thought that "I'm making $100,000 a year now, and that's as much as I ever thought I would make," then that becomes your self-fulfilling prophecy. You're placing a limit on your own growth.

> # KEY:
> **It's true for you IF "you say so."**

Where Have You Stopped Growing?

Where have you placed a limit on your growth in other areas of your life? Have you thought: "I only have one good friend but that's all I expect to have, so I'm never going to have more friends," or "I've got $5,000 in the bank, and I'm probably never going to have more than that," or "My car is five years old and that's all I get to have. I don't deserve a better or newer car or two cars or a car and a motorcycle." If you thought those or similar thoughts, then you're placing limits on your potential for growth. And they become your self-fulfilling prophecies. These thoughts become what you expect, and as we have talked about before: **we get what we expect**. We create those limitations. We can approach them, but is very difficult for us to exceed our own limitations. Growth is the natural order of the universe, remember? It's a natural law that things grow, and therefore, if you limit that growth, you are being unnatural. You're going against nature and the divine order. Why would you do that? If growth is the natural order of the universe, why would you limit your own growth and want to stay where you are? It's because it's safe! It's easier! You won't have to work as hard, or be afraid, or take a risk, or change. Nobody will make fun of you for moving forward and changing. You will never seem different, and people will always know what to expect from you. All the limitations of thinking that you have put in place become part of your belief system in order to play it safe, to protect you.

Remember in previous chapters we've talked about our inner self, our ego self and small ego. They really want us to have everything stay the same. That voice, your inner critic that's speaking to you and saying "Don't do that. You don't need that. You're not good enough, not strong enough. You're not ready for that." That's only the limitations you're putting on your own growth. If that voice was saying instead, "Go for it! You *are* strong enough, you *are* smart enough, you're big enough, you're ready and capable, you're able to do that and you can do anything you choose to do," then what would be possible for you? If your inner voice was saying those things you would be in line with the natural order of the universe. You would be growing! Your finances would be growing, your business, your relationship with other people, the amount of love you give and receive would be growing. Every area of your life would be growing and you would be learning every day. You would be like that giant Sequoia tree that starts out small and becomes one of the biggest living things on the planet. How would you like to be that powerful and strong? The Sequoia tree starts out from a seed that you can hold on the end of your finger, but it continues to grow. Growth is the natural order of the universe and only stops when you stop.

> ## KEY:
> Everything in your life wants to grow and expand and flourish unless you stop it or limit it! Don't get in your own way!

I want you to stop and notice. Where are you limiting growth? I want you to look into every area of your life. I want you to look at your financial life and your work. Do you enjoy your work? Is it fulfilling and rewarding? I want you to look at your spiritual life. Are you continuing to have a deeper and deeper spiritual connection with God and the universe, or with your own belief system? I want you look at your physical life. Are you happier and happier with your physical self? I'm not talking just about how many push-ups you can do and whether you can do more today than you could do last year, or how fast you can run. I'm asking how happy you are with your physical self at this given age. Are you healthy? I want you also to look at your family life. Are your family relationships better than they were five years ago, or better than they were one year ago? It's the natural order of those relationships to be growing and developing, maturing, changing. How about your relationship with your spouse or partner? Is that relationship improving? Is it deepening? Is there more love as the years go by? Are you feeling more supported and loved as you give more support and more love? Growth is the natural order, remember. I want you to look at your environment and your surroundings. Look at what you have—your cars, your clothes, the house you live in, and the things around you. Are you happy with those things? Are they improving? Are you getting more and more? Again, it's the natural order of things to expand and grow and for you to have more and more of everything.

I know that as you're reading this you may be thinking: "Well, that seems pretty greedy. It seems selfish, or not really fair." But again, if that's what you're thinking, I want to challenge your thinking because it means that you're still caught up in scarcity and you still think that if you have more it means that someone else has less. It's not true! It's not true at all, and it goes against the natural order of the universe. The natural order is for things to grow and expand. Everything can grow and expand just like the universe itself. There are no limitations! Only we impose limitations on what is possible. If you had more you would be able to give more, share more, help more, and would support the growth of many other people. That would be a natural consequence of your growing prosperity. If you chose to try to hoard all your gains for yourself, you would be stifling your own spiritual growth and going against the principle of stewardship and natural order of growth.

Did you ever notice that when a scientist has a breakthrough and makes an amazing new discovery, the scientist believes it is the next step, but they never believe it's the last step? Recently scientists discovered how to clone animals and how to duplicate an entire creature from a single DNA strand. It's taken us years and years to develop this knowledge. Do we now think that's the limit of our progress? It's easy for us to believe that in the area of knowledge and learning that there will always be more, and it doesn't seem greedy to want more. We all believe that in the area of science, there is always more to discover. Why don't we believe that for other areas of our lives? Why don't we believe that it's possible for the natural resources of the earth, or our own personal wealth, or relationships? Why don't we believe that things can continue to expand and grow and develop?

Universal Expansion

"But, if what you're saying is true, then as the Earth's population continues to grow, pretty soon we will run out of food, won't we? And we'll run out of water!" Where will the food and water go? They're not going anywhere! There isn't anything on this earth that has escaped. Things just recycle. It's important to recycle and I'm not suggesting that we don't take care of our home planet. I'm suggesting that there are always solutions. There are always means to deal with the expanding growth that is a natural part of the universe. At the same time the population increases, so will our knowledge, our consciousness, our technologies, and everything else we need in order to be able to cope with the expanding needs of the new population. There will be expansion and growth in every area across the planet—in fact, across the universe. If those things all expand there will be a natural abundance available to us because we are expanding all areas. We're not just expanding in one area. It's absolutely true that if we use all of our resources and expand only in the area of consumption and population we will definitely run into trouble. But the reality is that it is not the only area that is expanding. Technology is expanding. Science is expanding, conservation is expanding. Even recycling is expanding. It is the natural order of all things to grow, get larger, and flourish.

As we look at this concept, we have to ask ourselves how does that apply to us personally? Let's look at this issue of expansion and natural growth on a personal level. **Remember that growth is the natural order of the universe, which means it is the natural order for you and for everything in your life.** If you accept that simple principle, my question for you becomes: "Where are you not growing?" There may be areas where you have grown for years. Even so, you may admit to yourself that in some other areas your belief systems told you that you were as big as you were ever going to get. You may have limiting beliefs in small areas that have slowed your growth, or very large areas where you have stopped your growth entirely. Are you placing limitations on what's possible for yourself? Limitations themselves go against this principle of abundance that allows us to believe that growth and expansion are the natural order.

What would happen if you start to apply the principle of abundance and growth to your life? What's possible for you then? Or, better put, what's *not* possible? Maybe huge steps are not possible immediately because it may take you time to shift your beliefs. Remember what we talked about earlier with regard to time itself, things happen over time. Time is our creation! So everything is possible given enough time. Growth is the natural order, so look at your life and start noticing where you are not growing. Where are you stuck? Where are you frustrated or incomplete? Where are you unfulfilled or unhappy? I will tell you right now, with certainty, that these are the areas of your life where you have stopped growing. If it's in the area of finance, and your money world is completely stuck, then get unstuck by shifting your beliefs.

KEY:

Accept this principle of abundance and the idea that it's the natural order for you to have more and more. Believe it is possible for you to continue to get more and more wealth in your life and become one of the 20% who hold 80% of the wealth. Expand yourself. Continue to grow and develop.

If it's in the area of relationship where you're stuck, you may even have given up. I want to encourage you to not give up. Is the natural order for you to receive and give more and more love through your life. It's completely natural for you to find more and more people to be in close relationship with. If you notice yourself pulling back and playing it safe, then **get into *motion*. It is up to you to initiate *movement*.** We will talk about that in a future chapter, but for now just know that in every area of your life where you feel struck, you will need to create movement, and from that you will start to expand. Opportunities will show up as your beliefs change, and your life will start to expand in those areas. And yes, of course, all areas of your life can expand at the same time. In fact, expansion in one area will promote expansion in other areas. That then implies that many areas may be stuck because of the lack of growth in one key part of your life.

Challenge yourself, Notice what you really want and where you want to see expansion. Start breaking down those limitations and accept the simple principle of growth as the natural order. Don't try to figure out *how* to get it! Sometimes people get stuck in the details of "I can't do this because…" They come up with lots of logical reasons why it's impossible to create that much wealth, or impossible to deepen their relationships, or it's impossible to have their business succeed, because of blah blah blah blah blah. Don't try to figure it out! **Accept the principle and know that it's God's job to figure out how**. It's your job only to identify what you want and believe that it's possible. Don't get caught up in conversation with yourself or others telling you there isn't enough time, or there isn't enough money, or there isn't enough of this or of that. In other words, don't get caught up in excuses. Don't blame it on bad employees or bad marketing or whatever. Those are excuses for staying in *small thinking*. Shift that thinking and believe in abundance. Things don't naturally get smaller and smaller.

If things got smaller and smaller our planet would be gone by now.

If we accept the idea that growth is the natural order of the Universe, and that it's part of God's plan that everything gets bigger and grows, then the next question becomes: How do we encourage it? How do we nurture it? How do we support growth so that every area of our life is growing and moving forward and expanding? Again, let's look at the Sequoia tree or any other growing thing in this world, and ask ourselves specifically what it takes for them to grow. For most things, some form of support is needed. For instance, in the case of the tree, the giant Sequoia needs space to start, water, nutrition, sunlight, and air. If those things are taken away, the growth will stop.

KEY:

Natural growth requires the availability of specific things in order to occur.

How Do We Feed Growth?

If we look at one aspect or area of our life that is not growing, what might we suspect? We might suspect that some of the nutrition, or support, or some of the required elements are not there or maybe you have not made space for growth to start.. So what, to take one example, would some of those required elements be for a relationship? What would you have to give it? What does it need? Maybe it needs attention or your time. Maybe it needs your energy or support, or love or patience or understanding. The short answer is, it requires whatever you have been holding back for that particular area of your life to grow and thrive and flourish. I don't know what those things are for the specific areas of your life in which you would like to see growth. But you need to take the time to notice and ask yourself what's missing. If you continue to withhold those elements of required support, that area of your life will slowly get smaller and smaller until it goes away. Even relationships will slowly die and wither away. There may be areas of your life that you're doing that right now. If so, what's needed to reverse that cycle and starting growing again? Seeds in the desert may wait years for rainfall in order to germinate and grow. They just wait for the supporting element that they need. Right now some areas of your life are waiting for the rain so they can germinate, grow and expand. That area is waiting for your attention and support.

We're always moving forward or backwards. We're always either expanding or contracting, growing or shrinking. **If you're stopped and you believe you're not moving in any direction at all, you are, in fact, shrinking, and your relative position is getting smaller and smaller.** That's because everybody else is also either expanding or contracting, and if they are expanding, then your position is getting smaller, relative to them. Many people tell me that their lives are coasting. They've achieved what they want to achieve, and now they're in cruise mode. The problem is that they are coasting or cruising backwards, not forwards. When you stop feeding some areas of your life, whether it's financial, business, relationship, personal growth, or spiritual, that part of you will slowly die because of lack of support and nutrition. If it's dead or dying you are actually moving backwards, not forward. In earlier chapters we discussed the concept of being on a plateau and integrating your growth before moving on. There is a discernible difference in being on a plateau between growth periods as opposed to just dying or growing smaller, because you're not nurturing or supporting yourself in some area.

The principle that *the natural order of the universe is growth* is supported only by your free choice. You can choose to support that through feeding and nurturing those elements that are needed for growth, or you can choose not to support them and take away those elements. It's totally up to you! It is the natural order for things to grow. That means it's easier, it's less effort for us to allow growth than it is to fight it. It comes naturally to us to support growth, and yet many times we don't. Because of fear or limiting beliefs or our need to be safe, we take away the elements that are needed for growth. We take away the food, we take away the air, we take away the sunlight and our sequoias wind up as stunted seedlings instead of the magnificent trees God intended them to be.

So again, it's time to notice things in your own life. Which areas are you supporting and nurturing? Which areas are you feeding? Which areas are growing? In some areas it may be a kind of mature growth that is slow and steady, like the expansion at the edge of the universe. In other areas it's teenage growth, wild and sporadic, growing at breakneck speed, with some growth pains.

FOCUSED GROWTH EXERCISE:

Use the following list to identify which areas of your life will need your support, and attention, or just space to grow.

Physical Health
Relationships and Family
Environment and home
Business or Job
Investments and Finance
Recreation and Fun
Your Spiritual Life

In each of these areas, ask yourself: are you growing or shrinking? What is needed in this particular area to grow? And finally, what will you do to support yourself in this area? And when will you start?

Natural Limits And Impact

I have two final thoughts I want to share with you about growth and the natural order of expansion in the universe. First, **there is a natural growth limitation to many things.** There is a natural genetic code in human beings that stops our growth at a certain point. It's our natural size. There is a natural size to most things, but if circumstances change the natural size changes as well. In other words, trees grow to a certain height here on Earth, but if we put them in a place where gravity is reduced, the trees' height would probably increase correspondingly. So there's a natural limit to how far things should grow, but as long as we support it through nurturing and attention, it will grow to its *optimum* size. It doesn't matter if we're talking about a physical thing, or an emotional thing, or even something financial. **We should support growth to its natural limit.**

The second thing to observe is that **we can measure growth and see its result by looking at the impact** that it is having on the things around us. If we want to measure the growth of a relationship, we should ask "What impact is it having?" If that relationship is growing stronger and stronger, the impact is that we are have an improved lifestyle, improved communications with that person, deeper companionship, and the ability to work together better. All of those things are part of the impact that the growing relationship may be giving you.

The same thing is true in our financial lives. If we look at our accumulated wealth and ask ourselves what impact this abundance and wealth is having, we should see a positive impact. Larger things will have a larger impact. Greater wealth has a larger impact than small wealth. If it doesn't create a positive impact, then what's the point? Even if it's the natural order for things to grow, if it's not having positive benefit, then why bother with it? We've spoken before about the **responsibility that comes with increase.**

> # KEY:
>
> Notice if you're in a position of growing and gaining more but not having an impact. If that's the case, you are simply hoarding. If you are hoarding money, or relationships, or physical ability, then it has no impact and what's the point? The point of abundance is to share it.

This principle of growth as a natural and universal law is relatively simple, but I bring it to your attention because I constantly see people fighting this idea. If we can simply accept that this is a part of the natural order, then acceptance allows us to believe more is possible for us, and we actually will attract the opportunity for growth.

ACCEPTANCE AND CHOICE EXERCISE:

Here are three quick questions to ask yourself:

1. Do I accept this principle as a natural and universal law?
2. Am I seeing growth in my own life? If so, where?
3. Is that growth creating a positive impact, or am I hoarding?

Notice your own life, but also notice the lives of others around you. Are you growing, utilizing, sharing, spreading, and expanding other people's possibilities as well as your own? **The purpose of expansion and growth is impact—impact on you and the world around you**. As you grow you will show up larger and have a larger impact. It's one way you can leave a mark in this world.

So notice, what is the impact you're having? Notice as your personal abundance grows, what is the impact of your wealth or abundances. Many people don't ever attract wealth and abundance because they don't have any use for it; they're just storing and hoarding it. That's not being a good steward in what you've been given, and you will probably not be given more. **Growth is designed to be beneficial**, and it's a natural order of the universe. It will come to you in large measure as long as you use it wisely, and it can have a tremendous positive impact in your life and the lives of people around you as well.

Like so many other chapters, it's up to you. It's up to you to notice, shift your beliefs, and step up to your potential.

Chapter 20

LEVERAGE AND
MULTIPLICATION
OF EFFORTS

W e've all heard about the idea of leverage or *multiplication of efforts*. Sometimes people call this *amplification*. It' not quite the same as the principle of exponential growth that we talked about earlier. It's using other people's money or time or leveraging your own time to accelerate your growth. In this chapter we're going to examine how we can take the principle of leverage and apply it, almost like another layer over every other principle that we've talked about in this book. **Leverage is a very powerful tool for amplifying or magnifying the efforts that you're already making in any area of your life.**

Let's talk about leverage just briefly and see if I can challenge you to start leveraging every situation. Now, let's ask ourselves, is leverage always a good thing? Leverage is a good thing if what you are leveraging is positive. If your efforts are good and worthy efforts, then you get to multiply or magnify those worthy efforts. However, if your efforts are not worthy efforts and you're not doing good deeds, but doing bad deeds, then leverage amplifies those also. Often people talk to me about money and they say "If I had more money, I could do more good things," or "I know this guy who has a lot of money, and it's ruined his life. He's a bigger jerk than he ever was before." His behavior is *amplified* by money and it's true, money is one of the big leverage tools. If we have money, we can leverage our time and almost everything we do. It allows us to have a larger impact—for either good or bad.

Hiring someone to do something for us so that we don't have to do it ourselves, is a perfect example of how leverage can work to support us. If we can afford to, we can leverage ourselves by hiring employees, hiring people to work for us, hiring out tasks, and therefore, we don't have to do them ourselves. This became really clear to me the first time I ever hired an employee.

EXAMPLE:

Many years ago I was just out of my teens with my first business, and I was working for about $20 an hour. A lot of the work I did I didn't even enjoy very much, and it dawned on me one day that I could hire people, or even just one person, to do the things that I didn't enjoy doing. That way I would have more time to do the things that I did enjoy doing and the things that really made me the most money. And so, my decision to hire some assistants was a combination of a couple of principles. It was combining the principle of my being at my highest and best use, doing what I love doing, and also the principle of leverage or multiplication of my efforts. Minimum wage at that time was about $5 an hour. If I hired someone at minimum wage, and if they were as efficient as I was at the things I asked them to do—and remember, these were the things I didn't want to do anyway— then I actually profited about $15 per hour for every hour that they worked. So instead of my doing many things I didn't like to do and only using part of my time to do the things I did like, and making about $20 an hour on this mixed bag, I was now making $35 an hour and only doing the things that I liked and was best at. **When we apply the principle of leverage we become much, much more efficient!**

I work with many people in coaching who simply asked me "In order to grow my business, should I hire employees? I don't know if I should take that step, because it's an awful lot of responsibility." And I always go to the principle of leverage. The principle of leverage will show us really quickly the benefit, or lack of benefits, from hiring an employee. How can we possibly grow in abundance, and prosper, and multiply ourselves and our potential for income if we limit ourselves to the number of hours that we are able to work in a week? If there's no opportunity for multiplication or leverage we're just trading our time for dollars like any other wage earner. One of the huge advantages in being self-employed, is that you get to apply the principle of leverage to yourself and your business by using other people's time. You get to make those choices yourself. **When you're an employee someone else is leveraging their time through you**. Think hard about that. When you are an employee someone else is leveraging their time through you.

Hiring people is one example of how leverage works, and makes very good sense for us to take advantage of leverage and to place ourselves in those situations where we can take advantage of that principle. Again, if you are an employee, someone is taking advantage of you for *their* benefit, using the principle of leverage. They're leveraging their time through you. As you move into the self-employed position, at some point you get to hire people to work in your business. You especially get to hire people to do the things that you don't like doing, as I did for my first business. You also may choose to hire people with skills that you don't possess. Believe it or not, **some people can actually do parts of your business better than you can,** and when you hire them, you are leveraging their knowledge and expertise for your business. Ideally, at some point you have leveraged yourself right out of your own business. You have employees doing everything in your business, and you're still making profits from the business without having to work in the business. That's when you're a true business owner. You're not working in your own business anymore. Instead, you own the business and reap the rewards without trading your time for dollars. You're simply using the principle of leverage. That's how big this principle is!

Leverage Applications

The principal of leverage is easily applied in a business scenario, but it also has application in many other areas of our lives. For instance, let's look at how we might leverage our personal time. A very quick example is *multi-tasking*. You've heard about people who are great at multitasking or double tasking. These are people who can be talking to you on the telephone while they're doing the dishes, combing their daughter's hair and watching television. They may be doing all of these things at the same time. These are people who can be working in an office at a computer, and at the same time, they're thinking about a letter that they're going to write to a friend. These are people who are watching television while reading a book. They're leveraging their time through multitasking. They're making use of all that's possible for them at that moment. This example of leverage goes back to the idea of full engagement that we spoke about in chapter 18, filling the empty mental processing capacity to create free time.

One of the ways I want you to think about leverage, though, is to **think of leverage as moving things away from you**. One of the ways this shows up all the time is when I'm coaching people in the area of investment. Often they say to me, "I don't have enough money." One way to get money is to bring in a partner, right? A partner can provide the money and you provide the time. That's leverage. Lots and lots of real estate deals are done this way, with investors providing the capital and an operator providing the groundwork of putting the deal together, getting it closed, managing the property, and closing the sale when it's time to sell the property. **One person is leveraging their partner's time, while the other person is leveraging the other's money.** They're both using the principle of leverage to get what they want. One person brings the thing they have in excess to the table, in order to trade it for the other's item they have in excess. In some cases you may need to leverage your time, but in other cases you may need to leverage your money. Leverage is a simple way for you to partner with people and only have to be responsible for bringing half of the required components to the equation. You don't necessarily have to put up all the time and all the money.

What are the costs of leverage? In the scenario I just described, the cost of leverage is that you have to split the rewards, but on the other hand it may allow you to do something that you're unable to do otherwise.

Many people have started a business buying and selling homes using other people's money (OPM). When we read about people buying and selling homes with no money down, that's one example of the principle of leverage. The buyer may even use the house seller's money to buy the house itself. That's leverage! You say, "Well, that's like buying something for no cost." Exactly! That's the principle of leverage. Or, I may take the excess money that I have to invest and give it to somebody as a partner in some investment. I let them do all the work with managing the investment and we both profit. If we look at it objectively, we realize that our entire society is leveraged. When we left the caveman era and stopped gathering all of our own food, and making all of our own clothing, and killing our own bison, we moved into the area of leverage. People became specialized. The bison hunters became strictly hunters, and they traded the bison that they had killed for vegetables, clothing, and fire, for some of the cooked bison meat, and as soon as that happened everybody was leveraging their skills for mutual benefit. Everybody was doing what they did best and what they loved doing. Leverage allowed everyone involved to be more efficient.

One of the tricks is to identify not only what your best skills are but what you enjoy doing the most. At the end of this chapter I'm going to attach a list that I call the "good like list" which will help you identify the things that you should be doing in areas where you are highly efficient, as well as areas that you should use leverage by delegating to others.

Let's start leveraging our pleasure and enjoyment. Why spend our time doing things that we don't enjoy doing? I don't work on my car anymore. I don't like draining the oil from underneath my car and lying out in the gravel driveway, getting all greasy. I pay someone to do that. Do I feel that I have to do everything myself? No, I do not! I'm happy to leverage my time by using others, especially when it comes to the things that are not fun for me to do. There are probably many areas of your life that you've already leveraged for the same reason.

Why do I go out for dinner once in a while and pay someone to cook my meal? Why don't I cook all my meals myself? Because I want to leverage my efforts and have someone else do that for me. It's pleasurable for me to go out to eat and not have to cook. If I have to cook, it's not as fun to eat. Some of you may be thinking the opposite. Some of you may love to cook, and if so, then that's not an area of your life that you would want to leverage. Start noticing what's pleasurable and enjoyable to you. What do you enjoy doing? **Do more of what you enjoy and less of what you don't enjoy.** Use the list at the end of this chapter to identify those things, and then leverage your time and efforts accordingly. Leverage your enjoyment. You'll find that your life becomes more and more efficient, and you're working less while having more fun and making more money! Who doesn't want that?

Where Are You The Expert?

What do you get from leverage? You get the ability to be a specialist and expert at those things you do best. You don't have to hunt the bison, grow the vegetables, cook the meat, and make the clothing; you get to specialize. You're not a caveman anymore. Specialization means, first of all, noticing what you want to be special at. What are your gifts? What are your talents? We talked about this in chapter eight. It's time to master leveraging those gifts and talents that you identified before. Focus on what you do best and do more of that, and hire someone to take care of the other stuff, or delegate it to somebody on your team. Where do you make the most money? What part of your business is the most profitable? Focus on doing what you do best. That's an example of you leveraging you. What if you could spend all your time doing what you love doing the most and what you can charge the most for?

EXAMPLE:
I recently worked with a client and when we employed the ideas I'm sharing with you through leverage, his income went up 400% in six months and he actually worked fewer hours than before. Here's

what we did: first I asked him to call together a group of people that had similar skills to his, but that did not do the specific things that he was best at. He got their agreement to work for him in his company as subcontractors on all the work that my client did not want to do. That allowed him to focus on what he did best and could charge the most for. He immediately had more work because he was able to say "yes" to every job and delegate to his new subcontractors. For every hour that they worked he made money, and while he did not work as much as previously, his hourly rate almost doubled. Business more than doubled and his personal income went up exponentially.

Most of us don't make money while we sleep. On the other hand, it's difficult to leverage our sleep and have somebody else do that for us. Some of us have tried that, but we all need a certain basic amount of sleep. But beyond that there are many things in your life that you're still doing that you're not very efficient at. You may still be doing things that you're not very good at or that you absolutely hate doing. So, the question I have for you is: why do you do them? Why don't you leverage your efforts and have somebody else doing those things for you? If you would hire someone to do those things, you'd have more pleasure and free time, more energy, more happiness, and you would be able to spend your time doing the things that you really want to do, things that are pleasurable and that are part of who you want to be. You'll be doing things that you excel at, or in which you are an expert, or that you have specific skills or talents for. You will be operating much more efficiently and you will move ahead faster. Your life will be more pleasant, and therefore your attitude and your energy will go up as well. So find the things that you don't like doing and get rid of them. Shift them to somebody else. Leverage your time, leverage your pleasure, and leverage your money!

> # KEY:
> If you want to leverage your sleep time, hire a *virtual assistant* in an opposite time zone to do some of your work, assign the work to them before you leave your office and the results will be waiting for you the next morning because they worked through your sleep time.

In order to leverage yourself you must often be very creative. You must often be able to think differently than every other person to find a situation where you can trade one of your talents for another talent. You may bring money to the table but not time, or you may bring time but not money. You may bring ideas, but not involvement. You might bring expertise and leverage that to get what you want. There are lots of ways that people leverage themselves, and most often creativity is involved at some level. In previous chapters we talked about the principle of creativity versus competition, and that if we think creatively, then we have less need to be competitive. If the general mass of people tend to do things one way, then if we do things a little bit differently and leverage our thinking, we wind up leveraging ourselves. Through creativity we can differentiate ourselves and create opportunities to leverage ourselves away from competition by putting ourselves in a unique position. We put ourselves in a situation that's different than the situation of other people through creativity. **Creativity is allowing the differentiation.** Let me give you an example: have you ever seen a house that had a "For Sale" sign in the front yard for many months without being sold? After seeing that sign for so long as you drove by it each day, you began to think "That place must not be a very good deal. There must be something wrong with it. Surely if it was worth buying they would've sold it by now." And so most people tend to dismiss the property as not being worth buying because it's been on the market for a long time, or the price may be way too high or maybe there is something wrong with the property. Maybe there is something wrong with the layout of the house. If you can bring creativity to the deal, you leverage yourself. You put yourself in a separate category from all the other buyers looking at that property. Maybe the selling price is way too high and the seller is unwilling to come down—but maybe they're willing to sell if the person comes up with the right amount of money, even if you have to creatively adjust the terms. What you're doing is differentiating yourself from all the other buyers. Most people will say "That property is not worth as much on the open market right now according to the values of other homes in the area." Maybe they won't even consider it. But if you are able to bring a creative eye and a creative mind, then you leverage yourself through creativity and take all the other competition out of the picture. You're separating yourself from the need to compete. Maybe you're willing to pay the seller's price, but you're not willing to pay the seller on his terms. You may offer terms that leverage the price or give you some special advantage. Or, you may meet the terms, or even improve them, to be able to lower the price. In other words, you're leveraging the price against the terms or vice versa. Maybe you offer full price on the property but no money down, or with cash back at the closing, or with a balloon payment five years down the road and nothing out of pocket now. You may offer the seller something that gets them their full price, but gives you the terms that you need in order to be able to do the deal. You leverage yourself by giving them what they want in one area and taking what you want in the other area.

Leverage May Be A Simple *Trade*

Leverage often involves two things trading against each other. Often leverage involves trading one of the strengths or skills that you have for something that you lack. But you have to bring creativity to the equation in order to be successful. Creativity is the ability to bring fresh ideas and new thinking to something and to eliminate your competition. All of our lives are full of negotiation and creativity. We're always balancing what we have with what we want, and if you're good at it, you become very efficient at the process. That's what allows you to buy the house with no money down, or drive your car without ever having to work on it. That's what allows your business to grow through the efforts of other people. What you're actually doing is creating a deal, leveraging yourself, finding a way to make something happen where there is no competition because nobody is able to compete in your marketplace.

Perhaps you're looking for a job right now as you read this book. If you're looking for work right now, one thing you might do is leverage yourself by becoming very creative. It's important to differentiate yourself so that you appear to offer something more to employers than every other candidate who walks in their door. Take yourself out of the market that everybody else is in and separate yourself so you're not competing. Yes, you are still going for the same job they are, but by using your creativity you can actually create your own separate market and make yourself into a unique category as employee. It's important to recognize your strengths and skills, and where you have expertise. Where are you the expert? By being creative, you might look at the job hunt completely differently. Perhaps instead of looking for a job in the paper or on Craigslist, you actually put an ad in the paper or on Craigslist under "Job Wanted" and describe exactly what you want. Perhaps instead of looking for work on the regular 9-to-5 shift you offer to do something unique and different in terms of hours. Maybe you define it on your terms and find an employer that will match your terms. Remember, it's a creative negotiation and you are selling you. It's up to you to develop skills that nobody else has, and offer something nobody else is offering. The best salespeople in the world have done exactly that. They have created a niche where they are the expert and they have differentiated themselves. That's your job as well.

Imagine you want to open a hamburger business and that you're in a neighborhood with lots of fast food restaurants. There is a McDonald's, and a Wendy's, and a Burger King. If you open a hamburger restaurant with that same formula and the exact same sort of menu, it would be very difficult for you to compete against three other restaurants that were just like yours. However, if you opened a restaurant that was completely different, that didn't serve fast food or hamburgers, but a completely different type of food with a different presentation, then you would put yourself in a unique market. Through creativity you'd have eliminated your competition. You wouldn't be competing with McDonald's and Wendy's and Burger King. You'd just be competing for food, and if your food was unique in that market, then you would have have this huge edge on the market, and while the other restaurants competed against each other you'd have absolutely no competition in your particular market except for food itself. **Creativity will take you out of the competition.**

One of the things that make each of us unique, and gives each of us our own *brand*, is our own unique *way of thinking*. Each of us is able to think just a little bit differently than everybody else because our background, skills, training and so on have made us a little different than everybody else. If you're reading this and thinking "No, I'm just not able to think creatively," then I challenge you to believe that you just never tried it. You never trusted it. You never listened to that inner voice that is uniquely yours and has different ideas than everybody else. You just shut down that voice in the past. Maybe that part of you was always stomped on at school or at home. Our society, the media, our schools, and most of life around us, tells us to do it the way that everybody else does. Schools train us to be that way. But I'm challenging you with this principle of leverage to think creatively, to think differently, in order differentiate yourself from the pack, to use the principle of leverage to find what is uniquely you and come up with your own ideas. That's the edge that you have and that nobody else has. Nobody else is you! You have the opportunity to think like you and nobody else does. If you can think like yourself and express your true self, it will be a little different than everybody else on the planet. You will have differentiated yourself just by listening to yourself. That differentiation through creativity is a huge advantage. Start using that for leverage!

Finally in the area of creative leveraging, I want to challenge you to do one more thing. Let me say it just one more time, **leverage is trading what you have in excess for something which you lack** in order to get what you want without having to bring everything to the table yourself. I want you to use this principle of leveraging creativity and go back and review the other chapters in this book. Leveraging *creativity* is a layer that you can put over everything else you do that will give you a specific advantage that is uniquely you. I want you to ask yourself as you look back in previous chapters: "how am I leveraging this idea? How might I take this principle of leverage and leverage it in my life? How am I making an opportunity for myself or giving myself an edge?" How are you leveraging yourself as you develop your life puzzle? Are you leveraging yourself as you identify the level you're on and moving to the next level? How are you leveraging yourself as you play win-win?

There's a way to bring leverage to every situation that will allow you to move at an accelerated pace and achieve more in what you're doing, in a way that supports other people and takes nothing away from you. How can you leverage yourself with the idea of caring about and not caring for people? How can you leverage yourself with the principle of radical acceptance? Go back and revisit all of these chapters and ideas that we've talked about before. Now I'm challenging you to take this principle of leverage and add it on top of the other principal or principles. In other words, **I'm asking you to leverage the principles!** I'm asking you to **leverage ideas** and I'm challenging you to add to them. It's not *this* principle or *that* principle but instead, it's this principle in combination and multiplication with this principle.

Perhaps the principles in this book are a way for you to leverage what you now know. Knowledge may be the commodity that allows you to leverage yourself to be bigger and to do more than you were able to do before. Bringing creativity, negotiation, and differentiation to every situation will allow you to leverage yourself, and that leverage will allow you to move forward in life faster.

THE "GOOD-LIKE LIST" EXERCISE:

Take a sheet of paper and divide it into three columns. In the left-hand column write down all the things that you do in your life, both business and personal. Every task you do, whether you do it every day or just occasionally, from cooking and cleaning to bookkeeping or sales. write everything you do in this column. List each item separately; you may wind up with 50 to 100 items. In the second column, write yes or no if you have a specific talent or gift for doing what you wrote in the left column. And in the third column, write yes or no to indicate whether you like doing that specific task. In some cases you will have a yes/yes response. Those are the things that you enjoy doing and are good at doing. Some items will have a yes/no response in some items will have a no/no response. It's the no/no items that I want you to focus on. I want you to think about getting rid of them through delegation, or hiring someone, or just stopping that activity. I want you to stop doing them because they are taking away from your efficiency and your enjoyment of life. I want you to focus on the yes/yes items because they represent your special strengths and are also where you will find the most enjoyment. Those are also the things you should leverage.

Use this "good like list" as a starting point to examine where you need to leverage your business, your spiritual life, your relationships and family and all other areas. As you do this, it will set the direction of your movement and change your focus. In the next chapter we will look at the principle of movement and this principle of leverage will help you head the right direction!

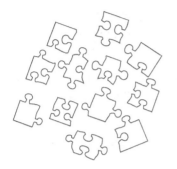

Chapter 21

BALANCE IS
ESSENTIAL

In this final chapter we'll talk about the principle that balance is essential, and that without balance in our lives our accomplishments are diminished. Without balance, our enjoyment is diminished, and so are our chances of success.

Extreme Balance

It has been said that we should strive for moderation in all things, including moderation. Balance does not mean mediocrity. Balance does not mean that we settle for things as they are. Balance means that occasionally it's good to have an extreme response, but keep in mind that extreme responses need to be balanced with extreme moderation or extreme calm, so that when we are extremely wild, we have at some point to be extremely calm to create the balance. **The universe wants to balance things out and keep things in that balanced harmony. That's also where success lies.**

Ever notice people who live in the extremes? A radical example would be a person who has a very wild lifestyle, maybe even into drugs and alcohol or other excessive behavior. At some point they will crash and all of that behavior will go away and they will go to the opposite extreme. They may be swinging back and forth from one extreme to the other. Very much like a pendulum. They must balance the wild times they have with extremely low times or down time. Manic depressive behavior is an example of this. If you have extreme manic times, you will have periods of extreme depression to balance them out. If this describes you and you want to avoid extreme depression and extreme manic times, you need to strive for a little more balance in your life. You need to learn to live in that center position.

The balanced position is where you will find your highest productivity. Balance is where you will find accomplishment. Now, let me say again, I'm not suggesting complete neutral balance without extremes. I'm suggesting that you start noticing what you are choosing. What is your behavior? Is it intentional? Is it what you want to create? Your behavior may include times of very hard work that need to be balanced with times of calm and restful recuperation. Your behavior may include emotional extremes, or physical or health extremes, but it's important to notice that each of these extremes need to be balanced out with its opposite. I'm not recommending living a milquetoast existence, although some people do. What I am recommending is to keep balance in your life. Have you ever known a person who was what you would call one-dimensional? They have extreme success in one area of their life but no success in other areas of their life. Often what it takes to create extreme success is to have some area of your life be all-consuming. Sometimes we have to go through that consuming process to get breakthroughs in one area of our lives. But what I want you to notice is that it comes with a price. The price is that we have to ignore other areas of our lives. Do you know anyone who is extremely successful in business? Perhaps they're very wealthy, and at the same time they're very unhappy. Perhaps they don't have a family life because they sacrifice that. Perhaps they don't have relationships in their lives that are functional. Perhaps they're spiritually hungry. Or, to go to the other extreme, do you know someone who is very spiritual, and yet they live at the poverty level? Some artists live this way. They are very talented, but that extreme talent keeps them from ever having financial success because they're focused on their art. They may never achieve financial success, business success, or personal relationship success.

They may achieve tremendous success as artists or highly creative people, but that success is limited to only their art.

What I'm saying here is that we are always given a choice. You can choose the lifestyle you want to live in. I'm saying that as you notice it, you can control it. Sometimes there may not be as much satisfaction in the mediocrity as there is in the extremes, and sometimes the opposite. For some of us, the extremes are where the action is, that's what's sexy and gets our juices flowing. This is not a judgment or preference for one position over another. It's not a condemnation or a recommendation, but it is about noticing. Where are you? What's your lifestyle? What gets things accomplished for you? Where do you function at your highest level? How are you most productive? What's the balance for you in life? Are you in complete balance even if it's in the extremes? These are great questions because they challenge you to notice and examine and to take stock of where you are. It's not about being right or wrong or a judgement, but it is about noticing and asking yourself "How productive is that?" Perhaps there's a huge area of your life where you're not being very successful. If you're not able to create success in that area, I suggest that it may be because you are out of balance. Earlier in this book we talked about creating space for things to show up. Balance is an extreme example of this, because when you create balance you are creating space for more things to come to you.

Balance looks at the overall picture and asks "Are we giving all of our attention to one thing and none of our attention to another thing? Is there a lifestyle extreme in one area and shut down in another area?" If some areas of your life are shut down, perhaps it's because you're living an extreme lifestyle in another area of your life to balance that out. Maybe you're living at the extreme swings of the pendulum, and it may benefit you to move into a less extreme position. It's important to look at yourself objectively and be able to identify what you're giving up in response to what you're taking. Often tremendous rewards in one area keep us focused on that, not noticing what we're missing in another area. Whether it's acknowledgment, recognition, personal satisfaction, or money, that reward may be so huge, and make us feel so good, that it overpowers our judgment and pulls us to the extreme. Some of the people who are most successful in business and finance are also very unbalanced. They've been pulled so far into that end of the spectrum that the other end of the spectrum has no activity.

BALANCE QUESTIONS EXERCISE:

My questions for you are simply these:

1. Are you a balanced person?
2. What is the balance point for you?
3. If you're always a balanced person, do you know how to live in the extremes?
4. What's the most radical thing that you've done lately?

This is not about choosing to be mediocre or average in any way. This is about noticing and identifying the areas where you've shut down and the areas where you're in the extreme. Where do you show up and what do you want? If you assume that you get to choose everything that happens to you, that everything brought you to this moment of your life as a result of the choices you've made up until now, then you must also assume that everything that's going to happen in your future is the result of the choices that you make from this moment on. If that's the case, you can further say "Okay, I'm responsible for my choices. I'm responsible for whether I live a balanced life or an extreme life or a shut down life.

We can look at our relationships with an eye toward balance. Some of you are reading this book and have had relationships in the extreme. What would be an example of an extreme relationship? Maybe it's a one night stand, or a lifestyle of having very superficial relationships so that people don't get too close. The extreme opposite of that would be the person who has no relationships, or only monogamous long-term relationships.

The concept of balance applies to every area of our lives. I encourage you to look at each of the seven segments of your life below and ask yourself: "Am I balanced in this area? Do I want to make a change? Do I want to become more balanced or more extreme? And what would that look like?"

Physical Health
Relationships and Family
Environment and home
Business or Job
Investments and Finance
Recreation and Fun
Your Spiritual Life

Your viewpoint and opinions about what you were created for will determine where the balance point is for you. Your balance point may be different than it is for anybody else. If you continue to examine the relationship metaphor, for example, you may see that for some people having a balanced lifestyle means having a long-term, loving and supportive relationship with the same person. For somebody else it may seem like an extreme position because it's an extreme commitment. So your viewpoint is critical to you and unique to you. I'm certainly not suggesting that everybody has to be the same or that we should all have the same values and opinions about what balance means. I'm not suggesting that we become robots or that we all live an average lifestyle. We don't all have to be married for 24.6 years and have 2.3 kids and live in a house in the suburbs with a white picket fence. We don't have to have an average income or average lifestyle or have an average education or drive an average car. That would be very boring and none of us would show up as individuals. The discussions we had earlier about what differentiates us would have no relevance. So it's not about being average or "normal." It is about you making choices for yourself. We started this book recognizing that it's all about you working on yourself because nobody else has the power to change you. Only you can notice and make the choices for your future.

So again, it comes back to choices. This is not about saying that a monogamous relationship for life is a good or bad thing or that the wild lifestyle is good or bad, or that extreme financial success is good or bad. I'm not making a judgment about any of those things. But I am asking *you* to make a judgment about those things in the determination of where you are in your own life, so that you are making conscious choices about creating balance in your life that will *support you moving forward.*

It's all about noticing and making choices. Where are you out of balance? Are you out of balance in the area of relationships? Are you out of balance in your spiritual life, or your physical life, or in your business or financial life? In what part of your life are you shut down? In what part of your life are you living in the extreme? For some people it's as simple as balancing their eating habits, and for some people it's a matter balancing sleep and wake time. For some people, balance can be determined for every area of their life and again even in the specific areas there is no right or wrong. It's about noticing and choosing like most of this book.

KEY:

If you are a result of the choices you have made and the choices you will make in the future, then those choices are important.

It's important how we choose. When you're confused about something or when you're not seeing the results you want in your life it may be important to come back and look at this issue of balance.

Balance is much like the *principle of leverage* from the previous chapter. These are general principles that can be combined with all the principles in this book. So we can look at the principle of leverage, possibly using our money and somebody else's time, and we can apply the principle of balance on top of that and find a balanced way to use leverage. We can go back and look at every principle in this book and apply them in a balanced way to our own lives. I know from personal experience that as you do that, you will have many choices to make that will serve you well.

Become conscious of where you're out of balance or living in the extremes and make conscious choices.

This simple principle is about your choices. **Now it's up to you!**

Summary

WHEN I INITIALLY STARTED writing this book, it was done for the purpose of gathering ideas and collecting my own thoughts in a way that made sense. It was a response to many coaching challenges I was having with clients, as well as many issues I was facing in my own life. I thought writing these ideas down and spending a little time thinking about them would help me clarify some of the choices that I was being faced with regarding those issues or principles. It did help, and it continues to help. I've also found that over the years these have been the principles that have had the most impact on my clients allowing them to look at things differently and make powerful choices that propel them forward.

My first need to organize these principles, and my ideas around them, expanded significantly as I worked with other people on these specific ideas. When I saw the breakthroughs that people could make by adopting a simple idea like *learning to communicate from your true spiritual self* and how that can effect every area of your life, I really began to see the power and importance of sharing principles and ideas with each other.

As I collected these principles and organized them, I was amazed to realize some fundamental truths that I had never even truly understood. I realized that I don't have the power to change anybody else. I can barely change myself. Yes, I can introduce ideas, but by just introducing ideas I'm not changing you,

I am only offering you an opportunity for choice or change like we talked about in chapter 12. It's totally up to you! As I said earlier in the book the most important thing is for you to work on yourself. **Only you have the power to change you!**

I also came to realize that this is just the tip of the iceberg, and that there are always many more levels, more complex, profound, more challenging levels that will show up for you and I when we are ready. It will be exciting to see what's next!

As I look back on it now I realize that I wrote this book for three fundamental reasons:

1. I had a fundamental belief that **ideas need to be shared**, and while none of these principles are uniquely mine, I did feel that in some way it was up to me to share them just as they had been shared with me. Many of them were pieces I added to my own personal puzzle and became part of my belief system as well. They were ideas on which I was able to build greater success in my own life. I hope that at least a few of these principles have had that effect on you. I hope they fit, and are appropriate in some way to what you're going through in life right now. I think that through sharing ideas we elevate each other. I think it's one of the fundamental ways that we learn and evolve. I love it when someone challenges me with an idea, because it either confirms what I already believe or challenges me to think something differently and adopt their opinion. If my opinions and ideas are strong enough, then the new idea simply confirms and strengthens my resolve and position. However, if their idea is able to shake me off a position, or change my belief, that's even better because I'm no longer the same. I have changed my beliefs and therefore *who* I am in the world also changes. That's a happy day! I think another basic part of this sharing of ideas is that I am responsible in some way to pass on what I've been given. It goes back to the principle of stewardship in chapter nine and knowing that I will be given more if I do a good job with what I've been given. That's true for you as well. If you've embraced some of these ideas and

taken them on as part of your beliefs, or if they have confirmed your beliefs about some idea, then you also have a responsibility to pass them on and share them with the people around you. I also realized that I simply had to get the ideas out of me. I don't know if you can understand what I mean, but I was spending too much time thinking about the same ideas. I needed a process for passing them on so they did not remain on my shelf. That leads to the second reason...

2.   **I wanted to receive more**, and I know that in order to receive more we sometimes need to create space as I talked about in chapter 14. So part of that process was for me to get this book off my shelf, and I'm already being presented with ideas for a next book. The next book will focus less on the physical opportunity for change and much more on the mental and spiritual opportunities for change. I want to challenge readers like you with a higher level of universal truths like the one that we alluded to in this book, that *it's impossible to make a mistake*. Ideas like that cause us to question our foundational beliefs that limit who we are at our core. Whether you believe an idea like that or not, your questioning of that idea causes you to evolve and change. Who you are is slightly altered even by the presentation of an idea, and even more altered by the presentation of a radical idea that is outside of your current belief system.

3.   Finally, and this is probably the most important reason, **I honestly wanted to share ideas that had the potential to create a positive impact** in other people—people like you. I know that the ideas and principles that were presented in this book may not have all resonated with you, but I hope that one or two of those principles caused you to question what you are doing, or what you think, or what your next steps might be. Almost at every moment, each of us is at a point where two paths diverge, and we are called on to make a choice, and the choices we make can *make all the difference*. Even the smallest experience or interaction can lead us on a totally different path, and when we take that path, our lives will morph into something totally different. Each of us is constantly at a point of decision where we get

to choose one path over another. I hope this book has helped you to make a few of those choices! I hope this helps you create a higher level of success for yourself, and that if you look back you will be able to point to some idea that was presented and say, "That principle or idea was really good for me because it helped me understand something, or it helped me believe, or helped me choose a path that has had a huge powerful impact in my life." I love being part of someone else's success! And to me that can best be measured by the results that you achieve. If even one principle I've presented changes your life for the better, then I consider this book a huge success, and worth all the time and effort it took to get it off my shelf and in your hands.

One of the hardest things about writing a book is that your experience with me is not directly with me. You are having an experience with me through this book, so I don't get to see the impact that these principles have had on you. With my coaching clients I get to see it in every conversation, and go through the process with them. I would love to share that experience with you.

Therefore I have one request:
Send me your stories. Let me know what happened as a result of reading this book. Let me know how your life was changed or what impact these ideas had on you and the people around you. I would love to know what results you experienced from reading this book, even if it was just one chapter that meant something to you or that caused you to do something slightly differently.

As a first-time author, I question the value that this book has to anyone and whether it's good or bad. Quite frankly, I can't tell, and I'm probably the last person to make that judgment. But I care very much about the impact of this book on you and others who read it. In the end, those results and the impact on you is the measure of this book's success or failure. So again, if this book has impacted you please send me your story and let me know.

You can reach me at:

Will Mattox

will@coachingservices.com

ABOUT THE AUTHOR

Will Mattox… Coach, Speaker, and Author

Over 40 years of entrepreneurial experience, coupled with an education degree and international certification as a business coach, give Will Mattox the ability to work with clients in a very direct and honest process to create accelerated growth toward their goals. "I love being a part of other people's success and feeling that I contributed in a positive way."

Will was an early pioneer in business and financial coaching launching Coaching Services, Inc in the mid-1990s where he developed the Directive Coaching model that is a blend of coaching, consulting, and mentoring. Will was Certified Nationally and Internationally in 1997 as a Business Coach and has coached thousands of entrepreneurial clients around the world in business startup, acceleration, and profitability, sharing his business success in manufacturing, construction, real estate, retail, and sales. This strong entrepreneurial background combined with his intuitive ability to get results quickly, place him as a leader in the coaching profession.

Will and his wife Virginia split their time between Lake Oswego, Oregon with their children and grandchildren, and Bucerias, Mexico where they recently built a home near the beach.

Contact Will at www.coachingservice.com

Special Offers

I have 2 special offers for you:

1. **There are 6 bonus chapters waiting for you as a FREE download!**
    Like the 21 chapters in this book, they are full of tools to help you as you go through change in life. They will add another layer of insight and power to what you have learned from this book and will help get off the plateau and on your way to your next level.

    1. Identify your next level
    2. Always play win-win
    3. Organization at all levels
    4. Care about, don't care for
    5. Five levels of learning
    6. Movement, Momentum, and Precession

On the website, simply click on the "free download" button on the right side. This will take you to another page where you will be prompted for your name and email address. Simply enter in your information and click download and enjoy!"

2. **FREE COACHING!** The principles I am sharing are the tools that you need for accelerated growth! These principles, like the ones in this book are a catalyst for change and IF you do the exercises will lead to an easier life and help you achieve your dreams. However, if you are having trouble implementing them in a specific area of your life or if you are not getting the results as quickly as you would like, then contact me for a **FREE 20-minute strategic coaching session** to accelerate the change and achieve your dreams even faster!

Book your free call at:
www.coachingservices.com/coaching
or scan the QR Code below.

Additional Resources:
All of my books, newsletters, and more are available at:
www.coachingservices.com/books
or scan the QR Code below to take you
directly to my site and other special offers.

Printed in the USA
CPSIA information can be obtained
at www.ICGtesting.com
JSHW022215140824
68134JS00018B/1076